CAMBRIDGE CLASSICAL STUDIES

General Editors: W. K. C. GUTHRIE, A. H. M. JONES, D. L. PAGE

TEXTILE MANUFACTURE IN THE NORTHERN ROMAN PROVINCES

TEXTILE MANUFACTURE

IN THE

NORTHERN ROMAN
PROVINCES

J. P. WILD

Lecturer in Archaeology
University of Manchester

CAMBRIDGE
AT THE UNIVERSITY PRESS
1970

CAMBRIDGE UNIVERSITY PRESS
Cambridge, New York, Melbourne, Madrid, Cape Town, Singapore, São Paulo, Delhi

Cambridge University Press
The Edinburgh Building, Cambridge CB2 8RU, UK

Published in the United States of America by Cambridge University Press, New York

www.cambridge.org
Information on this title: www.cambridge.org/9780521074919

First published 1970
This digitally printed version 2008

A catalogue record for this publication is available from the British Library

Library of Congress Catalogue Card Number: 74–77294

ISBN 978-0-521-07491-9 hardback
ISBN 978-0-521-10051-9 paperback

TO MY PARENTS

πλεοναχῶς δ' ὄντος τοῦ 'επίστασθαι,
πῶς ἕκαστα μεταδιωκτέον; ἀρχὴ
καὶ μέγιστον ὁ οἰκεῖος τρόπος

Theophrastus, *Metaphysics*, 22

CONTENTS

CONTENTS

TABLES

ILLUSTRATIONS

FIGURES (pp. 150–181)

xi

PLATES (*between pp. 184 and 185*)

PREFACE

Archaeologists are regularly heard to complain that the material which they have undertaken to synthesize and interpret is too small in amount or too uneven in distribution to allow any but the most tentative of conclusions to be based on it. Their professional caution causes no raised eyebrows; but their tale of woe no longer commands much sympathy. It has been heard too often. Yet in those fields where the material evidence is highly perishable, such complaints are fully justified. What, for example, would we know of wine and oil consumption in the Roman Provinces, if the pottery containers for these commodities had not survived? The problem is even more acute in the case of textiles, where the commonest textile implements, usually of wood, survive almost as rarely as the woven products.

I was fortunate to begin work at a time when, quite by accident, a number of important new groups of textiles were discovered. This book would have been far more sketchy, if it had been written even ten years ago. But even when textiles have been located in archaeological and other excavations, their handling and ultimate fate have often left much to be desired. One shudders to think how much in the past must have simply been missed or even jettisoned on the grounds that it was of no value.

It is a pleasure to recall and record the unstinting help which I have received from many scholars during the preparation of this work. My greatest debt is to Professor J. M. C. Toynbee, Lawrence Professor Emerita of Classical Archaeology in the University of Cambridge. Without her constant support and encouragement at all stages of production the work would never have been completed. Her advice and criticism have been of immense value to me. I have benefitted greatly from discussions of ancient textiles with Miss A. S. Henshall of the National Museum of Antiquities of Scotland, Dr Marta Hoffmann of the Norsk Folkemuseum, Oslo, Dr Walter Endrei of Budapest and Miss Elisabeth Crowfoot. I could not have attempted an account of Roman sheep breeds without considerable help from Dr M. L. Ryder of the Animal Breeding Research Organisation. His published work and much unpublished information which he has kindly allowed me to use form the basis of the opening section of the first chapter. For advice on linguistic matters I am indebted to Professor Dr K. H. Schmidt of the University of Bochum.

The published material relevant to the Roman Rhineland and the continental provinces was studied by me over a number of years in the library of the Rheinisches Landesmuseum, Bonn. I am grateful to Professor Dr Harald von Petrikovits,

Director of the Landesmuseum, for giving me ready access to this splendid collection. Much of the material for my study, however, was not fully published, and I examined it through the kindness of the directors and staff of many European museums. Of their number I wish to thank particularly:

Dr H. N. Savory and Mr G. C. Boon of the National Museum of Wales, Cardiff; Miss J. E. A. Liversidge of the Museum of Archaeology and Ethnology, Cambridge; Mr Robert Hogg of Tullie House Museum, Carlisle; Mr D. F. Petch of the Grosvenor Museum, Chester; Dr M. G. Simpson, Hon. Curator of Chesters Museum; Mr N. C. Cook and Mr R. Merrifield of the Guildhall Museum, London; Dr D. J. Smith and Mr C. M. Daniels of the University Museum of Antiquities, Newcastle-upon-Tyne; Mr C. Barnett of the Museum and Art Gallery, Newport; Dr I. E. Anthony of the Verulamium Museum, St Albans; Mr G. F. Willmot of the Yorkshire Museum, York.

M. G. Collot of the Musée Central de Metz; M. F. Pomarède of the Musée Historique et Lapidaire de Reims.

Professor Dr H. von Petrikovits and my colleagues in the Rheinisches Landesmuseum, Bonn; Dr P. La Baume of the Römisch–Germanisches Museum, Köln; the staff of the Mittelrheinisches Landesmuseum, Mainz; Dr Th. K. Kempf of the Bischöfliches Museum, Trier; Dr H. Cüppers of the Rheinisches Landesmuseum, Trier; Dr O. Roller of the Historisches Museum der Pfalz, Speyer; Dr G. Illert of the Städtische Kulturinstitute, Worms; Dr H.-E. Mandera and Professor Dr H. Schoppa of the Städtisches Museum, Wiesbaden.

Dr E. Thomas and her colleagues in the Archaeological Department of the Magyar Nemzeti Múzeum, Budapest; Dr Klara Pócszy of the Történeti Múzeum, Budapest.

Professor Dr H. Brunsting of the Rijksmuseum van Oudheden te Leiden; Miss M. H. P. den Boesterd of the Rijksmuseum G. M. Kam te Nijmegen.

Dr C. Clement of the Bernisches Historisches Museum, Bern; Dr H. R. Wiedemer of the Vindonissa-Museum, Brugg; Professor Dr E. Vogt of the Schweizerisches Landesmuseum, Zürich.

For perspicacious comment and helpful criticism of many details of the work I am under a considerable obligation to my wife. To the critical faculty of Mr W. K. Lacey of St Catherine's College, Cambridge, I owe much. Both of them very kindly gave me a great deal of their time. To the firm of Wild & Co. I owe the happy idea of transferring my family's traditional interest in the textile industry into archaeological channels.

ACKNOWLEDGEMENTS

Grateful acknowledgement is due to the following for permission to reproduce illustrations: the Museum of Antiquities and Society of Antiquaries of Newcastle-upon-Tyne for Fig. 76, Plates IX a, XII d; the Director, Bankfield Museum, Halifax, for Plates III a, XII b; the Direktor, Bischöflisches Museum, Trier, for Figs. 44–6; the Trustees of the British Museum for Plate III b; Cambridge University Museum of Archaeology and Ethnology for Plates I b, XII a; Fototeca Unione, Rome, for Plates IV a, IV b, XI a, XI b; Dr M. Hoffmann and the Norsk Folkemuseum, Oslo, for Fig. 54, Plates X a, X b, X c; Instituto Poligrafico dello Stato, Rome, for Plate II; the Director, National Museum of Antiquities of Scotland, Edinburgh, for Plates VI b, XII c; the Director, National Museum of Wales, Cardiff, for Plate V a; the Konservator, Rätisches Museum, Chur, for Plate VII a; the Direktor, Rheinisches Landesmuseum, Trier, for Fig. 34; the Directeur, Rijksmuseum G. M. Kam, Nijmegen, for Fig. 40; Dr M. L. Ryder, Edinburgh, for Fig. 2, Plate I a; the Direktor, Saalburgmuseum, who kindly lent the block for Plate V b; the Direktor, Schweizerisches Landesmuseum, Zürich, for Figs. 13, 14, 43, 47, Plate VIII; the Director, Verulamium Museum, St Albans, for Figs. 26–9; the authorities of the Vindonissa-Museum, Brugg, for Fig. 12, Plates VII b, IX b; Professor Rushbrook Williams for Plate VI a; Wiltshire Archaeological and Natural History Society for Fig. 9.

ABBREVIATIONS

For abbreviations cast in the form of author and year, see Bibliography p. 143 ff.

AA	*Archaeologia Aeliana*
Aarbøger	*Aarbøger for nordisk Oldkyndighed og Historie*
Acta Arch.	*Acta Archaeologica* (Copenhagen)
AJA	*American Journal of Archaeology*
AJP	*American Journal of Philology*
ANL	*Archaeological News Letter*
Ant. Class.	*Antiquité Classique*
Ant. J	*Antiquaries Journal*
Arch. Cant.	*Archaeologia Cantiana*
Arch. Ért.	*Archaeologiai Értesítö*
Arch. J	*Archaeological Journal*
Arch. Trajectina	*Archaeologia Trajectina* (Groningen)
ASA	*Anzeiger für Schweizerische Altertumskunde*
AuhV	L. Lindenschmit, *Die Altertümer unserer heidnischen Vorzeit*, 1858
BBCS	*Bulletin of the Board of Celtic Studies*
BCAC	*Bulletino della Commissione archeologica comunale di Roma*
BCH	*Bulletin de Correspondance Hellénique*
Ber. Rijksdienst	*Berichten van de Rijksdienst voor het Oudheidkundig Bodemonderzoek*
Birka III	A. Geijer, *Birka III, Die Textilfunde aus den Gräbern*, 1938
BJb	*Bonner Jahrbücher*
BM	British Museum, London
BM *Guide*	British Museum *Guide to the Antiquities of Roman Britain*, 2nd edition, 1958
BR-GK	*Berichte der Römisch–Germanischen Kommission*
Br.	Breadth (of an object)
BSA	*Annual of the British School at Athens*
Cat. Chester	R. P. Wright & I. A. Richmond, *The Roman Inscribed and Sculptured Stones in the Grosvenor Museum*, Chester, 1955
Cat. Devizes	M. E. Cunnington & E. H. Goddard, *Catalogue of the Antiquities in the Museum of the Wiltshire Archaeological and Natural History Society at Devizes* II, 1911
Cat. Leiden	J. H. Holwerda, *Catalogus van het Rijksmuseum van Oudheden te Leiden*, 1908
CIL	*Corpus Inscriptionum Latinarum*
CQ	*Classical Quarterly*
CR	*Classical Review*
C-R. Comm. Imp.	*Compte-Rendu de la Commission Impériale Archéologique de St-Pétersbourg*

CW	*Transactions of the Cumberland and Westmorland Antiquarian and Archaeological Society*
Dura (1945)	R. Pfister & L. Bellinger, *The Textiles, Final Report* IV, 1945, apud M. I. Rostovtzeff et al. *The Excavations at Dura-Europos*
Eburacum (1962)	Royal Commission on Historical Monuments, *An Inventory of the Historical Monuments in the City of York* I, 1962
Esp.	E. Espérandieu, *Receuil Général des Bas-Reliefs, Statues et Bustes de la Gaule Romaine*, 1922 with supplements
FO	Findspot (of an object)
Führer Rottweil	P. Goessler, *Arae Flaviae: Führer durch die Altertumshalle der Stadt Rottweil*, 1928
Germ.	*Germania*
Ges. Vindonissa	*Jahresberichte der Gesellschaft Pro Vindonissa*
Heddernheim	*Mitteilungen über römische Funde in Heddernheim*
IA	Iron Age
IG	*Inscriptiones Graecae*
ILN	*Illustrated London News*
JBrit. AA	*Journal of the British Archaeological Association*
JEA	*Journal of Egyptian Archaeology*
Jhb. DAI	*Jahrbuch des Deutschen Archäologischen Institutes*
Jhb. R–GZM	*Jahrbuch des Römisch–Germanischen Zentralmuseums, Mainz*
JRS	*Journal of Roman Studies*
Kat. Brugg	*Das Vindonissa-Museum in Brugg*, 1931
Kat. Xanten	P. Steiner, *Xanten*, 1911
KJb	*Kölner Jahrbuch für Vor- und Frühgeschichte*
Korr. bl. WZ	*Korrespondenzblatt der Westdeutschen Zeitschrift* (issued with *WZ*)
L	Length (of an object)
LMB	Rheinisches Landesmuseum, Bonn
LM Trier	Rheinisches Landesmuseum, Trier
Med. Arch.	*Medieval Archaeology*
Mitt. Anthr. Ges.	*Mitteilungen der Anthropologischen Gesellschaft, Wien*
Mschr. Ges. WD	*Monatsschrift für die Geschichte Westdeutschlands*
MZ	*Mainzer Zeitschrift*
NArch.	*Norfolk Archaeology*
Nass. Ann.	*Annalen des Vereins für Nassauische Altertumskunde und Geschichtsforschung*
NMA	National Museum of Antiquities of Scotland, Edinburgh
NStaffs. J	*North Staffordshire Journal of Field Studies*
Num. Chron.	*Numismatic Chronicle*
ORL	*Der Obergermanisch-Rätische Limes des Römerreiches* (ed. E. Fabricius et al.)
Oseberg I–III	A. W. Brøgger et al., *Osebergfundet* I, 1917; III, 1930

Oud. Med.	*Oudheidkundige Mededelingen van het Rijksmuseum van Oudheden te Leiden*
Ox.	*Oxoniensia*
P. Cair. Isid.	A. E. R. Boak & H. C. Youtie, *The Archive of Aurelius Isidorus*, 1960
P. Ox.	B. P. Grenfell, A. S. Hunt *et al. The Oxyrhynchus Papyri*, 1898
PPS	*Proceedings of the Prehistoric Society*
Proc. CAS	*Proceedings of the Cambridge Antiquarian Society*
Proc. Cott. C	*Proceedings of the Cotteswold Naturalists' Field Club*
PSAN	*Proceedings of the Society of Antiquaries of Newcastle-upon-Tyne*
PSAS	*Proceedings of the Society of Antiquaries of Scotland*
PSI	*Proceedings of the Suffolk Institute of Archaeology*
P. Teb.	B. P. Grenfell *et al. The Tebtunis Papyri*, 1902
PZ	*Prähistorische Zeitschrift*
R–E	Pauly–Wissowa, *Real-Encyclopädie der classischen Altertumswissenshaft*
Rev. Arch.	*Revue Archéologique*
R–G Mus.	Römisch–Germanisches Museum, Köln
R–GZM	Römisch–Germanisches Zentralmuseum, Mainz
Richborough I–IV	J. P. Bushe-Fox, *First (Second etc.) Report on the Excavations of the Roman Fort at Richborough, Kent, Report of the Research Committee of the Society of Antiquaries of London* I, 1926; II, 1928; III, 1932; IV, 1949
Schweiz. LM	Schweizerisches Landesmuseum, Zürich
S–Jb	*Saalburg-Jahrbuch*
Sussex AC	*Sussex Archaeological Collections*
Sussex NQ	*Sussex Notes and Queries*
TAQ	Terminus ante quem
TLL	*Thesaurus Linguae Latinae*
TPQ	Terminus post quem
Trans. AAS	*Transactions of the Architectural and Archaeological Society of Durham and Northumberland*
Trans. BAS	*Transactions of the Birmingham Archaeological Society*
Trans. BG	*Transactions of the Bristol and Gloucester Archaeological Society*
Trans. ERAS	*Transactions of the East Riding Antiquarian Society*
Trans. Woolhope FC	*Transactions of the Woolhope Naturalists' Field Club*
TJhber.	*Trierer Jahresberichte der Gesellschaft für nützliche Forschungen*
TZ	*Trierer Zeitschrift*
V & A	Victoria and Albert Museum, London
VCH Beds.	*The Victoria County History of Bedfordshire* II, 1908
VCH Bucks.	*The Victoria County History of Buckinghamshire* II, 1908
VCH Essex	*The Victoria County History of Essex* III, 1963
Ver. Inst. VF	*Veröffentlichungen des Instituts für Vor- und Frühgeschichte der Universität Köln*
WAM	*Wiltshire Archaeological and Natural History Magazine*

ABBREVIATIONS

Wroxeter I-IV	J. P. Bushe-Fox, *Excavations on the Site of the Roman Town at Wroxeter, Shropshire, Report of the Research Committee of the Society of Antiquaries of London* I, 1913; II, 1914; IV, 1916
WZ	*Westdeutsche Zeitschrift*
YAJ	*Yorkshire Archaeological Journal*
ZAK	*Zeitschrift für Schweizerische Archäologie und Kunstgeschichte*
Zeitschr. Christ. Kunst	*Zeitschrift für Christliche Kunst*
ZMdV	*Zeitschrift für Mitteldeutsche Vorgeschichte*

I

INTRODUCTION

Clothing manufacture must have been carried out in some guise in practically every household in the provinces. In studying it the archaeologist is seeking to regain knowledge that many Romans must have possessed. But because he is, as it were, a bystander, he may be able to form in his own mind a better overall picture of processes and products than any individual Roman could have done.

Many trades and crafts which were once a familiar part of the lives of the inhabitants of the northern Roman provinces were still in being up to a hundred years ago. But most have now been transformed out of all recognition by the rapid advance of modern science and technology. The layman has a reasonable excuse for pleading ignorance of them. But the archaeologist cannot afford to neglect any aspect of the work of the ancient craftsman simply because he does not immediately understand it on the basis of his own experience.

Roman textiles, in contrast to the less easily perishable artefacts such as pottery and metalwork, have not received their fair share of attention. Sixty years ago Hugo Blümner analysed with exemplary thoroughness the literary evidence for Roman textile manufacture in the framework of his masterly and still unsurpassed survey of Greek and Roman technology. Little was known in his day of the archaeological evidence for textiles and textile implements and it would be unjust to criticise him for mentioning them rarely. In recent years a number of important contributions to our knowledge of prehistoric spinning and weaving in Europe have been made, notably by Dr Margrethe Hald, Dr Marta Hoffmann, Dr Agnes Geijer, Miss Audrey Henshall, Mrs Grace Crowfoot, Dr K. Schlabow, Professor H.-J. Hundt and Professor Emil Vogt. Their work has been based largely on archaeological material.

The Roman Empire in the period since Hugo Blümner wrote has been neglected. Professor R. J. Forbes's volume on the textile industry in his series on ancient technology is a very useful secondary source of information, but should be regarded as a card-index rather than a synthesis of present knowledge. Several groups of Roman textiles have been discovered in the cities of Roman Syria and in the Dead Sea region and their publication has been a major event. A selection of the more interesting cloth-fragments from Roman Britain has been published and discussed by Mrs Grace Crowfoot and Miss Audrey Henshall. But no attempt has yet been made to bring Blümner's survey up to date in archaeological terms and offer a connected account of Roman textile manufacture based on all available sources.

Since it was desirable to examine personally all the material which is the basis of this account, my attention has had to be limited geographically to the area which in the fourth century formed the provinces of Britain, Belgica I and II, and Germania I and II. This comprises in modern terms the British Isles and the land on the Continent bounded by the Channel coast, the Rhine and a line drawn from Basel to the mouth of the Somme. The cultural connections between the Belgae in Gaul and Britain and the strong trading contacts between Britain and the Rhineland give this area a certain unity. I have included some important items which were found just beyond these boundaries. The present account cannot claim to be valid for a wider area than its title suggests, but some of my conclusions may be found to have a wider application.

I have limited myself in time to the period from Caesar's conquest of northern Gaul (57 B.C.) until the withdrawal of the Roman administration in the early fifth century. This time-span, however, is in a sense arbitrary; for, as I hope to show in the following chapters, the arrival of the Romans seems to have had little immediate effect on textile techniques. At the end of the Roman occupation the Franks inherited and fostered several fields of Roman technology and it may eventually be possible to establish and trace continuity in the textile industry too.

My account of textile manufacture is based on the extant cloth-fragments (most of which are recorded here for the first time) and on the implements. These have been interpreted in the light of the ancient literary sources and modern parallels from primitive communities. The latter have been of particular value for understanding the implements which can still be seen in use.

Most textile fragments are minute; and the only complete garments in the western provinces, those from Les-Martres-de-Veyre, lie outside our area. I have discussed these at length in an article in *Bonner Jahrbücher* on provincial-Roman clothing.

I have searched through the bulk of the periodical literature and monographs relating to the northern provinces for facts and material; and I have visited most of the major and many of the minor museum collections, either in the knowledge that they did, or the hope that they might, contain something relevant. The bibliography on page 143 ff. lists mainly the primary sources, both archaeological and linguistic, including works from which I have drawn parallels.

I have not attempted a general assessment of the status of the provincial-Roman textile industry in economic and social terms. I hope to do so at a later date, but at the present moment it would not have a great deal of point. Many archaeologists do not yet seem to have realised that economic history is more than a list of known imports and exports. Some effort must be made to assess the volume and balance of trade across provincial boundaries, even if the result at first is largely a series of disappointing question-marks. Until this has been done, there is no background against which an individual industry could be measured. Fieldworkers, perhaps understandably, are inclined to attribute greater significance to those commodities for which there is abundant physical evidence than to those for which the evidence on the ground is meagre.

The place of textile technology in a study of the process of Romanisation in western Europe is a more satisfactory question. I have drawn attention, wherever possible, to the origins of the various techniques and implements, so as to give some impression of Rome's contribution in this field. But it is noteworthy that the two major textile-producing centres in the Roman world lay at opposite ends of the Empire in Northern Gaul and Syria. The heart of the Roman Empire contributed remarkably little in the way of either textile output or technical ideas. In this respect Rome probably gained more from the area under scrutiny in this book than she gave to it.

II

TEXTILE FIBRES

The logical starting-point for a study of textiles and their manufacture in the northern provinces is a consideration of the fibres known to have been available in the area, whether they were produced at home or imported. Textile fibres can be classified as being of animal origin (wool, silk) or of vegetable origin; and the latter category can be further subdivided into fibres from the stalk of a plant (bast) (linen, hemp) or from the seed (cotton). Curiosities such as the mineral asbestos also occur occasionally too.

1. ANIMAL FIBRES

WOOL

Sheep were among the earliest animals to be domesticated, probably before the end of the Mesolithic period in south-west Asia.[1] In addition to meat, milk and manure, they supply what has long been the staple textile fibre—wool. In the Middle Ages, manure and milk were important by-products (sheep are still kept for milk in Germany); but in prehistoric times the increase of the sheep population after the beginning of forest-clearance in the Bronze Age is clearly related to the rise of the woollen industry.[2]

The special properties which wool possesses[3] include:

(1) *Warmth.* The natural wave of the wool fibres (crimp) helps to form air-locks in woollen cloth which give good insulation.

(2) *Elasticity.* Woollen garments are crease-resistant and quickly regain their shape after rough wear.

(3) *Felting.* The crimp of wool fibres enables them to interlock easily in spinning and imparts maximum stability to the woven cloth.

(4) Wool is water-repellent.

---

[1] I am heavily indebted to my friend Dr M. L. Ryder of the Animal Breeding Research Organisation for considerable advice during the preparation of this account of wool. Mesolithic: Ryder (1959). See Ryder's reports on wool fibres in my tables of textiles, p. 89 ff.

[2] Clark (1947), 130.

[3] This information is derived from literature issued by the International Wool Secretariat.

The nature of wool

The wool fibre has a thin outer covering known as the cuticle composed of over-lapping scales within which lies the bulk of the fibre, the cortex (fig. 1). Coarser wool fibres have a central hollow core known as the medulla, and in hairs and kemps this becomes increasingly wider until in the coarsest kemps it occupies most of the width of the fibre.[1]

The sheep's fleece grows from two types of follicles, primaries and secondaries.[2] The primaries produce the coarser fibres of the outer coat, while the secondaries grow the more numerous finer and shorter fibres of the undercoat. Dr M. L. Ryder has recently demonstrated that the pattern of the grouping of these primary and secondary follicles in relation to one another, which he has studied in skin samples taken from modern sheep or from parchments, can give information on the development of fleece types (fig. 2). Progressive improvement of the breed results in a narrowing of the primaries, while the secondaries move from their original position between the primaries (as in the wild sheep) to a point to one side of them (fig. 2).

The secondaries are almost always wool fibres in the strict sense, while the primaries in primitive breeds are coarse fibres known as kemp, or in some cases, hair. Kemp is brittle and characteristically pointed at both ends; it is the rough fibre which sticks up on the surface of Tweed cloth. The precise definition of hair *vis-à-vis* kemp and wool is as yet unresolved, but it seems to hold an intermediate position between the two as regards character, origin and growth.[3]

Modern domestic sheep grow little or no kemp. The presence of comparatively large amounts of it in the fleeces of the most primitive sheep of the Bronze Age was at first not understood by scholars and gave rise to bitter controversy.[4] It was held that kemp represented an admixture of reindeer hair; but it was in fact merely the protective outer coat of the wild sheep.

The wool grown in the provinces

Our knowledge of sheep breeds in the Roman provinces is growing rapidly through the work of Dr M. L. Ryder on fibre-diameters and the follicle-patterns in skin. At least two breeds can be detected in Roman Britain. The first is the Iron-Age type, a small brown sheep with a generalised medium-fine wool fleece (see below),

[1] J. W. S. Hearle *et al.*, *Fibre Structure* (1963); Ryder & Stephenson (1968).
[2] Ryder (1962), 168 ff.; cf. *idem* (1964 *b*), 397.
[3] *Nature*, 178 (1958), 781–3.
[4] Schlabow (1939); von Stokar (1939–40); Schlabow (1941–2).

exemplified in the modern Soay breed of St Kilda. The second is the improved Roman breed, white in colour, with a true fine-wool or generalised medium-fine wool fleece (fig. 3). It was probably imported into Britain and perhaps crossed with the Soay type.

The above statements are supported by the distribution map of British sheep breeds for 1800.[1] Scotland and the western parts of Britain, Wales and Cornwall produce sheep with white or tan faces of which only the rams are horned (e.g. the Cheviot). This sets them apart from the black-faced hairy breeds of eastern and northern Britain, and from the hornless short-woolled Down types. The low gene frequencies of haemoglobin A in the white-faced breeds may be another distinguishing feature.

The white-faced breeds, notably the Shetland, bear a resemblance to the Soay and their distribution on the Celtic fringe suggests strongly that they are descendants of the sheep of Roman Britain. Apart from the intrusion, possibly in Viking times, of the black-faced breeds, brought from Scandinavia, the distribution pattern of 1800 probably reflects approximately the situation at the beginning of the Middle Ages. The mediaeval fine-woolled sheep, on the other hand, which are known from the analysis of samples of dated parchments, are likely to have had a Roman fine-woolled ancestry.

The information gleaned from the map is supplemented by fibre measurements of yarns in Roman provincial textiles. The details are set out below, where the textiles are individually described (tables A, B). The evidence for sheep of Soay type with a generalised medium-fine fleece and for the true fine-woolled sheep in small numbers is convincing.

The Soay or Iron-Age sheep

The Soay of St Kilda off the Outer Hebrides resembles so closely the sheep of Britain in the prehistoric period, in fleece-type and skeletal structure, that it has been accurately described as a living fossil.[2] Cut off from the mainland, the breed is thought to have remained undisturbed in a semi-wild state since pre-Viking times.

The Soay sheep is a small animal (plate I a) standing perhaps 2 feet high at the shoulder. The rams have strong, down-curved horns, while the ewes are often hornless. The creature has a slender frame, but is amazingly agile and in this respect deserves the epithet 'deer-like', which is often applied to it. The short tail (thirteen

---

[1] Ryder (1964 a), 65 ff.; Youatt (1837) for breeds.

[2] Williamson & Boyd (1960), 77 ff.; Boyd et al. (1964); Curle (1911), 371 f. I am grateful to Dr Ryder for allowing me to examine the Soay sheep at the Field Laboratory of the Animal Breeding Research Organisation at Roslin, Midlothian.

vertebrae against twenty in modern breeds) and the throat-fringe of black hair on the rams are primitive characteristics.

The coat is usually a deep chocolate-brown colour, with a lighter patch on the rump and under-belly. The muzzle and legs are darker. Williamson and Boyd[1] reckoned that two-thirds of the Soay sheep in the St Kilda group have this colouring, while the remaining third are of a lighter fawn shade. Jet-black and reddish-brown animals are also found occasionally too. It is useful to compare this colour-range with that of the closest-related improved breed, the Shetland.[2] There, lighter colours are slightly commoner and reddish-brown (moorit) fleeces are also represented. Undyed yarns in shades such as these were often used in antiquity for patterned textiles (see p. 53); but the darker shades had a tendency to fade.

The fleece type of the Soay is a generalised medium-fine wool (that is, mostly of medium-fine fibres, but with a few hairs and kemps in the coat) and is not completely primitive.[3] Some of the animals on St Kilda, however, have a hairy coat with kemps, showing them to be more primitive and closer to the Moufflon. The Iron-Age sheep may have had a greater percentage of coarse fibres. The diameters of the fine secondary follicles of the Soay range from 15 to 25 μ (mean 20 μ) (1 μ = 0.001 mm.) and of the primary follicles 30 to 50 μ (mean 40 μ). The staple length is 7–10 cm. and the wool is soft to handle.[4]

The fleece moults in the summer and the wool can be plucked off, leaving the hair, which falls out naturally in the autumn. But only wool already loosened after the onset of moulting can be plucked; and much of the fleece is unavoidably lost in the fields. The weight of the plucked wool from a single sheep is about 1–1½ lb. as contrasted with the 1½–2 lb. of the Shetland. This is comparable with mediaeval and even Bronze-Age Cretan fleece weights.[5] There is no evidence as to whether the Soay type of sheep were shorn or plucked in Roman Britain.

[1] Williamson & Boyd (1960), 78 ff.
[2] *Sheep Breeding and Management*, Bulletin no. 166, Ministry of Agriculture and Fisheries, 1964, 27 f. A similar range is visible in the North Ronaldsay sheep of Orkney (Ryder in *Scottish Studies* forthcoming).
[3] Mr J. I. Murray (of Keddie, Gordon and Co. (Galashiels)), who has successfully spun and woven a medium-fine 2-over-2 twill cloth from Soay wool, observed (private communication) that the wool was very dirty and low-yielding. But it was equivalent to fine Shetland in quality, and spun without difficulty to a count of 7,000 yards per lb. He noted the tendency to fade.
[4] Ryder (1966).
[5] Killen (1963), 75; but see now *Kadmos*, 4 (1965), 111 ff.

Improved breeds

The sheep with improved fleeces probably had the same woolly primitive ancestors as the Soay, but had been bred on a selective basis.[1] They were physically similar to the Soay, except for having a longer tail.[2] The bulk of the fibres in the coat were fine, but a small number of medium fibres put the fleece into the category of generalised medium-fine wool. The true fine wool, which had been developed in Asia Minor before the first century A.D.,[3] lacked the medium fibres. Both the generalised medium-fine wool and the true fine wool were present in the northern provinces, as analysis of the textiles shows.

Textiles have shown that the colour of the Roman sheep was probably white. In any case natural pigments can be eliminated by selective breeding. This distinguishes them from the brown sheep of the Iron Age and earlier prehistoric periods. They were probably both crossed with the Iron-Age breed and kept as pedigree flocks on the lowlands. It is difficult to estimate to what extent they replaced the earlier breed.[4]

Certain of Ryder's measurements hint that the distinction between the later long-woolled breeds (e.g. the Leicester Longwool)[5] and the short-woolled (e.g. the Down breeds) was beginning to develop in the Roman period (fig. 3). But it is difficult to be sure. The improved sheep were probably shorn, not plucked.[6]

The value of bones to distinguish breeds of sheep is still in dispute.[7] Some scholars assign the prehistoric sheep of Switzerland (the first to be studied seriously) to two breeds differentiated by body size and horns, while others assert that such differences are merely signs of sexual dimorphism in the same breed. Bones found on many sites in the Roman provinces have been examined[8] and compared with those of the Soay, but both the Iron-Age and the Roman sheep were skeletally of Soay type. Bones, it appears, can give no facts about fleece types relevant to a study of textiles.

[1] The wild sheep of Europe, the Moufflon, is generally considered to be the main ancestor of the early British breeds; see Ryder & Stephenson (1968).
[2] See for instance *Atlas of the Early Christian World* (1958), nos. 514–19.
[3] *Nature*, 182 (1958), 781; 204 (1964), 556.   [4] Ryder (1964 a), 66, fig. 11.
[5] *Nature*, 204 (1964), 558; Trow-Smith (1957), 145.   [6] Pliny, *N. H.* VIII. 190.
[7] Zeuner (1963), 187 f.; Boessneck (1958), 88.
[8] Bokerly Dike: Pitt-Rivers (1892), 233–4; Newstead: Curle (1911), 371 f.; Eardarloch Crannog: *PSAS*, LXXVI (1941–2), 63; Mumrills: *PSAS*, LXIII (1928–9), 569; Bar Hill: *ibid.* XL (1905–6), 529; for the continental provinces see Boessneck (1958), 88 ff.

The distribution of flocks

Entries in the Edict of Diocletian and the *Notitia Dignitatum* referring to the two Germanies and Belgica indicate that sheep farming must have played a leading role in the economy of the western provinces, at least in the third and fourth centuries (fig. 4). The wool of the Ambiani, the Atrebates, the Nervii and the Treveri was famous; and the siting of the army's weaving-mills at Reims, Tournai and Trier suggests that some of the wool was channelled into army supply-lines in the fourth century.[1] The estates enclosed by the Langmauer in the South Eifel perhaps supplied wool for the emperors' private weaving-mill at Trier; for the soils which the walls enclosed would be suitable for sheep.[2] There is no denying that the chalk soils of Champagne would be ideal for the large-scale sheep-farming envisaged by Roman agricultural writers.

In Britain the Breckland heath of East Anglia was certainly used for raising sheep as the finds of iron wool-combs there prove (table C).[3] This is the best-attested Roman sheep country in the province. The wool-combs cannot be dated accurately, but may be third-century.

R. G. Collingwood's famous thesis that the downland of southern England was converted into ranches in the fourth century is now under fire. On Cranborne Chase sheep were an important part of a probably mixed farming economy.[4] But the idea that agile animals like the Soay sheep could have been penned into enclosures which some scholars have described as sheep-pens is fanciful.[5] Although the Chase is indeed ideal sheep-country, Collingwood's suggestion still needs proof.

The siting of the *Venta* where an army weaving-mill was established in the fourth century cannot be settled on present evidence,[5] but Winchester on the Wessex Downs is still the best candidate. The downs are likely to have been the home of the improved breeds of sheep; and if two unnamed Panegyrists of the early fourth century are to be trusted,[6] they must have borne a large sheep-population. The *byrrus Britannicus* (cape) and the *tapete Britannicum* (rug),[5] on the other hand, were probably supplied by the most primitive breeds in Britain, roaming the northern uplands; for these garments must have been of particularly hard-wearing wool.

[1] *Edictum Diocletiani*, XIX. 60; XXV. 9; XIX. 32, 54; *Notitia Dignitatum Occidentis*, XI. 56–8.
[2] *TZ*, 6 (1931), 41 ff., 51 f.; cf. *Arch. J*, CIV (1947), 27 ff. But perhaps less of the Eifel was open country than Steinhausen thought.   [3] Manning (1966).   [4] See n. 8, p. 8
[5] I have discussed this question in *Latomus*, XXVI (1967), 648–76; see now Taylor (1967). The absence of liverfluke on downland may have been another factor influencing flock-distribution (Fox (1932), 84).
[6] *Pan.Constantio Caes.* V. XI (A.D. 297): 'tanto laeta numero pastionum'; *Pan Constantino Aug.* VII. IX (A.D. 310) 'pecorum mitium innumerabilis multitudo ... onusta velleribus'.

Strabo notes[1] that the Romans kept 'jacketed', i.e. fine-woolled, sheep in Gallia Belgica, which were probably a legacy from the Belgae. Fine-woolled sheep wore jackets for protection (see below). In Britain also the Belgae may deserve the credit for improving the fleece of the Iron-Age breed and introducing what I have called above the Roman improved breed. The Romans are likely to have added to the flocks of improved sheep by importation from the continental provinces.

Wool in the Mediterranean world

The quality and quantity of the wool available for textiles in the northern provinces was such that little yarn needed to be imported from outside. There was in fact a lively export trade of the valued Gallic wool and Gallic textiles into Italy which increased as time went on.[2] Our knowledge of sheep in the Mediterranean area is limited, since few textiles have been microscopically examined. Literary evidence, although more abundant, is also vaguer and more subjective.

The Tarentine breed (also called 'Greek sheep') probably originated in Asia Minor and had the finest wool in the ancient world.[3] Both generalised medium-fine wool and true fine wool would come under this heading. Sheep of this strain wore 'jackets' or sacking ('*pellitae*') to protect their fleeces, and, according to Columella, required special care in their management. The improved flocks in Britain would belong to this breed.

Flocks with pure-white wool were raised in the first century in northern Italy at Parma, Padua and Mutina.[4] Spain was famous for both jet-black[5] and tawny fleeces, and some breeds in Asia Minor were dark red (moorit?) in colour.[6] Grey sheep (*pulli*) are also mentioned by writers of the early Empire.[7] The colour range is typical of the Soay (p. 7), with the addition of the pure-white wools of the improved breeds.

SILK

The most expensive and highly regarded of the textile fibres known to the ancient world was silk. It was available only in limited quantities, but was greatly in demand, because it possessed the unique quality of sheen.

[1] IV. 196: ἱκανῶς ἀστείας ἐρέας. His information, perhaps from Poseidonius, dates from the latter half of the first century B.C.

[2] See n. 1, p. 9.

[3] Columella, VII. IV. I.

[4] *Ibid.* VII. II. 3–4, 6.

[5] Pliny, *N. H.* VIII. 191.

[6] Columella, VII. II. 4.

[7] *Ibid.* II. 4, 6; Pliny, VIII. 191.

The nature of silk

Silk is the name given to the filament spun by many varieties of insect, but particularly the larvae of moths.[1] They spin it to form a cocoon in which to rest while undergoing transformation from the larval stage into the fully grown insect.

The fibre thus produced is classified as (i) cultivated and (ii) wild silk.

Cultivated silk is spun by the mulberry silk-worm (*Bombyx mori* L.), which is native to the Himalayas and China. It was domesticated in China in the third millenium B.C., but did not reach Europe until the sixth century A.D. During the larval stage it is reared indoors in shallow trays or racks and fed intensively on white-mulberry leaves. The grub shows no inclination to leave the racks and spins its cocoon there after five or six weeks as a larva.

Deep inside its body the grub has twin systems of glands and reservoirs, which make and contain the silk fluid. This is led by two glands to a single aperture in the grub's lower lip, where it issues forth as a double filament. A single grub can spin up to a 1000 metres of silk without a break.

Wild silk is spun by the larvae of many moths of the family Bombycidae, but it lacks some of the special properties of cultivated silk. In many cases the cocoons are too small to be of commercial value. The commonest of the wild silk moths is the *Antheraea mylitta* Drury, native to India, which gave its name, Tussah, to the whole class of wild silks.[2]

There are two European silk moths, the *Pachypasa otus* Drury and the *Saturnia pyri*, which are at home in the central and eastern Mediterranean. It has been argued, but not conclusively proved, that these two moths spun the famous Coan silks.[3] The larva of the *Pachypasa* feeds on the leaves of the ash, cypress, juniper, pine and various types of oak. The *Saturnia pyri* prefers ash and apple. The cocoons are larger than those of the *Bombyx mori* (7–9 cm. long) and form a loose, soft, woolly web. The grub cannot be fully domesticated, but can only be reared near the owner's house on a supply of the right kind of leaves. *Saturnia pyri* spins the finer thread.

The structure of silk thread consists of an inner core of *fibroin* (the actual silk) and an outer coating of *sericin*, the gum which holds the cocoon together.[4] The fibre must be de-gummed in hot water before it can be unwound from the cocoon. Wild silk is flattish in section, with surface striations, while cultivated silk appears somewhat rounder: both have a double filament.[5] The fibre diameter of true silk is

---

[1] *CIBA-Review*, 53 (1946), for full account; cf. Murphy (1911), I, 60 ff.
[2] Pfister (1934), 56.
[3] Pfister (1934), 55, quoting Demaison. Pfister objects that *Pachypasa* is extremely rare; cf. Forbes (1930), 25.
[4] *CIBA-Review*, III (1955), 4025.   [5] Pfister (1934), 55.

reckoned by Pfister to lie between 8 and 15 μ; that of *Pachypasa* measures 12–18 μ and of *Antheraea mylitta* (Tussah) 40–50 μ. It is thus possible to classify the silk of ancient textiles roughly on the strength of fibre measurements. The natural colours of *Bombyx* silk are white, yellow, brown or green.[1]

The special properties of silk

(1) *Sheen or lustre*. Unlike most textile fibres, silk has few surface-irregularities and so reflects light. Its lustre can be accentuated by pattern-weaving.

(2) *Warmth and smoothness*. Although it has a cold handle superficially and lacks the insulating properties of wool, silk is ideal for garments worn next to the skin.

Silk in the north

Silk is rarely found in the northern provinces, but was an object of trade from the earliest times. Sericulture in Europe is a relatively modern introduction. The first dated find of silk is of the late sixth century B.C. One of the Hallstatt *Fürstengräber* of the Hohmichele in Württemberg (*c.* 500 B.C.) contained a woollen textile embroidered with what Professor H.-J. Hundt tentatively identified as silk.[2] A second find of the same period from Rheingönheim confirmed this.[3] These surprising discoveries show that silk was known even to the prehistoric communities of northern Europe.

In the Roman period silk has been found in a second-century grave in Bavaria.[4] Remains of three damask silk textiles were recovered from the coffin of St Paulinus at Trier (late fourth century) (table B, 86–8) and in a burial of late-Roman date at Conthey in the Wallis (table B, 85). Both fabrics had spun warps, which points to their having been woven within the Empire (silk thread was not spun in Han China, see p. 51). A Latin embroidered factory-mark on the Trier fragments has been thought to indicate a workshop in Italy as the centre of production (see p. 51 and table B, 86). Woollen cloth from an early fourth-century grave at Aquincum-Budapest was embroidered in silk, definitely identified as *Bombyx* silk.[5] The Latin loanword *serica* in Old Welsh shows that silk was known in Britain also.[6] This appears to be

[1] *CIBA-Review*, 111 (1955), 4014; 53 (1946), 1906.

[2] Riek & Hundt (1962), 206 ff.

[3] Unpublished information from Professor Hundt. Miss Richter suggests that the *amorgis* of Aristophanes is a wild silk (*AJA*, XXXIII (1929), 27), but the passages she quotes seem to refer to a fine *bast* fibre, perhaps *Malva Silvestris* as others have supposed.

[4] Unpublished information from Professor Hundt.

[5] *Arch. Ért.* 91 (1964), 192–3; cf. also *Acta Antiqua*, XIII (1965), 259 ff.

[6] Jackson (1953), 78.

confirmed by the discovery that cloth fragments from a Roman barrow at Holborough in Kent (probably dated to the third century) are probably damask silk (table A, 51).

Silk in the Empire

Aristotle's succinct description of the life-cycle of the wild silk moth does not give enough information to permit identification of the species with accuracy.[1] Other ancient accounts of the origins of silk are hopelessly garbled.[2] The Aegean island of Cos, the best-known centre of sericulture, appears to have declined in importance after the first century A.D., perhaps because it could not compete with the imported silks.[3] Analysis by Pfister of the fabrics found at Palmyra (before c. A.D. 276) has shown that many varieties of wild silk, as well as the thread of the *Bombyx mori*, were imported from India and China.[4] The Hadrianic *Periplus of the Erythraean Sea* lists both silk yarn (νῆμα) and woven silk fabrics among Roman imports from the Far East.[5]

It is difficult to judge how much silk was available in the Mediterranean world. There is no need to believe that Elagabalus in the early third century was the first to wear a garment of pure silk,[6] for there seems to have been an abundant supply 200 years earlier. There can be little doubt from the entries in the Edict that the silk trade was even brisker in the late Empire.

2. VEGETABLE FIBRES

LINEN

The most important of the bast fibres, linen, is known to have been used for textiles as early as the seventh millenium B.C.[7] It has qualities which wool does not possess, and so it survived in face of competition from the more versatile animal fibre.

---

[1] Aristotle, *H.A.* v. 19; Forbes (1930), 25, suggests that he is referring to both types of European wild silk-moth. [2] See Forbes (1956), 50 ff.

[3] The Edict of Diocletian (XXIII. 2; XXIV. 13) suggests that the unravelling and spinning of wild silk continued in the eastern provinces until the introduction of the *Bombyx mori* in A.D. 513–514.

[4] Pfister (1934), 55–6.

[5] *Periplus M.E.* 39; for the date of the document see *Num. Chron.*[7] 4 (1964), 271 (Hadrianic) against *Journal Asiatique* (1961), 441 ff. (early third century). I cannot follow A. Dihle (1965) in his return to a first-century dating.

[6] SHA, *Elagabalus* 26. 1; cf. Tacitus, *Ann.* II. 33. 1. The abundant Roman coin-finds in India probably represent in part payment for silk.

[7] At Çatal Hüyük in Anatolia: *ILN*, 9 Feb., 1963, 197; Ryder (1965), 175 f.; but see *Archaeology*, 16 (1963), 33–46. Present evidence favours Ryder's identification of the fibre as flax.

The nature of linen

The flax plant supplies both a fibre, linen, which is stripped from its main stalk, and linseed oil, which is crushed from its seed-bolls.[1] Cultivated flax (*Linum usitatissimum*) developed from one of the several varieties of wild flax, such as were used for textiles in the Neolithic period in the Swiss Lake-Dwellings. Before the Roman period cultivated flax had established itself everywhere.[2]

The flax plant has a single erect stem up to 1 metre tall (fig. 7), which branches only at the top, where it bears a number of small flowers.[3] Narrow lanceolate leaves sprout from alternate sides of the stalk. It is best suited to a temperate climate, with little sun and moist winds, and demands a rich, deep soil.[4] Well-drained and tilled alluvial deposits are ideal for it. It is said by Pliny to exhaust the soil, but doubt has recently been cast upon this statement.[5]

The flax seed, according to Columella, should be sown between October and December,[6] but Pliny observes that the Gauls do not sow it until March.[7] The seeds are scattered thickly to encourage a tall stalk.[8] The plant ripens five to six months after sowing, and is reaped before the seeds are fully ripe.[9] Harvested too early, the plant gives soft and weak fibres, while late reaping allows the woody core to harden. It is pulled by hand, not cut.

The stem of flax is made up of a thick woody core surrounded by an outer bark: between them, parallel to the core, lie the linen fibres. The actual fibre is hexagonal in section with a central channel or lumen. It has an even diameter throughout its length, but is interrupted at intervals by knots which break its regularity (fig. 6).[10]

The properties of linen

(1) *Tensile strength and durability.* Linen is particularly valuable for sail-cloth.

(2) *Fineness of fibre.* It is possible to weave exceedingly fine cloth.

(3) *Smooth handle.*

(4) *Whiteness (bleached).* Linen fabric is often praised in antiquity because whiteness has associations with purity and cleanliness.

---

[1] Bradbury (1920); *CIBA-Review*, 49 (1945), 1773 ff.; *RE* VI, 2 (1909), 2435–84 for full references.

[2] La Baume (1961), 36 f.

[3] Plutarch, *Is. et Os.* 4; cf. Murphy (1911), I, 96.

[4] Pliny *N.H.* XVIII. 165, quoting Varro.

[5] Pliny *N.H.* XVII. 56, quoting Vergil *Georg.* I. 77; cf. Bradbury (1920), 28 f.

[6] Columella II. x. 17 (1 October–1 December).   [7] *N.H.* XVIII. 205.

[8] Columella, II. x. 17.   [9] *N.H.* XIX. 16 ff.

[10] Bradbury (1920), 9; von Stokar (1934), 313, Abb. 3.

Linen in the northern provinces

The linen industry of the northern provinces does not appear to have been on a large scale. Supplies may have been augmented by imports from Italy and southern Gaul.

Two Bronze-Age sites in Britain have yielded flax seeds, which indicate that flax was grown there at that time.[1] Seeds from wells at Silchester and Pevensey described as probably of flax are the sole direct evidence for the Roman period.[2] Glass linen-polishers found at South Shields (Co. Durham) (fig. 76) and Hees near Nijmegen on the Rhine suggest the presence of an industry in those parts.[3]

Flax grows well near the sea-coast[4] and it is interesting to note that the Morini (Pas-de-Calais) and the Caleti (Le Havre) were famous for linens in the first century A.D., according to Pliny.[5] Remains of linen textiles are relatively common (tables A, B); but they may have been spun and woven anywhere within the western Empire (see p. 44).

The nearest large centre of flax-growing from which supplies could be drawn was in the Rhône valley. There was an imperial linen-mill at Arles in the fourth century and linen-merchants were operating from Lugdunum (Lyon) at an earlier date.[6] The neighbouring Cadurci and Ruteni are found in Pliny's list of linen-growers.[5] Flax was grown on the sea-coast and in some of the major river valleys of Spain, while further afield the Po valley was the most important Italian source.[7] Linen of the highest quality was exported from Syria and Egypt; and eastern linens appear to have monopolised the entire imperial market in the late third and early fourth centuries.[8] It is doubtful if their products reached the north in significant quantities (see p. 44).

HEMP

Hemp was a textile fibre of secondary importance in antiquity. It was more suitable for ropes and sail-cloth than for articles of clothing, and it never proved a serious competitor to fine linens. Its value as a narcotic was possibly discovered first.[9]

[1] Jessen & Helbaek (1944), 55 ff. The flax may have been raised for linseed oil only.
[2] *Archaeologia*, LVII (1898), 254; *Arch. J*, LXV (1908), 135.
[3] South Shields: PSAN⁴, 6 (1934), 355-7 (University Museum of Antiquities, Newcastle-upon-Tyne); Hees: Brunsting (1937), 184 Vondst. 25, Nr. 7 (Rijksmuseum G. M. Kam, Nijmegen, B.C.I. 121). Both are third-century.   [4] Bradbury (1920), 21.
[5] Pliny, *N.H.* XIX. 8. He states vaguely that all the Gauls wove linen and the Germans knew it too.
[6] *Notitia Dignitatum Occidentis* XI. 62; *CIL*, XIII. 1995. 1998.
[7] Pliny, *N.H.* XIX. 8-10.   [8] *Edictum Diocletiani*, XXVI-XXVIII.
[9] Good accounts of hemp in *CIBA-Review*, 5 (1962), (by L. Castellini); 49 (1945), 1779 ff.; *R.E.* VII, 2 (1912), 2313-6; Godwin (1967).

The nature of hemp

The plant hemp (*Cannabis sativa* L.) was at home in the lands south and east of the Caspian Sea, where it still grows wild. Its progress westwards was slow, but it seems to have preceded the Roman advance in areas that were later incorporated in the Empire.

Hemp is dioecious; that is, the male and female plants are separate.[1] It is characterised by a tap-root and a long hollow stem, the lumen of which is partitioned at intervals by woody knots. The leaves (which are absent on the lower stalk when the plants are grown close together) vary in shape, but resemble in general outline a hand with fingers outstretched. The stem branches only at the top, where it bears clusters of minute flowers. The plant may grow as much as 5 metres (15 ft. 6 in.) high; 'as high as a tree' in Pliny's words.[2]

Hemp requires much the same climate and soil as flax does, although it needs a higher summer temperature. Rich soil, deep and well tilled, is ideal; and it should be moist, but not waterlogged.[3] The seed is sown in spring, densely scattered to stimulate upward growth.[4] The plants grown for fibre are not allowed to become fully ripe before being harvested (see p. 29) and are usually pulled at the height of the summer. Pliny, however, in his brief but excellent account of hemp-growing, implies that an early autumn harvest was usual in Italy in the first century A.D.[5]

The fibre bundles which form between the bark (cortex) and core (medulla) vary in fineness.[6] The primary fibres nearest the woody parts (as Pliny notes[4]) are longer than (8–23 mm.), but not so fine as, the secondaries (2–4 mm. long). The primaries show an irregular polygon in section, while the secondaries are more regular. The knots in the individual fibres do not block their hollow centres.

Hemp in the northern provinces

Hemp advanced westward from its homeland along two distinct routes. It reached the Germanic peoples before the completion of the first Germanic sound-shift, well before the Roman invasion.[7] This suggests a line of penetration north of the Danube. On the other hand Athenaeus[8] (writing *c.* A.D. 200 about an event in the mid-third

---

[1] *CIBA-Review*, 5 (1962), 4.
[2] Pliny, *N.H.* XIX. 174.
[3] *CIBA-Review*, 5 (1962), 9.
[4] Pliny, *N.H.* XIX. 173.
[5] Pliny, *N.H.* XIX. 173; Columella, II. X. 21.
[6] *CIBA-Review*, 5 (1962), 12; von Stokar (1934), 313 f.
[7] Godwin (1967); Walde & Hofmann (1938), *s.v. cannabis*. The *terminus ante quem* for the completion of the first sound-shift varied from area to area; see Weisgerber (1966–7), 209 f.
[8] *Deipnosophistae*, v. 206 f.

century B.C.) says that hemp was grown in the Rhône valley, where flax later flourished. It was probably planted there by the Greek colonists, with whom it had travelled along the sea-routes of the Mediterranean.

Ropes of hemp, mentioned frequently by ancient writers, have been recovered from wells in the Roman forts of the Saalburg and Zugmantel on the Upper-German Limes[1] (the rope from the Antonine fort at Bar Hill has now been shown to be of elder[2]. It was used as sewing thread by a cobbler at Köln.[3] A fragment of plain-weave fabric, perhaps the lining of a purse, from Alzey (table B, 36) was identified as hemp by von Stokar. The yarn is Z-spun (see p. 44), and may be a northern product; there is no other evidence for clothing of hemp or for the cultivation of the plant in the North. Asia Minor, particularly the towns of Alabanda and Mylasa in Caria,[4] supplied the Roman world with the highest-quality fibre, but it is likely that hemp was grown in many places on a small scale for local needs.

COTTON

Cotton is the only fibre from the seed of a plant which was of commercial value in antiquity. Recent finds suggest that it was more widely used than was hitherto imagined.

The nature of cotton

Theophrastus' excellent description of cotton-growing in India can serve as an introduction.[5] (His facts were collected in the late fourth century B.C., probably from members of Alexander the Great's entourage.) 'The plants from which they [the Indians] make their clothes have a leaf which is like the black mulberry, but the whole plant resembles the wild rose. They plant it in rows in the plains, and so, when viewed from a distance, they look like vines.' Of cotton-growing in Bahrein in the Persian Gulf he writes: 'These cotton-plants have a leaf like the vine, but smaller, yet bear no fruit. The capsule which contains the wool is as big as a spring apple when closed up; but when it is ripe, it unfolds and puts forth the wool, from which they weave fine cloth, some cheap, some very expensive.'[6]

There is little to add to Theophrastus' account.[7] The cup-shaped flowers are purple,

[1] References in R-E VII, 2 (1912), 2315; Jacobi (1897), I, 161, 166; S-Jb, III (1912), 67. I am grateful to Mr A. C. Sanctuary of Bridport-Gundry for discussing hempen ropes with me.

[2] PSAS, XL (1905–6), 531. I owe this information to Professor H. Godwin.

[3] Germ. 10 (1926), 49 (c. A.D. 150–250).   [4] Pliny, N.H. XIX. 174.

[5] Theophrastus, H.P. IV. IV. 8.

[6] Ibid. IV. VII. 7.

[7] Brown & Ware (1958), 33 ff.; CIBA-Review, 95 (1952), 3402 ff.

and after pollination develop seed-capsules (bolls), *c.* 3 cm. in diameter (fig. 5). Two species of the genus *gossypium* were known in antiquity, *Gossypium arboreum*, tree-cotton, which is native to India and the Sudan and grows to 2 metres in height, and *Gossypium herbaceum*, which is at home in the Nile valley and grows only 60–120 cm. high. Both are perennials.

The fibre grows on the seeds within the boll, and when the capsule splits in the summer, the seeds and cotton-wool are picked out by hand. The fibres are classified as *lint* (the long, single-cell, hairs) and *fuzz* (the short hairs, of little value for textiles). The structure of the lint fibres resembles a hollow tube, which dries out in the final days of ripening and twists itself into irregular spirals. The staple length is 2–2.5 cm.

The properties of cotton fabrics

(1) *Attractive handle.* Cotton lacks the harshness of linen, and is softer to the touch.

(2) *Lightness.* This quality is particularly relevant in the hot climates where the cotton plant flourishes.

Cotton in the provinces

Cotton has rarely been identified among the textiles in Britain and the Rhineland. The only find so far is a piece of cotton thread from an early-fourth-century well near Chew Stoke in Somerset.[1] The mummified body of a woman of fourth-century date was found on the Táborberg near Aquincum-Budapest, wrapped in a series of strips of a cotton and wool union-fabric.[2] A similar mummy was found recently in a tomb on the Via Cassia near Rome; this, too, had a cotton winding-sheet.[3] There is a possibility of direct oriental influence in each case.

Cotton was grown, woven and worn in the Sudan in the Roman period,[4] and the contemporary papyri from Egypt mention cotton clothing comparatively frequently.[5] But it forms only a small proportion of the textiles found at Dura-Europus and Palmyra in Syria.[6] The *Periplus of the Erythraean Sea* gives the impression of a brisk import trade in Indian cotton fabrics, which must have been highly priced when they reached the Mediterranean.[7]

Cotton was grown at Elis in Achaea in the late second century A.D., according to

[1] Biek (1963), 148. It was identified by the Shirley Institute, Manchester; information from Dr Biek, who kindly states that it is S-spun.
[2] Nagy (1935), 33 ff. with microphotographs.
[3] Castellani (1964), 140 (no evidence cited).
[4] Griffith & Crowfoot (1934), 5–12.
[5] Winter & Youtie (1944), 249–58, citing texts of papyri.
[6] *Dura* (1945), 53 no. 262; Palmyra: Pfister (1937), 15 f.   [7] *Periplus M.E.* 41, 48.

Pausanias;[1] and a semi-wild form of the plant still exists in Greece. The literary evidence for the use of the fibre in Europe is unsatisfactory; for the terms *carbasus* and *byssus* can refer to any fine cloth of vegetable origin.[2] Cotton is not mentioned in any of the surviving fragments of the Edict of Diocletian.

To sum up: cotton, when and if it occurs in the northern provinces, must be classed as a rare luxury fabric.

3. MISCELLANEOUS FIBRES

The five fibres described in the preceding part of this chapter are the only ones which were of economic importance to the Empire as a whole. In the individual provinces additional sources of spun thread of local origin were exploited. The complete list of all the textile fibres mentioned in the literature is of formidable length and provides proof of considerable ingenuity on the part of the provincials. I have chosen for discussion a certain number of the more important of these fibres which are relevant to the northern provinces.

ANIMAL FIBRES

Rabbit hair

The Latin word *lepus* covers both the hare and the rabbit and where no explicit description of the animal is given it is difficult to distinguish them.[3]

The rabbit (properly *cuniculus*, but more often *lepus*) was native to, and exceedingly common in, the Iberian Peninsula and the Balearic Isles. The soft, silky hair was difficult to spin, Pliny says,[4] because of the shortness of the staple. (The modern Angora rabbit, improved by selective breeding, grows hair up to 10 cm long.)

Because of the confusion of the terms, it is hard to decide whether the fibres of the hare were used too. The Cappadocian *lepus*, which was responsible for the *vestes leporinae*, is more likely to have been a hare than a rabbit, unless the rabbit was more widely known than ancient writers lead us to suppose.[5]

The Edict of Diocletian lists a number of body garments as *leporinus*; and *lana leporina*, rabbits' wool, is relatively expensive.[6] The fact that such fabrics are noted

[1] Pausanias, VII. 26. 6. Flax, hemp and *byssus* (cotton ?) are here listed as plants grown in Elis; cf. Pliny, *N.H.* XIX. 20.   [2] *TLL s.v. carbasus, byssus.*

[3] Walde & Hofmann (1938), *s.v. lepus.*   [4] *N.H.* VIII. 219.

[5] *Descriptio Totius Mundi*, 40; for date and credentials of the document see *Seminarium Kondakovianum*, 8 (1936), 1 ff.

[6] *Edictum Diocletiani*, XIX. 62; XXV. 7; cf. *BCH*, LXXVIII (1954), 358 f.; Mommsen & Blümner (1893), *ad loc.*

in the Edict at all suggests that in the late Empire they had a certain economic value.

No fragments of *vestes leporinae* have been found or identified in the northern provinces, but an insole-sock from Basel (table B, 97) was made of hares' wool. The hare and the rabbit (either wild, or reared specially in *leporaria*) were probably among the fauna of Roman Britain.[1]

Goats' hair

Garments made of coarse hair are not comfortable to wear: hair-shirts are traditionally associated with asceticism. Goats' hair falls into this category, and while it was used for ropes, tents and sails,[2] few people except the very poor wore it.[3] It was used for sacking[4] and was found in some quantity at Dura.[5] No trace of its use in the North has come to light; but the goat was ubiquitous as a domestic animal and it would be strange if its fibres were *not* used.

Pinna

The discovery in a grave at Aquincum-Budapest of small fragments of textile woven from the fibres secreted by the *pinna nobilis* (a variety of mollusc) provides confirmation of the literary evidence for this practice.[6] Blümner, commenting on the ἐρέα θαλάσσια of Diocletian's Edict, cites the relevant passages and gives good grounds for believing that Diocletian's 'marine wool' is the product of the *pinna*.[7]

The *pinna nobilis* is an elongated member of the mussel family, whose habitat is the Mediterranean[8]. It grows up to 40 cm. in length and like the rest of its family exudes a fibre (now called *byssus*), with which it anchors itself to any firm object. The *pinna* has an extensible 'foot', with a groove running across it from the byssus gland. By alternately cupping and relaxing its 'foot', it spins many short lengths of fibre which may eventually cover the whole area of the hinge between the two halves of the shell. The filaments are 40–60 μ in diameter, yellow, vitreous and without visible structure.[9] They have been woven until recently in southern Italy.

[1] The skeletons of a rabbit and a hare were found in a mid-third-century pit (7 ft. 6 in., 2.25 m., down) at the villa on Hambledon Down, Bucks. (*Archaeologia*, 71 (1920–1), 164). The rabbit could be a later intrusion.

[2] Columella, VII. VI. 2, quoting Vergil.

[3] Pliny, *N.H.* VIII. 203.

[4] *P. Cair. Isid.* 74. 9 (A.D. 315): σάκκος τριχίνος.

[5] *Dura* (1945), 56 ff., nos. 267–88.

[6] Nagy (1935), 37.

[7] Mommsen & Blümner (1893), 159 f., 167 f.

[8] L. A. Borradaile and F. A. Potts, *The Invertebrata*, 2nd ed. (1951), 583.

[9] Pfister (1934), 34. Pfister's objections to Blümner's interpretation of θαλάσσιος are based on the erroneous idea that the Edict only applied to the eastern provinces; see now Lauffer (1964).

BAST FIBRES

Experiments were made to strip the bast fibres from the stalks of many varieties of plant and weave them into fabrics.[1] In the following paragraphs I shall mention two of them.

Mallow

Isidore states that *vestis molochinia* is woven from the stalk of the mallow plant (*malva*);[2] the *Periplus* includes mallow cloth among the imports from the port of Barygaza in the Dekkan.[3] Both tree-mallow (*Lavatera arborea* L.) and common mallow (*Malva sylvestris*) belong to the flora of the northern provinces. The former grows 2–3 metres in height, the latter 45–90 cm.[4] While there is no direct evidence that mallow cloth was woven in the north, it is worth adding on account of the bast fibres listed in the textile catalogue which remain unidentified.

Nettles

No classical author refers to nettles as a source of textile fibre, but they have been popular in the North since the Bronze Age. The earliest known fabric of nettle was found in a Late-Bronze-Age cinerary urn at Voldtofte in Denmark.[5] Margrethe Hald, who gathered much curious information about the uses of the plant,[6] states that nettle cloth was highly prized in Scandinavia in the seventeenth and eighteenth centuries. So far, no Roman finds have come to light.

THE MINERAL ASBESTOS

A late-Roman burial in Köln contained the remains of a cloth, or perhaps cushion stuffing, made of asbestos.[7] Strabo and Pliny both attest its use for table-napkins which could be burnt clean instead of washed. They regarded it as a curiosity.[8]

Amphibole asbestos, which corresponds best to the colour mentioned in antiquity, occurs in veins as slip-fibres or cross-fibres up to 3 cm. in length. The individual fibres can easily be loosened from the mass and are polygonal in cross-section.[9] Pliny comments that they were difficult to spin because of their shortness. Quarries near Carystus in Euboea seem to have been the main supply centre in the Roman period.[8]

[1] Forbes (1956), 58 ff.   [2] *Origines*, XIX. 22. 12.
[3] *Periplus M.E.* 48; cf. Pfister (1934), 21.
[4] A. R. Clapham *et al.*, *Flora of the British Isles* (1952), 369, 372; cf. *Archaeologia*, LVII (1898), 254.
[5] *Aarbøger* (1943), 99–102.   [6] *Folk-Liv* (1942), 28–49.
[7] *KJb*, 6 (1962–3), 155. It was examined at the Botanisches Institut der Universität, Köln. For Hallstatt asbestos see *Germ.* 30 (1952), 36.
[8] Strabo, X. 1. 6; Pliny, *N.H.* XIX. 19.   [9] W. Lindgren, *Mineral Deposits* (1933), 394 ff.

III

PREPARATION OF TEXTILE FIBRES
FOR SPINNING

None of the fibres described in the preceding chapter is immediately ready for spinning. All of them require a greater or lesser amount of preparation to separate them from the animals or plants of which they were once a part and to remove any impurities from them.

1. WOOL

The shearing of sheep by hand on the moorland farms of northern Britain at the present day corresponds closely to Varro's description of the practice as it was carried out in contemporary Italy. My own account is based on these two sources.[1]

(Columella advocates a preliminary washing of the fine-woolled sheep,[2] but did not consider it necessary for any other breed.)

Shearing takes place in northern Europe in late spring or early summer; but the precise time will depend on the region and the weather. A sunny warm day is chosen, so that the fleece will dry out quickly from the morning dew and the grease (lanolin, *oesypum*) runs easily. The flock is gathered into stone-built pens or contained within hurdles, and the animals are taken out for shearing individually.

At this season the spring growth of wool at the base of the fibres (the 'rise'), about 1 cm. in length, is practically free of crimp and can be readily distinguished. The clipper shears the winter wool off, leaving the rise behind to give the sheep some protection. The animals are seldom scratched, but if they are, Varro advised that a solution of pitch be dabbed on the cut.

Sheep-shears consist of two blades hinged with a simple spring (fig. 8) and they have not changed their shape since the earliest times. The clipper grasps them in his right hand at the point where the blades join the handle. To shear efficiently, he must apply oblique pressure while drawing the two blades together, so that the cutting edges are always in contact with one another. The most satisfactory length for the cutting edge is about 15 cm. While it is difficult to recognise ancient sheep-

---

[1] Varro, *R.R.* II. 11. 6–9. I am grateful to Mr Leonard Scarr of Bainbridge, Wensleydale, for allowing me to take part in his shearing.

[2] Columella, XI. II. 35.

shears by their shape alone, it is fairly certain that shears with blades much longer or shorter than 15 cm. are not for clipping sheep.[1]

The older and less effective method of plucking rather than shearing had died out almost everywhere in Italy before the end of the first century A.D.[2] It may have continued among the mountain flocks of the North; but it is reasonable to assume that shearing was normal in Britain and the Rhineland. The great advantage of shearing is that the entire fleece can be removed in one piece (the 'clip', πόκος). It can then be easily rolled up into a compact bale for transportation and no wool is lost.

The freshly clipped fleeces (*lana sucida*) were submitted to a preliminary scouring (*putare*) to remove the bulk of the lanolin and impurities.[3] There is little known about the process, but it was probably carried out in tubs, for the lanolin was sometimes recovered and sold as a medicament.[4] The root of the plant soap-wort (*Saponia officinalis*) was employed as a cleansing agent to loosen the grease, but impurities such as burrs (which the Tarentine sheep in their jackets avoided) would have to be plucked out by hand.

It was normal in antiquity to dye wool in the fleece before spinning; the recipes for purple contained in the *Papyrus Holmiensis*,[5] together with many indirect references, make this clear (see pp. 79–80). A Roman terracotta model of a bale of raw wool found in the Broch of Dun an Iardhard on the Isle of Skye bears traces of green paint as if it were meant to represent green-dyed wool[6] (plate XII c). Wool, however, was dyed in the piece as well. I have included a discussion of the dyeing and colouring processes in a later chapter on cloth-finishing. The different coloured yarns for check fabrics (*scutulata*) must logically have been dyed before weaving, the indigo-dyed Thorsberg check *Mantel* being a case in point.[7] On the other hand, un-dyed yarns in natural colours may often have been used for fabrics such as the Falkirk tartan (table A, 42): these had the advantage over dyed yarns of being fast to washing.

[1] I have not compiled a table of the sheep-shears in the northern provinces because of the difficulty of identifying them. But four identical pairs of shears from a depot-find of the late third century at Wald-fischbach (Kr.Pirmasens) (length 27 cm. overall, cutting edges 15 cm.) may be sheep-shears (Sprater (1929), I, 65, Abb. 59; Historisches Museum der Pfalz, Speyer).

[2] Pliny, *N.H.* VIII, 191. In Roman Egypt there were semi-professional sheep-shearers (my note in *Hommages à Marcel Renard* (1969), 817–9).

[3] Varro, *R.R.* II. 2. 18; cf. Columella, XI. II. 35.   [4] Pliny, *N.H.* XXIX. 35.

[5] Lagercrantz (1913) for recipes for a number of dyes.

[6] *PSAS*, LXVI (1931–2), 289–90, fig. 2 (NMA). Miss Henshall kindly informed me that the colour overlies a thin layer of stucco. A similar object in the BM (1953 . 10–6 . 1) was found in a garden at Sible Hedingham, Essex (unpublished information from Mr K. S. Painter).

[7] Cf. Wild (1964); Schlabow (1951), 176 ff., 180.

The final stage in the preparation of wool for spinning is represented by the two operations of 'carding' and combing. Knots, tangles and the remaining impurities are removed in this way from the scoured wool.

Carding, if it existed at all in the modern sense, would have been subsidiary to combing. The basic modern distinction between the thicker *woollen* yarns of carded wool and the fine *worsted* yarns, composed of long fibres lying parallel to one another, was not made in antiquity. But Pliny knew that short-stapled wool is unsuitable for fine cloth.[1]

CARDING AND TEASING

Wool of which the fibres were too short to be effectively combed had nevertheless to be freed from knots and tangles. From the early Middle Ages onward[2] this was done with a pair of hand-cards—small square boards with handles, set with little metal hooks. A handful of wool was placed on the hooks of one card, while the other card was drawn across it repeatedly in the same direction, drawing the wool out flat and removing any knots. By reversing the direction the wool could then be rolled up into a long sausage, which could be wound round the distaff ready for spinning. The name *card* (from *carduus*, thistle) was transferred from an older implement set with teazle-heads which was used for raising the nap on cloth during finishing (see p. 83); but as an implement for the preparation of wool the card was unknown before the fourteenth century.

It would be natural to look for an analogous process in the Roman period; but there is little direct evidence and there are no archaeological remains. Varro, the most helpful source, explains the rare verbs *carminare* and *carere* as 'to draw out (*deducere*) the wool and free it from impurities'.[3] The guild of *lanarii carminatores* of Brixellum (Brescello) may have had a function parallel to that of the *lanarii pectinarii* (woolcombers)[4] of Brixia (Brescia). To employ the word 'carding' of a process in the Roman period is probably an anachronism; but it seems that an operation was practised which was not combing, yet succeeded in removing by some method most of the foreign matter. What it was precisely we do not know. It may have amounted to little more than teasing the wool out by hand.

[1] *N.H.* VIII. 190.
[2] Singer Holmyard (1956), II, 193 f.; cf. Hoffmann (1964), 287 f.
[3] Varro, *L.L.* VII. 339 (54).
[4] Brixellum: *CIL*, XI. 1031; Brixia: *CIL*, V. 4501; cf. *CIL*, V. 4504, 4505. *Lanarii* in the Edict of Diocletian (XXI. 1–4) were probably preparers of wool, *pace* Mommsen & Blümner (1893), *ad loc.*

COMBING

Long-stapled wool is at the present day combed to remove any short wool (noils) and draw the long fibres parallel to one another. A finer, more even, thread can be spun with combed wool than with uncombed because fewer fibres are needed to form a stable yarn. Combing, however, was not confined to long-stapled wool in the Roman period. A number of flat iron combs with long teeth similar to, but not identical with, the wool-combs of modern times provide adequate evidence that wool-combing was carried on in the northern provinces.

The five combs found in East Anglia (table C) belong to a regional type which has at one end 22–23 teeth and at the other two broad prongs which may have been slotted into a wooden framework or post (fig. 10; plate I *b*). A commoner type of similar size found on the Continent has long teeth at both ends and there are approximately the same number of teeth in each row (fig. 9; table C, 4–6).[1] Both varieties of comb are cut from a flat piece of iron measuring 25–35 cm. by 10 cm. The teeth are cut with a saw and are often irregular. Although the combs from Straubing, Uranje, Waldfischbach and Worlington were found in hoards of iron-work, there is no complete example.

It is reasonable to assume from their shape, on analogy with the mediaeval specimens, that the comb was set in, or firmly attached to, a post. The East Anglian type may have been set with the teeth pointing upwards. A wall-painting from the workshop of Verecundus at Pompeii shows (unfortunately somewhat indistinctly) three seated male figures who are combing fibres, probably wool[2] (plate II). The combing-post behind which they are sitting seems to extend at the top into a (metal?) device which grips the two-ended comb at the centre and allows it perhaps to pivot on a horizontal axis. One set of teeth points upward, one downward. Spinazzola has discussed the scene at length with reference to a group of combs found at Pompeii. He thinks that the combs have teeth at only one end.

Modern wool-combs[3] (fig. 11) have 3–6 rows of pointed teeth set behind each other in a wooden base. They are rooted in a layer of horn which covers the head of the tool to make them more elastic. A wooden handle is attached to the head at 90° to the plane of the teeth; and the whole is clamped to a wooden post so that the teeth point upwards or sideways (plate III *a*). This style of comb was already in

---

[1] Mr. W. H. Manning has kindly drawn my attention to another two-ended comb from Ewell (Surrey). A second-century contract from Egypt refers to 'A pair of iron combs, complete, brand-new, with teeth all the same length (ἰσάκμον)' (*P. Ox.* 1035; A.D. 143). Probably they had two rows of teeth. Wipszycka (1965), 28, 35, seems confused about the purpose of the combs.

[2] Spinazzola (1953), I, 190 ff., Tav. d'agg. 2.   [3] Ling Roth (1906).

use in the Viking period.[1] The more rigid Roman examples where teeth and base are a single entity, would have been less satisfactory to operate,[2] but these are what Verecundus' men are using.

Woolcombers in northern England in the last century had various methods of working the raw wool which differed from place to place. No description survives of how the Romans managed their combs, and a detailed reconstruction would be impossible. All that can be seen of Verecundus' woolcombers is that they are seated behind the combing-post, working the fibres through the comb with their fingers. A second comb holding fibres lies on a low table in front of the post, together with a series of knife-like implements, the purpose of which is uncertain.[3] They may have been used to remove the shorter fibres which gathered at the base of the teeth. A small pedestal-cup, probably containing water to keep the fibres moist, stands on one of the tables.

The modern woolcomber used a pair of combs, one fixed to a post, the other held in the woolcomber's hand.[4] Both combs were heated in a special warming-pot and the wool was kept moist throughout the operation (plate III a). The heat and moisture combined to make combing easier and to keep the fibres together. The woollen fibres were first impaled, a small quantity at a time, on a fixed comb in one direction and in this position are slowly combed out by repeated strokes of the free comb. During this process the fibres transferred themselves to the free comb and were then worked back on to the fixed comb by a change in the direction of the strokes. The combed wool was drawn off into sausage-shaped sleevers (slivers), which were combed out a second time in the same way and dried before they were ready for spinning. The short fibres which gathered at the base of the teeth could be removed and spun separately.

The result of combing and 'carding' (teasing?) would be wool which could be fastened to the distaff and spun at once. The rovings or slivers of combed wool mark a half-way stage to spun thread, but no attempt may have been made to prepare rovings from teased wool.

2. SILK

The mulberry silk-worm spins a thread which requires very little treatment before being woven. In mediaeval China, as at the present day, before the moths emerged the cocoons were dropped into a copper of boiling water, which both killed the

---

[1] Hamilton (1956), 122, fig. 57, no. 8 (from Jarlshof); see Hoffmann (1964), 381, note 27.
[2] Juvenal (VII. 224) mentions an *obliquum ferrum*, Claudian (*Carm.* XX. 380–5) a *pecten uncus*.
[3] Spinazzola (1953), I, 194, fig. 227.   [4] Ling Roth (1906).

pupa inside and loosened the gum which held the fibres. By brushing or beating the floating cocoons with a stick the loose ends of silk were picked up and could be reeled off on to a spool.[1]

The wild silk-moths on the other hand, which may not spin an unbroken filament, usually succeed in eating their way out of their cocoons, leaving a mass of short fibres behind. These have to be freed from gum, and then worked into a fluffy mass for spinning as in the case of short-stapled wool. The details of how this was done in the eastern Mediterranean in the Roman period or earlier are unknown.

Aristotle describes the Coan silk-workers as 'loosening (the threads from) the cocoons (ἀναλύουσι)' and 'reeling them up (ἀναπηνιζόμεναι)'; he was evidently thinking of cocoons largely undamaged by the pupa.[2] The Edict of Diocletian likewise mentions the unreeling (λύειν) of raw silk.[3] It is likely that complete cocoons (of wild silk?) were imported into the Empire, perhaps from India.

The older commentators believed that imported silk cloth was often unravelled in the Mediterranean area and rewoven as union-fabrics with wool or linen warp or weft. The authority of Pliny (who thought that silk grew on trees!) and of the poet Lucan were cited.[4] Blümner and Pfister have refuted the theory.[5]

3. LINEN

To separate the bast fibres of flax from the woody core and bark demands as many as seven different operations. Flax is the most difficult of all fibres to prepare for spinning. Fortunately Pliny has left an account of how flax was treated in his own day, an account which agrees in detail with what is known of modern peasant practice in Italy and Ireland.[6] The implements found in the neolithic *Pfahlbauten* (Lake Dwellings) in Switzerland (where only wild flax was worked) show that methods have remained unchanged over the last four millennia.[7]

Flax is pulled up by hand at the height of summer before it becomes over-ripe. The labourer pulls the stalks with his right hand and gathers them into bundles ('beets', *fasciculi manuales*) in the crook of his left arm. Pliny says that the bundles were then hung up in the sun to dry, so that the seeds (linseed) fell away or could

[1] *CIBA-Review*, 11 (1938), 370. [2] *H.A.* v. 19. 551ᵇ 14.
[3] XXIII. 2; XXIV. 13.
[4] *N.H.* XI. 76–8, quoting Aristotle in part; for a wild story see *N.H.* VI. 54; cf. Claudian, *Carm.* I. 179–80; Lucan, *Pharsalia*, X, 141–3.
[5] Mommsen & Blümner (1893), 162–3; Pfister (1934), 58.
[6] Pliny, *N.H.* XIX. 16–18; *CIBA-Review*, 49 (1945); Scheuermeier (1956), 231 ff.
[7] Vogt (1937), 47, Abb. 72.

be shaken out. According to earlier Egyptian accounts the peasants combed the dried flax with a rippling comb to remove the seeds.[1]

Three semicircular wooden combs, 10–14 cm. long by *c.* 10 cm. wide with teeth *c.* 7 cm. long, came to light among the objects from the first-century rubbish-dump (*Schutthügel*) at Vindonissa (table D; fig. 12). The teeth are so roughly shaped and widely spaced that they could only have been used to comb extremely coarse fibres. They may be rippling combs, although I cannot cite an exact parallel to them which was certainly used for this purpose. The hole through the base of each comb (if it is not merely to hang them up by) suggests that they may have been fixed to a stand and the stalks drawn through them: alternatively, the flax could have been laid on a bench and combed.

Rippling is not a vital stage in flax preparation, as Pliny shows; and if these combs can be demonstrated to have a purpose other than the one I have suggested, then there is no evidence for rippling in the north in the Roman period.

The retting of flax after rippling is attested everywhere. The stems are submerged in stagnant or gently flowing water and weighted down with stones for a period of two to three weeks. Pliny notes correctly that a warm pool speeds the process of bacteriological decay whereby the outer bark is loosened from the bundles of bast fibres. The stalks are then dried thoroughly in the sun and are ready to undergo a series of operations designed to remove the bark and woody core.

First the stalks are broken—that is, pounded on a flat stone with a wooden mallet (*stupparium malleum*). This loosens the fibres from the bark and core and breaks the latter into short lengths. Pliny names a mallet, but any blunt instrument would serve the purpose. In the second part of the process (*scutching*) the stalks are bent over a narrow object and beaten with a flat wooden blade to dispose of the remains of the bark. Pliny does not mention scutching; but a wooden scutching-knife (*swingle*) (34 cm. long by 4 cm. wide) was found in the *Pfahlbauten*, and a similar, slightly longer, instrument is still in use in Italy.[2] The provincials in the North were probably familiar with it (fig. 13).

The final stage in the preparation of flax is hackling (*ars depectendi degerendique*: also described as *carminare* by Pliny). The stalks with fragments of core and bark still clinging to them are drawn in present-day Italy across a hackle, a board (*c.* 45 by 15 cm.) set with several rows of iron spikes of graduated sizes.[3] The bast fibres are thus combed free of the remaining portions of the flax stem and separated from each

[1] Forbes (1956), 30. The evidence on which this conclusion rests, particularly the tomb-paintings, is not entirely satisfactory.

[2] Vogt (1937), 47, Abb. 72; Scheuermeier (1956), 242 f.   [3] Scheuermeier (1956), 249, figs. 450–4.

other. The hackle which I have described here is a sophisticated implement. Details of the comb or hackle which the Romans used are given by Pliny, but have been expunged from most texts by unintelligent emendation.[1]

A semicircular wooden board (fig. 14), 15 cm. long, probably with a handle, was found in a Neolithic context at Lattrigen (Kt. Bern).[2] The straight edge has a cordon on it and the whole surface of the board was set with about 270 groups of thorns, three to a group. Emil Vogt interprets it convincingly as a hackling-board. This, or an improved version of it with metal 'thorns' as described by Pliny,[1] may have been in use in the northern provinces. It is operated on the same principle as is the Italian hackle mentioned in the preceding paragraph. It is interesting to note its similarity to the mediaeval cards for wool-working. Moreover, Pliny uses the verb *carminare* (in Varro, of wool) to mean 'hackle' in his account of flax.

The prepared fibres were probably wound into coils ready to be attached to the distaff.

4. HEMP

The series of operations which are described in the foregoing section on flax are basically the same as those used in the treatment of hemp. The character of hemp, however, which has a longer and tougher stem than flax, is responsible for the occasional variations in method.

Hemp was pulled (*vellitur*), according to Pliny,[3] in the early autumn after the seeds had been stripped off. The male plants ripen before the female and must be plucked first. Retting follows in pools or streams. The old practice of dew-retting, by which the stalks are simply left lying in the fields until winter begins, survives widely in modern times. This method is effective, but slow.[4] The retted fibres are then thoroughly dried out.

Pliny sums up the next stage of treatment as *lucubrationibus decorticata purgatur* ('the hemp is cleaned and stripped of its bark in the evening by the light of candles'). In the country districts of Italy the bast fibres are still freed from the woody parts and bark by hand; and the womenfolk who carry out this task work together by lamp-light.[5] The middle finger of the left hand is crooked at a sharp angle and the whole length of each stalk is pulled round it several times. The dry and brittle woody

---

[1] See Wild (1968).
[2] Vogt (1937), 47, Abb. 72.
[3] Pliny, *N.H.* xix. 173; cf. *CIBA-Review*, 5 (1962); 49 (1945).
[4] *CIBA-Review*, 5 (1962), 15 ff.
[5] *Ibid*, 49 (1945), 1784; Scheuermeier (1956), 236.

portions crack across the stem throughout its length, breaking loose from the bast fibres which surround them. The core and bark can then be stripped away without difficulty.

The final process, hackling, requires the same tools and techniques as does the hackling of flax fibres.

5. COTTON

Any cotton which found its way into the northern provinces would have come as finished textiles or yarn; for there is no question of cotton being spun in the north. No ancient writer reveals any knowledge of how cotton fibres were prepared, although this knowledge must have been available in Egypt (see p. 18).

When the cotton seeds are ripe, the boll containing them splits open and the cotton-wool spills out. The seeds, and the fibres attached to them, were picked by hand until recently.[1]

How the lint (cotton hairs) was separated from the seed to which it adheres is unknown. It was probably removed by hand as in present-day Sudan.[2] The most primitive mechanical device, the roller-gin, was invented in India, but probably not until the Middle Ages. The rotation of its two, closely set, rollers drew the lint between them, but stopped the seed itself from passing through. The hairs were thus plucked from the seed. Cotton fibres are carded in modern times before being spun; but there is no evidence as to how this was done in Roman Egypt, if indeed it was done at all

[1] Murphy (1911), I, 87 ff.   [2] Crowfoot (1931), 40.

IV

SPINNING

The quality of spun thread depends on three factors of varying relative importance: prepared fibre of high quality, a skilful spinner, and suitable tools. The most important of the three is the spinner herself; for a skilled operative is capable of spinning yarn of consistently high quality which is hardly inferior to the best machine-spun yarn. The raw materials which she has at her disposal are only one degree less important, but the actual spinning implements in a peasant society are so simple that the quality of their construction is unlikely to be reflected in the final product.

1. IMPLEMENTS

DISTAFF

The hand-distaff (*colus*, in the North *conuclus* (*-a*)[1]) is basically a short stick, 20–30 cm. in length, which is grasped in the left hand. It serves to hold a convenient amount of the prepared raw fibres which are gradually converted into yarn and transferred to the spindle during the operation of spinning.

The simplest type of distaff is a short forked stick, the prongs of which support the fibres. It is more practical than the ornamental distaffs discussed below and is still popular in parts of Italy and the Balkans.[2] The coffin of a young woman buried at Les-Martres-de-Veyre (near Clermont-Ferrand) contained an example of this type, still bearing a mass of long-stapled white wool (table E, 19): another example was recovered from the first-century rubbish-dump at Vindonissa in Upper Germany (Brugg, Switzerland) (table E, 18). It was probably much the commonest form of distaff in the Roman provinces, but, being highly perishable, has only survived under exceptional circumstances.

In modern Italy hand-distaffs are often made of bulrushes:[2] the stem is slit at one end longitudinally to form a number of strips which can be drawn outwards into a cage to hold the fibres. Ammianus Marcellinus, writing in the fourth century, observes that distaffs of cane with cages were used in spinning flax fibres.[2]

A number of examples of ornamental distaffs of jet and amber have been noted

---

[1] Fr. *quenouille*; It. *connochia*; OldHG. *chuncula*.
[2] Scheuermeier (1956), 261, fig. 462; cf. Ammianus Marcellinus, XXIII. 4. 14.

31

in Britain and the Rhineland (table E, 1–11). In almost all cases they formed part of the grave-furniture of a late-Roman burial, and wherever the sex could be determined the burial was of a female. They can be paralleled exactly in many modern peasant communities[1] and Roman art confirms that they performed the same function in antiquity.[2] They consist of a lower shaft (the handle) and an upper shaft to which the fibres are tied, each of approximately the same length. The division is sometimes marked by a decorative central disc or cube and the tip may be carved with a similar embellishment (fig. 15).

The distaffs of jet were carved from a single piece, while those of amber were made up of a series of drilled amber segments mounted on a bronze pin. The source of the jet was probably Whitby in East Yorkshire, and it seems likely that the distaffs found in the Rhineland were imported from Whitby as finished articles.[3] An unusual specimen in a different material from Verulamium (St Albans) consists of an iron pin which holds a series of flat octagonal shale discs (table E, 15). It is paralleled by a bone distaff of similar shape from Aquincum-Budapest.[4]

Distaffs over 1 metre in length, carried under the arm or tucked into the belt, were the standard type of the Middle Ages,[5] but were rare, if not unknown, in the northern Roman provinces.

SPINDLE

The hand-spindle (*fusus*) has retained the same shape in Europe from the earliest times until the present day (plate III *b*). It is essentially a narrow rod of wood or bone, up to 30 cm. in length, which has a symmetrical thickening near the lower end to hold the spindle-whorl. The northern provincial examples vary between 12 and 25 cm. in length; the diameter of the bulbs is rarely more than 1 cm. They are precisely similar to those still in use in southern Italy;[6] and they are occasionally discovered with a whorl or fragment of wool still attached to them.

The great majority of ancient spindles must have been of wood, but the permanently waterlogged conditions (see p. 42) which are necessary for their survival exist only in a few places, notably the rubbish-dump at Vindonissa and the bed of the Walbrook

[1] See n. 2, p. 31.   [2] Esp.5518 (sarcophagus from Strassburg).

[3] *JRS*, LIII (1963), 241, with literature. The majority of jet objects in the Rhineland are found near Bonn and Köln. (Many in the Rheinisches Landesmuseum, Bonn, are unpublished.) No continental finds of waste jet fragments are recorded. While this suggests that most of the objects were imported from Britain in a finished state, necklaces found in Köln, which consist entirely of small irregular jet chips, may have been made up from waste material.

[4] *Arch. Ért.* 91 (1964), 180, Abb. 5 *a–d*.

[5] Singer & Holmyard (1956), II, 203.   [6] Scheuermeier (1956), 258 f.

in London. The rubbish which accumulated during only a century of legionary occupation at Vindonissa contained at least sixty spindles of wood against nine of bone. In A.D. 301 Diocletian fixed the price for a spindle of box-wood with its whorl at 12*d*, equivalent to the cost of twelve eggs or a pound of pork. It was expensive.[1]

The same type of spindle would have served for all the classes of fibre spun in the North, although a coarser yarn requires a heavier spindle. In the Aegean a specially light spindle made from a reed or rush was used to spin the Coan wild silk.[2]

A spindle-whorl (*verticillus*) adds momentum to the rotation of the spindle and is essential to its successful functioning. The whorl is a disc-shaped weight, pierced with a central hole so that it can be impaled on the lower end of the spindle and rammed tight on the thickened bulb. Spindle-whorls in every kind of material are found in large numbers on most habitation-sites in the northern provinces. Those made of cut-down sherds of pottery are the commonest type, but ornamental whorls in stone, lead, jet, shale and bone[3] are known too. They rarely have a diameter greater than 5 cm. A catalogue of the whorls found would shed no new light on methods of spinning and no attempt has been made to list them. Among the more noteworthy is a whorl from Trier (Löwenbrücken), cut from a sherd of black pottery, which bears the inscription IMPLE ME (above), SIC VERSA ME (below), 'load me (the spindle) up' and 'give me a twist'.[4] Another from Langres says SALVE TV PVELLA.[5] Inscribed whorls may have been traditional in the North; for a Viking example in the National Museum of Antiquities of Scotland in Edinburgh bears a Runic inscription.[6]

In the Near East the spindle whorl was, and still is, stuck on the upper end of the spindle; and the spinners in ancient Egyptian tomb-paintings and the peasants of of the Sudan at the present day follow precisely the same practice.[7] But in most of Europe the spindle-whorl hung below the yarn on the spindle at all periods of history.[8]

[1] *Edictum Diocletiani*, XIII. 5; cf. prices of eggs (VI. 43) and pork (IV. 1 *a*). Box grew wild in northern Europe (Christ (1913)).

[2] Pliny, *N.H.* XI. 78; Sidonius Apollinaris, *Carm.* XXII. 197–8.

[3] See for example the list in Wedlake (1958), 247, from Camerton (Somerset); wooden whorl from Les-Martres-de-Veyre, Clermont-Ferrand (Audollent (1922), 33, item 32, pl. VII,12).

[4] *CIL*, XIII. 10019/17, in Rheinisches Landesmuseum, Trier, 9231.

[5] *CIL*, XIII. 10019/19.

[6] *PSAS*, XXXII (1897–8), 321 (this example does not stand alone).

[7] Crowfoot (1931), 22 ff.

[8] See for example *MZ*, 29 (1934), 96, Abb. 24 (stele from Aquincum-Budapest); Esp. 5815 (Menimane); Scheuermeier (1956), 258 f.

BOBBIN

A bone implement, generally regarded as a bobbin, is common among the weaving appliances found in the Iron Age village at Glastonbury, Somerset.[1] This is known to have been an important centre of the woollen industry. The same tool is found as part of the closely related cultural assemblage of the broch-dwellers along the Atlantic coast of Scotland, who flourished during the Roman Iron Age.[2] So far as I know, no examples of the implement have been discovered outside Britain, but few, if any, belong to the Roman period within the province. They seem to be purely native (table G).

The implement is simply the metatarsal or metacarpal of a sheep or goat, pierced transversely through the centre of the shaft (fig. 16). Some examples have a hole drilled longitudinally into the proximal end, in which in one case at Glastonbury there are the remains of a bronze pin. No specimen is drilled at both ends, and for this reason Bulleid and Pitt-Rivers' attempts to visualise the tool as the spool from a shuttle cannot be accepted.[3] The most plausible explanation is that it carried spun yarn at some stage between spinning and warping (see p. 63); perhaps the contents of several spindles were wound on it. The end of the thread could be fastened through the central hole.

There is no evidence for bobbins in bone or in any other material in the Rhine-land. The commonest practice in the Roman period seems to have been to wind the wool from the spindle when it was full into a ball (see below)—a process which required no bobbin. Balls of this type have been found in the Swiss *Pfahlbauten*.[4] One of the stock scenes of Roman (and Greek) funerary relief sculpture shows the deceased spinning, with a basket (*quasillus*) full of balls of yarn at her feet.[5] *Quasil-lariae* was the name given to slave girls whose occupation was spinning.[6]

Forbes and Schwarz have concluded on remarkably little evidence that the reel was used in classical antiquity and earlier.[7] The stick-reel consists of a single rod with cross-bars or pegs at either end, round which skeins of wool or flax were

---

[1] Childe (1947), 234 ff.; Bulleid & Gray (1917), II, 422 ff.

[2] Childe (1935), 238, fig. 71, 5, 239. For current work on the brochs see Euan MacKie in *PPS*, XXXI (1965), 93 ff.

[3] Bulleid & Gray (1917), II, 426. Perhaps the unusual bronze pin in the Glastonbury example is the remains of a handle? It is difficult to explain convincingly.

[4] Vogt (1937), 48, Abb. 73–8.

[5] The best British example is on the tombstone of Regina from South Shields (Toynbee (1963), pl. 85, cat. no. 87); cf. Garbsch (1965), 152, Nr. 114, Taf. 12, 2.

[6] *CIL*, VI. 6339–45, from Pompeii.

[7] Forbes (1956), 166; A. Schwarz in *CIBA-Review*, 59 (1947), 2130 f.

wound. Marta Hoffmann suggests that the mediaeval Latin term for a reel (*trahale*), which is not recorded in classical Latin, may nevertheless have been in use earlier.[1] I cannot, however, find any good archaeological or philological reason for believing that the reel was known in the Roman period.

2. PROCESS OF SPINNING

The first action of the spinning process is to fasten the prepared fibres to the distaff. There is little information about what form the fibres had at this stage. In all probability the combed wool and flax formed long loose slivers or rovings, which were wound round the upper part of the shaft of the hand–distaffs and perhaps held in place by a band.[2] Wool which had not been combed, but simply teased out, could best be held as a loose mass on the forks, or in cages formed from the twigs, of simple stick-distaffs (see table E, 18–19). Although a distaff is not absolutely essential to the process of spinning, there is no hint in the relatively abundant literary references that it was ever dispensed with.

Quasillariae (spinning-girls) were assigned a certain weight of wool to work: *pensum* denoted both the raw wool and the ball of spun yarn.[3]

The actual operation of spinning consists of two basic steps—drawing (or drafting) the fibres and twisting them. The method of spinning practised most frequently in Roman Europe was what Grace Crowfoot classified as 'suspended-spindle spinning'; that is, spinning with a free hanging spindle.[4] It is at once the most efficient and speedy method to be developed prior to the invention of the spinning wheel. My account is based on a detailed passage in Catullus' *Marriage of Peleus and Thetis*,[5] supplemented by first-hand information collected by modern observers among the peasants of Italy and Egypt.[6] The facts culled from these two sources tally exactly. It should be noted that while the commonest fibres were all spun by this method, a more delicate fibre might require a lighter spindle and short-stapled fibres are more difficult to spin than are long-stapled ones.

The distaff with its accompanying fibres is grasped in the left hand ('laeva colum retinebat'). Seizing a few fibres from the bottom of the mass on the distaff between the (wetted) forefinger and thumb of her right hand, the spinner simultaneously twists them together and draws them gently downwards ('dextera tum leviter

---

[1] Hoffmann (1964), 290.

[2] Regina from South Shields appears to be holding in her left hand a distaff with laterally wound rovings (Toynbee (1963), pl. 85). [3] Tibullus, II. I. 63; from Pompeii: Overbeck (1884), 486.

[4] Crowfoot (1931), 20 ff., Type 6. [5] Catullus, LXIV. 311–19.

[6] Scheuermeier (1956), 258; Crowfoot (1931), 20 ff.

deducens fila supinis/formabat digitis'). When she has drawn out and twisted in this manner a long enough thread, she ties it to the top of the spindle; then, taking the tip of the spindle between her forefinger and the ball of her thumb, she gives it a vigorous twist to set it rotating and lets go ('tum prono in pollice torquens/libratum tereti versabat turbine fusum').[1] The thread, with the free rotating spindle on the end of it, thus hangs perpendicularly from the mass of fibres on the distaff. With the fingers of her right hand the spinner then continues to draw out a controlled number of fibres from the distaff, which are twisted by the action of the spindle into a thread. At the same time the weight of the spindle stretches the thread as it is being formed, and makes it finer. The simultaneous drawing and twisting continue without a break until the spindle reaches the floor and stops. At this point the spinner has to halt, pick up the spindle and, using it as a bobbin, wind up the spun thread. She makes the thread fast on the top of the spindle again, gives the latter a twist and continues the operation as before. When the spindle is full of yarn, she breaks off the thread and re-winds it into a ball or on a bobbin.

Sometimes the spinner is shown seated[2] (plate IV*a*), sometimes standing; Pliny says that it brings ill-luck to spin while walking—which implies that it was done in Roman times.

Catullus refers to the habit of biting-out with the teeth any irregularities or impurities in an otherwise evenly spun thread.[3] To learn to control the evenness of the yarn is one of the most difficult lessons which the beginner has to master in hand-spinning.

A necessary part of the operation of spinning is to secure the yarn which is being drawn out to the top of the spindle before setting it in motion. It is clear from a passage in Plato's *Republic* that the Greeks sometimes used a hook;[4] but the majority of the spindles of Roman date have a completely plain tip (for exceptions, see table F,10,14). A few have an ornamental terminal, but this would not catch up the thread without a knot (plate III *b*). Wolfgang La Baume has demonstrated that the yarn can be wound once (or twice) round the end of the thumb (probably of the left hand) and slipped off directly over the top of the spindle to make a knot which will be kept tight by the weight of the spindle[5] (fig. 17). Scheuermeier has shown that this method is practised by peasants in parts of modern Italy.[6] It is likely, however, that

---

[1] In the Roman period only twirling with the thumb and forefinger is mentioned; for other methods see Crowfoot (1931), 21, 31.

[2] Seated: Toynbee (1963), pl. 85; cf. Crowfoot (1931), 37; Herodotus, v. 12; Pliny, *N.H.* xxviii. 28.

[3] Catullus, LXIV. 315–7; cf. Forbes (1956), 163, fig. 16 (early-fifth-century Greek vase painting). Nineteenth-century Yorkshire woolcombers did the same (Ling Roth (1906), 9).

[4] *Respublica*, x. 616 *c*.   [5] La Baume (1931), 71–3, Abb. 1, 2.   [6] Scheuermeier (1956), 258.

as an additional safeguard the yarn was wound once round the bottom end of the spindle beneath the whorl before it was knotted on the upper end.

The mode of spinning with a suspended spindle described above is not the only one known in primitive communities; but to judge from the abundance of spindle-whorls and the types of spindles represented, suspended-spindle spinning must have been regular in the northern provinces. Warp-threads, especially for the warp-weighted loom, need to be particularly strong, and for this suspended-spindle spinning is ideal. On the other hand, for special fabrics a more loosely spun weft was sometimes required. Hence other methods may have been adopted occasionally, when it was felt that the weight of the free-rotating spindle and its whorl might be too great for the yarn to bear.[1]

Jerome contrasts the spinning of woollen warp (probably on a suspended spindle) with the spinning of weft, where the spindle rotates with its lower end resting on a saucer (alveolus).[2] Mrs Crowfoot notes that this type of spinning ('supported-spindle spinning') is used widely for fine muslin in the East.[3] There is no other mention of it in antiquity, but many of the textiles in the North have a weft-system more weakly spun than the warp-system. The method cannot be discounted entirely in the North, but even weakly spun wool could be spun more easily with a free spindle. It is interesting that a graffito from Pompeii, recording the weights of wool (pensa) distributed among a number of slave-girls, states whether they were spinning warp or weft yarn.[4] This would suggest a difference in the quality of the thread, but perhaps not a difference in spinning techniques.

The operation of rope-making as shown on a sarcophagus from Ostia[5] was carried out with a long heavy spindle, rolled on the thigh (Crowfoot type 5 A, 'supported spindle'). Whether the process of spinning individual strands or plying them together ('doubling') is represented here is uncertain. This method of spinning is suitable for particularly tough fibres.

The spinning of thread for cloth described as pexa (see p. 84), soft-finished stuff, was a well-paid specialist occupation in Diocletian's day, perhaps carried out by men.[6] Pexa probably required a loosely spun weft, perhaps a variety of slub yarn. It may have been spun by the supported-spindle method.

[1] For spinning with a reed spindle see Pliny, N.H. XI. 78.
[2] Ep. 130. 15. For a representation of this see R. Habelt, Archäologischer Kalender (1968): early Byzantine ivory pyxis in the Staatliche Museen, Berlin.   [3] Crowfoot (1931), 19, Type 5 B.   [4] CIL, IV. 1507.
[5] This sarcophagus was kindly brought to my attention by Dr Graham Webster (IG, XIV. 929; for poor photograph see Blümner (1912), 289, fig. 94. It is in the Museo Nazionale, Rome.
[6] Edictum Diocletiani, XXIV. 16; Wild (1967 a). It is unfortunate that the figures for the wages of other spinners in this section are missing; the masculine participle should perhaps not be taken literally.

3. SPIN-DIRECTION

Yarn spun with a spindle rotating clockwise is referred to as Z-spun or right-hand-spun yarn, since the central bar of the Z corresponds to the direction in which the fibres in the thread lie. Likewise S-spun yarn (left-hand spun) requires a spindle twirled anticlockwise (fig. 18). Wool and silk can be spun equally successfully in either direction, the fibres having no natural preference. Of the bast fibres linen (flax), when moistened, rotates naturally to the left (S); but while it was S-spun in the eastern provinces, it was regularly Z-spun in the north in Roman times. Cotton, on the other hand, was regularly Z-spun in the East, and although it exhibits no marked preference by nature, experiments have shown that Z-spun cotton disintegrates less easily during washing than S-spun cotton does.[1] In fact, however, the natural direction of spin played little part in spinning in the north.

A comparison of the textile groups discovered in the eastern provinces (e.g. those from the Cave of Letters in Palestine (A.D. 132–135 (?)) and from Dura-Europos in Syria (before c. A.D. 256)[2] with the material from the north shows that both wool and linen were almost exclusively S-spun in the eastern provinces at all periods, but Z-spun in the northern provinces, at least in Roman times. I have discussed this conclusion in greater detail below (p. 44).

In the pre-Roman Iron Age in Scandinavia and North Germany left-hand spinning (S) was the regular method, but in the Roman Iron Age (almost certainly *independently* of developments within the Empire) right-hand spinning became normal.[3] However, woollen cloth of late-Hallstatt date (sixth century B.C.) from Württemberg has two Z-spun systems.[4] When one system is S-spun, the other Z-spun, a firm cloth with good felting properties results; and this is not uncommon among Roman finds, both inside and outside the frontiers. In the Bronze Age and later special pattern-effects were created by combining differently spun yarns in the same system.[5] On present evidence, therefore, it is unsafe to use the direction of spin as a dating criterion, although this may be valid in a strictly local context such as Denmark.

The strength of doubled or plied yarns was appreciated by both Romans and natives. The finds demonstrate that sewing-thread was often doubled: S-spun yarn was Z-plied and vice versa for added strength. Yarn was probably plied on a free rotating spindle, drawing from two or more balls of thread. There are no precise details available as to how the provincials did this.

---

[1] Forbes (1956), 150 f.; *Dura* (1945), 1 ff.; Pfister (1937), 40 f.   [2] Yadin (1963); *Dura* (1945), *passim*.
[3] Hald (1950), 435, 439 (English résumé).   [4] Riek & Hundt (1962), 210.   [5] Schlabow (1962), 45.

4. GOLD THREAD

The popularity of gold and silver brocade within and without the Empire is reflected in the literature and in the material remains (see table H). While fragments of gold thread have frequently come to light in the northern provinces, none has yet been satisfactorily recorded or published; for archaeologists are generally unaware of the relevant details to note. The fact that with one exception the Roman finds are dated to the last two centuries of Roman administration in the north is probably a pure accident of survival. Most of them were contained in sarcophagi, where such fragile material is more easily preserved and observed. Until the Antonine period cremation was the normal rite; and the material in cremation burials is far less likely to survive and be noticed.

Agnes Geijer,[1] in publishing the textiles from the Viking graves at Birka (Sweden), classified the gold and silver thread according to construction under three heads:

(1) *Gold wire (Drahtgold)*. The wire is round in section and manufactured by being drawn out. No textile fibre is associated with it. 'Thread' in this technique is rare except at Birka; and it is not found or mentioned during the Roman period.

(2) *Spirally spun gold wire (Spiralgold)*. The wire, drawn out by the same method as in class (1), circular in section, is wound in tight regular spirals round a textile (usually silk) core.

(3) *Spirally spun gold ribbon (Gesponnenes Gold)*. A flat, narrow band of gold or silver is spun spirally round a textile core. The width of the band in Roman finds varies between 0.25 mm. and 0.8 mm. (see table H, 1, 11) and the core may be silk, wool or a bast fibre.

We can add to Agnes Geijer's list:

(4) *Gilded membrane*. A narrow band of organic membrane is gilded and spun round a silk core. This has been found only at Palmyra, as an import from Han China, and in Rome (locally made?) (table H, 18, 20). It was popular in the Middle Ages.

The literary sources often refer to spun gold without distinguishing between wire and ribbon.[1] The practice of drawing out the gold before spinning is mentioned by Jerome and Claudian;[2] and Sidonius Apollinaris refers explicitly to the yellow silk core.[3] But in view of our lack of knowledge of how such fine gold was prepared and spun in antiquity, we cannot conclude that gold wire was drawn, while gold

---

[1] *Birka*, III. 68 ff.; *CIBA-Review*, 3 (1961); Vergil, *Aen.* III. 483, x. 818; Ovid, *Met.* VI. 68.

[2] Jerome, *Ep.* 22. 16 (ed. Migne, 22. 403); Claudian, *Carm.* I. 177–82.

[3] *Carm.* XXII. 198–9.

ribbon was beaten and cut: gold ribbon was probably drawn, beaten *and* cut.[1] The few finds which have been analysed suggest that gold-ribbon was commoner than the other types.

Sidonius' words indicate that the gold ribbon was wound round the fibre core with the aid of a spindle in the manner of doubled yarn. In this case, however, the spindle would probably have to be rolled manually on the thigh (Crowfoot type 5 A, 'supported-spindle') and the gold band gradually paid in from the right or left at an angle to the fibre core. It was a well-paid man's job in the fourth century.[2]

It is surprising how common gold brocade is in Hallstatt contexts north of the Alps;[3] and although it would be more natural to suppose that the yarn or fabrics themselves were imported from the Mediterranean world, this cannot be proved. The tumulus at Lexden near Colchester, which may be the tomb of Cunobelinus or of a notable contemporary of his, contained a quantity of gold-ribbon thread (table H, 15). The taste for brocade with gold thread interwoven[4] or embroidered on a plain fabric had evidently developed before the arrival of the Romans. The lack of finds in the first and second centuries may be due to the metal having been melted down or re-used. In the fourth century the imperial circle at Trier was supplied by the barbaricarii working there.[5]

[1] An eighth-century Italian document states that gold ribbon was first drawn, then beaten, then cut; the process was repeated twice (*Aarbøger* (1915), 41–2).

[2] *Edictum Diocletiani*, xxx. 6.

[3] Filip (1960), 43 ff.

[4] Vergil, *Aen.* III. 483, with Servius *ad loc.*

[5] *Notitia Dignitatum Occidentis*, XI. 77; *Latomus*, XXII (1963), 806 ff. For Anglo-Saxon and Frankish gold thread see now *Med. Arch.* XI (1967), 42 ff.

V

PRESERVED TEXTILES

Contrary to popular belief, the body of material available for a study of Roman textiles is considerable and, more important, is a representative selection of the ancient fabrics. The purpose of this chapter is to bring together, discuss and assess the significance of the facts and observations recorded about the individual textiles. The contemporary material from the rest of the Empire will be used for comparison; and I shall try to show how the techniques of prehistoric Europe continued in the Roman era.

1. CIRCUMSTANCES OF PRESERVATION

The climate of western Europe with its alternating periods of cold and wet, hot and dry, leads to the rapid disintegration of artefacts composed of organic substances. Sections cut through the Overton Down Experimental Earthwork two years and four years after its construction showed that the cloth under the turf stack had deteriorated badly, but was slightly better preserved in the chalk layers.[1] Wool had suffered worse than linen fibres.

In the western provinces the majority of textiles owe their preservation to being submerged in water or buried in permanently humid layers. The clothes from the bog-burials of northern Europe (Early or Roman Iron Age in date) are the best known examples of this class. They owe their survival to the group of acids referred to as 'peat-acids' (*Huminsäure*), which permeate organic material lost or deposited in the bogs. Walter von Stokar collected the results of scientific investigations into the character of the peat-acids. He estimated that under ideal conditions, with a constant temperature, flax would take 200 years to perish completely, bone 600, wool 1800 and horn 3,400.[2] Thus wool is the only fibre to survive under these conditions.

Woollen cloth is usually stained a shade of brown by the peat-acids, and few traces of the dyes are left. It is sometimes possible on the basis of the lighter and darker

[1] *Antiquity*, xxxix (1965), 136; *PPS*, xxxii (1966), 325 ff., with tables vi–viii.
[2] Von Stokar (1938), 14 f.; *idem* (1934), 310. He may have put too much emphasis on the humic acids and not enough on the simple anaerobic conditions. This was pointed out to me in discussion after a paper which I gave in November 1967 to the Society of Antiquaries of London.

yarns to reconstruct the pattern effects (see p. 53). The structure of woollen fibres is astonishingly well preserved, but they tend to become brittle if they dry out.

The only notable British bog-find was made on Grewelthorpe Moor (Kirkby Malzeard) in Yorkshire in 1850. The corpse was reported to be wearing a green toga, scarlet tunic (?) and yellow stockings; but he was unfortunately reinterred and only two portions of a stocking survive. One is in plain weave, one in half-basket weave, and both are of Z-spun woollen yarns, giving no clue to date. There is no positive reason for thinking them Roman.[1]

The late-Roman town of Mainz in Upper Germany enclosed an area of marshy land into which a large number of pieces of cloth, together with other rubbish, had been thrown in the early Roman period. This is the most extensive group of woollen goods from any site of Roman date in the western provinces.[2] The legionary rubbish-dump at Vindonissa in Upper Germany yielded a smaller group of textiles all of first-century date (plate VII b). The shallow Walbrook, a tributary of the Thames within the city of London, was frequently used for depositing refuse until the mid-second century. All three sites may in the future add to the total number of surviving textile fragments.[3]

Roman wells were often turned into refuse pits, and where the water-table has remained at its original level the chances of discarded rags, both linen and wool, surviving are good (plate V b). The largest single piece of cloth in Roman Britain was salvaged from a well at a signal station at Huntcliff (table A, 43). A small piece of linen in a good state came from a well at Rugby (table A, 23).

The dry atmosphere of the deserts in the Near East is unfortunately unique to that area. The nearest approach to it is the air-tight coffin. The woollen and silk fabrics from the late-Roman tombs at Conthey (table B, 85, 90) and from the coffin of St Paulinus at Trier (table B, 86–88) are possibly examples of survival in dry conditions. In both cases other factors, perhaps metal oxides, may have played a subsidiary role.

The present state of the contents of the wooden coffins found at Les-Martres-de-Veyre (Puy de Dôme), with their fully preserved garments and dried fruit, may represent a condition akin to that obtaining in the East. The excavators, however, were unable to explain the precise reasons for the preservation and favoured the

---

[1] *The Ripon Millenary Record* (1892), preface to part II, p. ix. The stocking is in the Yorkshire Museum, York, where I examined it through the kindness of Mr G. F. Willmot.

[2] Topography: Baatz (1962), Beilage 1. Most of the material from the mid-nineteenth century has not survived.

[3] Vindonissa: Staehelin (1948), 240; recent work: *Ges. Vindonissa* (1955–6), 35 ff.; Walbrook: Wild in *Beiträge zur Textilgeschichte des Altertums und Asiens* (ed. S. Lauffer and W. Rau) (forthcoming).

theory of carbonic acid, a well-attested property of the local soil. They complained in 1893 of 'émanations irrespirables'.[1]

Perhaps the commonest method by which small fragments of cloth are preserved is by contact with metal objects, the corrosion-products of which they absorb. Bronzes can keep small pieces of linen which are in direct contact with them in a relatively good condition, but are not so protective towards wool (plate VI*a*).[2] Usually the wrapping of bronze utensils or the lining of purses will have been of linen in any case, so that the preponderance of linen surviving in these circumstances is not solely due to the selective action of the oxides.

Iron oxide converts cloth into an iron compound, preserving the shape while destroying or changing the composition of the fabric (diagenesis). Analysis of such textiles, except by purely visual means, is impossible. The Corbridge hoard of iron-work contained a large collection of woollen textiles, but they survive only as a hollow shell (table A).

The preservative properties of lead salts may account for the fragments of cloth which are often found within lead sarcophagi. The best example of this type is probably the linen from the lead canister of the pipe-burial at Caerleon (table A, 10). Its state of preservation is remarkably good (plate V *a*). A number of other conditions are known in which cloth survives, including pickling in salt—(the Hallstatt salt-mines have yielded many cloth fragments)—and charring. These need not detain us here.

It is important to establish whether the extant textile remains form a representative cross-section of the whole range of Roman fabrics. According to the circumstances of their deposition, the remains may be classed as selected or rejected material. The shrouds and offerings in rich burials (e.g. that of St Paulinus at Trier), or the wrappings of buried valuables, count as selected material. The pieces of cloth from the Walbrook, from the Vindonissa rubbish-dump and from Mainz, on the other hand, were certainly rejected by the owners. Textiles which had merely been lost accidentally appear to be only a small proportion of the finds. It is reasonable to suppose that most types of cloth known in antiquity would have fallen into one of these three categories, so that the remains which we possess are probably representative. From a technical point of view, in our examination of fibres and weaves, there are no gaps in the material which we might expect once to have been filled.

[1] Audollent (1922), 50 ff.   [2] Von Stokar (1938), 16 f.

2. SPIN-DIRECTION

The mechanical aspect of spinning has been discussed in a previous chapter (p. 31 ff.), where attention was drawn to the natural direction of rotation of the fibres—flax to the left (S) and wool in either direction (fig. 18). It remains to consider the wider significance of the spin-direction of the yarns in northern provincial textiles.

The majority of yarns throughout the Roman period in Britain and the Rhineland, whether of wool, hemp or linen, were spun to the right (Z) in both warp and weft. A number of woollens have Z-spun warp and S-spun weft, but this represents a deliberate attempt to produce a firmer cloth, closely interlocked. The same technique is to be found all over the Empire and beyond. Only three woollen fabrics have S-spun yarns in both systems (table A, 44, 46; B, 23) and only one piece of linen (?) (table B, 46). The latter was probably imported with the silks in the coffin of St Paulinus at Trier.

The textiles in wool and linen from the provinces of Syria, Palestine and Egypt, a large number of which have been published, show precisely the opposite direction of spin (S) at all periods. The finds of the late-first century from Qûmran Cave I,[1] of the period of the Jewish revolt (A.D. 132–135) from the caves of Bar Kokhba and Murabba'at[2] and of the early third century from Dura-Europos in Syria[3] tell the same story. The spinners of Egypt from pre-Dynastic till Arab times preferred to spin to the left.[4]

The local preferences for left- or right-hand spin were put forward by Pfister in 1934 as a criterion in establishing the centres of production of groups of textiles.[5] He showed that most Iranian and Indian yarns were Z-spun (right) in contrast to the S-spun fabrics of the eastern Roman provinces. Unfortunately he tried to apply this criterion too rigidly to individual textiles and lost sight of the fact that cloth need not be woven where the yarns have been spun. The idiosyncrasies of individual spinners must also be reckoned with.

For groups of textiles his basic principle is probably sound; for it is clear that the spinners of Gaul and Britain favoured right-spinning (Z), while those of Syria and Egypt spun to the left (S). It is not surprising that the two major centres of the Roman imperial textile industry,[6] northern Gaul and the Levant, should have followed

[1] Crowfoot (1955), 21. [2] Yadin (1963), 182; Crowfoot (1962), 56.
[3] *Dura* (1945), *passim*.
[4] Pfister (1937), 40 f. But a group of tenth-century textiles from Ghirza in Libya which I hope to publish shortly contains predominantly Z-spun yarns.
[5] *Revue des Artes Asiatiques*, VIII (1934), 81; see J. Beckwith in *CIBA-Review*, 133 (1959), 4, 8–9.
[6] Jones (1960–1), 185 ff.; cf. *Edictum Diocletiani*, XIX. *passim*.

independent modes of spinning. It is, moreover, a firm indication that the majority of textiles found in Gaul and Britain were manufactured there and not (with obvious exceptions) imported. Few fragments of cloth from southern Gaul,[1] Italy or Greece[2] have yet been published, so that it is impossible to state what local variations were to be found in the area between the two outlying regions mentioned above.

The contrast between East and West in this particular respect was of long standing. In Dynastic Egypt linen (the major fibre) was regularly S-spun, while the wool and linen yarn of Iron-Age date from the salt-mines of eastern Austria and from the *Fürstengräber* of Württemberg is predominantly Z-spun.[3]

Margrethe Hald has pointed out that in Scandinavia and North Germany yarn was almost always left spun (S) in the pre-Roman Iron Age, but right spun (Z) in the Roman Iron Age.[4] Since the fashion in parts at least of the La-Tène cultural zone seems to have been for spinning to the right before the Roman conquest, there is no need to assume direct Roman (Italian) influence to account for the change to Z-spinning in northern Europe.[5] The Belgae may have been responsible for it, if an outside cause is necessary at all. Roman technology had little to contribute at first to the already flourishing textile industry of Gaul and Britain.[6] It should not be used as a *deus ex machina* for changes in neighbouring areas.

The plying of yarns for extra strength was the normal practice in the La-Tène period; two Z-spun yarns were often S-plied together, particularly for the warp.[7] While S-plied woollen yarn was used for sewing thread in the Roman period, there is no evidence that plied yarns were woven.

3. WEAVES

The key fact to be noted in recording an ancient textile is its weave. In cases where the weave is at all complicated a draft of the weaving-plan giving exact details of each successive shed is required. Unfortunately a draft is seldom published. The following account therefore is of necessity based on an examination or re-examination of most of the surviving textiles in the western provinces; and the details listed in the catalogue have in most cases not been previously recorded.

[1] The woollens from Les-Martres-de-Veyre apparently contain Z-spun yarns despite the phrase 'à gauche' in Audollent (1922), *passim*.

[2] Z-spun linen at Koropi, Athens, from fifth century B.C.: *ILN*, 23 January 1954, 114.

[3] Hundt (1961), 24.   [4] Hald (1950), 435 ff., 442.

[5] *Pace* Geijer (1939), 190; Hald (1950), 443; cf. Hoffmann (1964), 246.

[6] Pliny, *N.H.* VIII. 196; Childe (1947), 234 ff.; Bulleid & Gray (1911), I; (1917), II, *passim*.

[7] Hundt (1960), 149.

PLAIN-WEAVE

Textiles in plain-weave—at once the simplest and commonest of all weaves—form about sixty per cent of the fabrics which have come to light in the western provinces. The principle of the weave is that each weft-thread passes under and over a single warp-thread.

Plain-weave was used regularly for all classes of woollen goods, particularly for bands and girdles. The relative counts of the threads in the two systems may vary, but girdles are characterised by warp set closer than weft (table B, 8–16). Yarns spun from bast fibres are almost always plain-woven. The linen shrouds from York and Trier (one made out of a fringed towel; table B, 49) can serve as an example. Some scholars call plain-weave 'linen-weave' for this reason.

The search for parallels for provincial-Roman plain-weaves would add little to the discussion. It is, however, worth noting that the neolithic textiles both from Çatal Hüyük in Turkey (dated to the seventh millennium B.C.)[1] and from the Swiss *Pfahlbauten*,[2] the linen from Dynastic and pre-Dynastic Egypt[3] and the Bronze-Age woollens from Scandinavia and Britain[2] were all woven in plain-weave. It is clear that plain-weave had a long tradition. Two other weaves which can be classed with plain-weave occur on occasion in the provinces. The first is basket-weave (hopsack) (table A, 11, 24; B, 37; fig. 22; plates VI*a*, VII*a*) where two threads are taken in place of one in both warp and weft. This weave is represented in material from the Hallstatt period in Austria,[4] but is otherwise rare before Roman times. It seems to have been quite popular in the eastern provinces for linen.[5]

Half-basket-weave (table A, 9; fig. 19), where one system consists of single, one of double yarns, is commoner than full basket-weave both in the Roman period and before. A few examples from the neolithic period in western Europe,[6] from the Hallstatt period[7] and from the Roman Iron Age in free Germany can be quoted.[8] In some cases the pairs of threads may represent the warp, in others the weft (table A, 5).

[1] *ILN*, 22 February 1964, 275, figs. 12, 17, 23.
[2] *CIBA-Review*, 54 (1947), 1960.
[3] See, for example, the linen cloth from various Ancient Egyptian sites in the University Museum, Manchester, and the Ashmolean Museum, Oxford.
[4] Hundt (1960), 143 f., Nr. 38, Abb. 8.
[5] Yadin (1963), 193, 250 (Cave of Letters, A.D. 132–5). There is a quantity of basket-weave woollen cloth from Pompeii in the Museo Nazionale, Naples, on exhibition.
[6] Latdorf (Kr. Bernberg): *ZMdV*, 43 (1959), 107, Gruppe D.
[7] Hohmichele (Württemberg): Riek & Hundt (1962), 204, Abb. 5, Taf. 33, 34; 206 f., Taf. 36–9.
[8] Marx-Stapelstein (Kr. Wittmund): Hahne (1915), 48, Nr. 3, Taf. xxvii, Abb. 3.

2-OVER-2 TWILL

The discovery of how to weave twill cloth was a significant advance in textile technology which took place before the end of the Bronze Age in northern Europe.[1] For 2-over-2 (or four-shaft) twill each weft-thread passes over and under two warp-threads at a time; and the passage of each weft-thread is staggered consistently to left or right of its predecessor (fig. 20; plate VII *b*). The increased stability of twill cloth amply compensates for the slightly more complicated knitting of the heddles and manipulation of the rods (see p. 64).

A considerable proportion of woollen cloth was woven in 2-over-2 twill weave during the Roman and pre-Roman Iron Ages in Europe, and its popularity was high in the Roman provinces.[2] The origin of 2-over-2 twill is in dispute, but its frequent use in the West before and after the Roman conquest contrasts strongly with its almost complete absence in the East in textiles until the third century A.D. Twill matting, however, was being made in Iran as early as the seventh millennium B.C.[3] Although the finds from the caves on the Dead Sea (dated *c.* A.D. 132–135) were the property of rebels, not of the wealthy, one might have expected more twill, if it had been a well-known textile weave.[4] At Karanis in Egypt only a minute proportion of the cloth fragments (mostly late-fourth or early fifth-century in date) are woven in 2-over-2 twill:[5] at Dura-Europos in Syria (before *c.* A.D. 256), on the other hand, they may have been slightly more popular.[6]

Twill is the ideal weave for woollen fabrics, since it exploits to the full the felting properties of wool. This may to some extent account for its rarity in the East, where flax was the main fibre. Two pieces of cloth composed of bast yarns (linen?) in 2-over-2 twill were found in the salt-mines at Hallstatt (late-Hallstatt or early La-Tène period)[7] and linen shin-guards in (irregular) 2-over-2 twill came to light at Dura;[8] they may both have been experimental.

Plain twill is the basis of several types of pattern-weave. The first of these is herringbone twill. The herringbone strip can occur in either weft or warp, the

[1] La Baume (1955), 100; von Post *et al.* (1924). This vital piece is dated by pollen-analysis to the Middle Bronze Age (von Post (1924), 17 ff.).

[2] Hald (1950), 145 ff.; Hundt (1961), 22. There is 2-over-2 twill from Pompeii in the Museo Nazionale, Naples, and in the local Antiquarium at Pompeii.

[3] *PPS*, XXXIII (1967), 177.

[4] Yadin (1963), 251 (no 2-over-2 twill); Crowfoot (1962), 55, nos. 3, 4, 7 (but Z-spun yarns—imports?).

[5] Wilson (1933), 16, nos. 11–12, pl. I; 17, no. 13, pl. II; 46, no. 16, pl. IV.   [6] *Dura* (1945), 3.

[7] Hundt (1960), 129, Nr. 26; 130, Nr. 27, Taf. 15.

[8] *Dura* (1945), 59, no. 292; cf. Pfister (1934), 35, fig. 5, L 17.

first reversing in slope on an axis parallel to the weft (weft-chevron), the second parallel to the warp (warp-chevron).

To weave weft-chevron twill, the weaver simply reverses the order in which the heddle-rods are lifted; she may reverse on a point (sheds 123/4/321, etc.) (fig. 62) or with displacement (sheds 1234/2143, etc.) (fig. 62). The Hallstatt weft-chevron twills from the salt-mines all have point repeat,[1] the three from Roman Britain (from Falkirk (table A, 42; fig. 23; plate VI b), Huntcliff (table A, 43; fig. 25), London (table A, 44)) have displacement. The Huntcliff cloth is peculiar in the whole Empire in having paired warp (i.e. two adjacent warp-threads worked as one): there is a precedent for this at Hallstatt[2] and a parallel at Karanis.[3] In the Falkirk tartan the reverse in the slope of the weave was emphasised by a change in the colour of the weft (see p. 53). Warp-chevron twills are planned during the knitting of the heddles, but I know of none in the Roman Empire. Herringbone twills appear to be even rarer than plain twills in the East.[4]

The Gerum mantle, dated on pollen analysis to the Bronze Age, is the earliest evidence both for the weaving of 2-over-2 twill and for the most advanced form of it, diamond (lozenge) twill.[5] Diamond twill is a combination of the thread-up for warp-chevron twill and the reversed order of sheds in weft-chevron twill; and it is the most complex pattern-weave in 2-over-2 twill which can be woven with four sheds.

The Roman diamond twills from Britain (table A, 45–9) may be considered medium or medium-fine in quality (8–20 threads per cm. in each system), and all have displacement in both systems (fig. 24). The two diamond twills from Les-Martres-de-Veyre (second century A.D. ?) fall into the same category.[6] One of the four pieces from Mainz (table B, 76), however, is a fine fabric (26 threads per cm.); this and one other (table B, 78) have point repeat in the weft direction (figs. 39, 40).

The diamond twills woven within the Roman frontiers in the West followed the traditions of the pre-Roman weavers. A glance at the Scandinavian twills from Karlby and Gerum[7] and many similar fabrics from the Roman Iron Age in North

[1] Hundt (1959), 76, Nr. 13, Abb. 6; idem (1960), 130, Nr. 29, Abb. 2.
[2] Hundt (1959), 75, Nr. 12, Abb. 5, Taf. 19, 1.
[3] Wilson (1933), 16, no. 12.
[4] A herringbone twill from Antinoe (third century?) is in the Musée des Tissus, Lyons; both systems are Z-spun (Hoffmann (1964), 374, note 71).
[5] Hoffmann (1964), 191–3; dating: von Post et al. (1924), 17 ff., 47 ff.
[6] Audollent (1922), 103, Étoffes nos. 10, 11.
[7] Hald (1950), 41 f., no. 26, fig. 141; Hoffmann (1964), 191 ff.

Germany[1] will offer ample proof of this. All have full displacement in both systems[2] and a fairly low count of threads per centimetre.

An exceedingly fine diamond twill from the tomb of Elahbel at Palmyra in Syria (before *c.* 276) (warp 26, weft *c.* 160 per cm.) is evidence of an independent eastern tradition.[3] The fibres of the weft are as fine as the finest modern merino wool[4] and are dyed with murex- (true) purple.[5] Unusually for the eastern provinces, both systems are strong Z-spun. This piece was probably woven in Syria, although its origin is a thorny problem.[6] Fabrics such as this seem to have been the models for the weavers of western and northern Europe in the early Middle Ages. Trade links with Byzantium or with the Franks probably provided the material.[7]

2-OVER-I TWILL

Marta Hoffman has argued[8] that the types of 2-over-2 twill weave discussed above were developed on the warp-weighted loom, where the natural shed and the even division of the warp between two rows of loom-weights played an important role. 2-over-1 (or three-shaft) twill, on the other hand, is closely associated with a loom where the warp was not evenly divided, probably the two-beam loom (see p. 70).

2-over-1 twill is very rare indeed before the advent of the Romans in western Europe. I know only of one piece of Iron-Age date from Bastheim (Ldkr. Mellrichstadt).[9]

---

[1] Vejen Moss, Denmark: Hald (1950), 63, no. 38, fig. 49; Bernuthsfeld (Kr. Aurich): Hahne (1915), Taf. xxxx, Nr. 40; Gjeite, Nord-Trøndelag, Norway: Hougen (1935), 62 f., Fig. 13, Taf. x, 5. For counts see Hoffman (1964), 373, note 60.

[2] A piece from Marx-Etzel (Kr. Wittmund) (Hahne (1915), Taf. IX, Abb. 1 (plan); Taf. VIII, Abb. 1 (photograph)) appears from the photograph, but not from Hahne's weaving-plan, to have point repeat; cf. Hoffmann (1964), 189 f.

[3] Pfister (1937), 24, L 43, fig. 8, pl. VI a; cf. *ibid.* L 44. If the figures for the count are accepted—and they agree with the fibre-range of the yarn—it is unlikely that the weft is in fact the warp (*pace* Hoffmann (1964), 251); the shed could hardly be changed with 160 warp-threads per cm.

[4] Range 11–18μ (mean 15μ); cf. merinos listed in *Australian Journal of Science*, 25 (1963), 500.

[5] Pfister (1934), 61 f.

[6] The presence of murex-purple suggests that the wool was dyed on the Mediterranean coast; but a Z-spin-direction is unusual for ordinary fabrics in that district. The fineness of the wool, however, tips the balance in favour of Roman Syria, both for the spinning and the weaving. There may have been exclusive workshops run by specialists in Syria, where yarns were Z-spun. Other Z-spun twills come from the Cave of Letters (Yadin (1963), 251, pl. 88), from Dura-Europos (*Dura* (1945), no. 36), from Palmyra (Pfister (1934), 35 L 17) and from Antinoe (Hoffmann (1964), 374, note 71; cf. *CIBA-Review*, 133 (1959), 8–9).

[7] Hoffmann (1964), 250 f. She deals here at length with the fine twills from Birka in Sweden.

[8] *Ibid.* 200 ff., 202, 251.

[9] Hundt (1964). The linen yarns are Z-spun.

In Britain 2-over-1 twill of medium quality (perhaps a coloured cushion cover) was among the material deposited under a floor near the principia at Corbridge during the Trajanic withdrawal (table A, 50; fig. 21). At Mainz six fairly coarse fragments have been discovered (table B, 79–84). These finds, in both cases associated with the Roman army, stand alone until pagan Saxon England. In northern Europe they are unparalleled until the Vikings.[1] We may reasonably view them against the background of new looms (p. 69).

The deposit in the Cave of Letters near the Dead Sea (A.D. 132–135) contained only one piece of 2-over-1 twill with wide-set warp (3 per cm.) and double weft-threads (10 pairs per cm.). The Z-spin-direction of the yarns suggests that it was not locally woven. In the caves of Murabba'at there were two pieces, unfortunately without dated context.[2] After the end of the second century 2-over-1 twills in S-spun yarns are more common, notably at Dura-Europos.[3]

On present evidence—which is admittedly not much—the Romans do not seem to have attempted to weave herringbone or diamond 2-over-1 twills. But this may merely reflect our current lack of information. The Alamanni of South Germany on the other hand appear to have done so[4] and we should not be surprised to find later that they were continuing an already existing tradition.

FANCY WEAVES

The earliest textiles in a pattern-weave more complicated than diamond twill can be assigned to the third century A.D., when weavers in the Near East began a series of experiments with new weaves on new looms. Many of the experiments will have taken place within the boundaries of Roman Syria (as they stood in the third century), but the shifting political frontiers of the Partho-Persian and Roman Empires are unlikely to have hindered the free movement of technical ideas, and may even have helped it. The group of twills provisionally accepted as Syrian (p. 49) may point to the centre for these experiments.

The two lines of development in weaving which I shall plot in this context are suggested by the few textiles in fancy weaves which are at present recorded or have been seen by me. The sequence of the various stages in each line is mainly theoretical

---

[1] Hoffmann (1964), 200, 204.

[2] Cave of Letters: Yadin (1963), 251, pl. 88; Murabba'at: Crowfoot (1962), 55, nos. 5–6.

[3] *Dura* (1945), 44, nos. 188–198; from the Crimea: *C-R. Comm. Imp.* (1877–9), 141 f.; *Atlas* (1878), Taf. VI, 4 (late Roman according to Rostovtzeff (1931), 239).

[4] But see the complex 2-over-1 twills of Alamannic date from Niederstotzingen and Marktoberdorf: Hundt (1966), 101; *idem* (1967), 8, 12, Taf. 13, 14. There is no indication that they were imported.

and developments were clearly taking place simultaneously in both lines. This theme is not more than marginally relevant to the northern provinces and I hope at a later date to be able to write a fuller account when more late-Roman dated textiles are recorded. The outline below, accordingly, should be treated as an interim report.

The first series of experiments to be described was based on 2-over-2 twill, the second on 3-over-1 twill. The products of both are to be found in the western provinces.[1]

DAMASK CLOTH IN 2-OVER-2 TWILL

The literary evidence for silk damasks (*scutulata*)[2] is provided with a fitting commentary by two pieces from Trier (fig. 44) and one from Conthey (table B, 85; fig. 43; plate VIII). They differ little from one another in weave and pattern, both being relatively simple checks. All three are late-fourth-century in date. One of the Trier fragments has the workshop mark FL]ORENTIA OF embroidered on one corner with a sliver of hide. Whatever the correct reading of the mark may be,[3] it indicates that the silk was woven in a Latin-speaking area, perhaps in Italy. The connection of this workshop with Syria is clear from the fact that the warp is Z-spun in all three fragments, the weft unspun. As Pfister has shown, this is a characteristic of Near Eastern silks, not of Chinese.[4]

Nothing more complex than these checks seems to have been essayed in 2-over-2 twill and further developments towards sophisticated damasks take place in 3-over-1 twill and related weaves.

DAMASK CLOTH IN 3-OVER-1 TWILL

The first 3-over-1 twills may have been inspired by attempts to exploit the two-colour effects of simpler 2-over-1 twill (p. 50). The simplest example is a plain check damask in silk from Palmyra (before *c.* A.D. 276),[5] not far removed in general appearance from the damasks in 2-over-2 twill. The checkered elements of the design are alternately warp-faced and weft-faced. The pattern owes its effect to the

---

[1] Wild (1965 a) (note misprint: *unlikely* for *likely* on p. 248).

[2] See Wild (1964), 263 ff.

[3] The reading *FL]ORENTIA OF(FICINA)* may be the best. *FL]ORENTIA* would on analogy with provincial-Roman potters' stamps (e.g. on samian ware) be a personal name, although a genitive would be expected here. *FL]ORENTIA* may be an adjectival form of a name from the root *FLORENS*; for confusion in antiquity over *-ens* stems see Pliny, *Epist.* II. 17. 1. The reading *FL]ORENTI(N)A OF(FICINATRIX)* (*Zeitschr. Christ. Kunst*, XXIII (1910), 347) is less plausible; for specialist weavers were regularly men.

[4] Pfister (1937), 35 ff.; cf. *ZAK*, 18 (1958), 121 ff.   [5] Pfister (1937), 35, S 38, fig. 16.

light reflected from the silk threads at different angles, depending on which system predominates in each square. This effect is heightened if warp and weft are in contrasting colours.[1]

Slightly more complex versions of the same check pattern-weave have been found at Holborough, Kent (table A, 51; fig. 41) and at Palymra (fig. 42). These two are strikingly alike and perhaps come from the same workshop. The Palmyrene piece has blue-dyed warp and golden-brown weft[2] and there is a hint that the warp and weft of the Holborough fragments were dyed too. The workshop was probably Syrian.

The wealthy eastern merchants who settled in the Danube valley were buried, mummified in costly fabrics. From Brigetio, dated to *c.* A.D. 280–300, comes a 3-over-1 silk damask which probably belongs to the same series as the Holborough and Palmyra fabrics. It is too badly preserved to reconstruct its full repeat-pattern.[3]

COMPOUND CLOTH

The compound weft-faced cloths to be discussed next may belong to the same technical milieu as the 3-over-1 twill check damasks. But they represent a new dimension in pattern-weaving.

Four sheds only are required for the simplest compound cloth (fig. 45). The shots of weft lie alternately under 3 and over 1 warp-thread and under 1 and over 3. Odd-numbered weft-threads (shot 3/1) are of one colour, the even-numbered ones (shot 1/3) of another. As a result, one colour predominates on one face of the cloth, the other on the opposite face. The warp is invisible. By careful knitting of the heddles simple patterns can be achieved, the colours of which are reversed on opposite faces of the fabric.

The earliest piece in this technique is a silk fragment from Dura-Europos[4] which has a reversed key pattern in red on an undyed silk background. Its Z-spun yarns may indicate Syrian manufacture.

It is surprising how complicated check and lozenge patterns could apparently be woven with just four heddle-rods. Grace Crowfoot analysed and published several Coptic (undated) compound cloths in wool and found that, although the

[1] The Theodosian Code in a decree dated A.D. 393 (xv. 7. 11) distinguishes *sigillatae sericae* (figured silks) from *scutlatae et variis coloribus sericae* (check and coloured damasks).

[2] Pfister (1934), 42 S 6; *idem* (1937), 36, fig. 17.

[3] Hajnal (1965), 259–66; 262, fig. 5. I examined this material through the kindness of Fr. Hajnal and Dr E. Thomas in the Magyar Nemzeti Museum, Budapest.

[4] *Dura* (1945), 53, no. 263, pl. I, XXVI, F.

thread-up (knitting of the heddles) is involved, there are only four sheds. A similar piece in wool (probably late-Roman) was found in the Crimean *hypogea*.[1]

A number of compound cloths have a free or curvilinear pattern which would have required many individual sheds in the weaving (fig. 46). One might suppose that these sheds were mechanically opened (the design is a regular repeat), but not by a series of heddle-rods, since too many rods would have been needed. These textiles may be the first evidence for the introduction of a draw-cord device for raising a succession of different sheds (see p. 77).

The most important textile of this class is a silk fabric found in the coffin of St Paulinus at Trier and securely dated to *c.* A.D. 395 (table B, 88; fig. 46). The Z-spun warp is indicative again of a Syrian workshop. The story of the translation of the saint's body from Phrygia in its coffin of cedar of Lebanon supports the technical considerations about the origin of the silk.[2] Parallels for the pattern of circles and crosses can be readily found among the early Byzantine silks. There is no evidence that compound cloth was woven within the western provinces. None of the draw-loom silks imported direct from Han China (such as have been found in quantity at Palmyra) have yet come to light in the West as imports before the end of Rome's political control.[3]

4. COLOUR EFFECTS

The Gauls were fond of multi-coloured checks, according to Diodorus Siculus, but the Romans in Italy regarded tartans with suspicion. Pliny states categorically that the Gauls invented them.[4]

A single piece of tartan woollen cloth was found in Britain, at Falkirk (fig. 48; plate VI b; table A, 42), while several pieces came to light in Upper Germany, at Mainz (fig. 35). They are made up of dark and light (undyed?) woollen yarns. The Falkirk tartan has a simple check design (fig. 48), while one of the Mainz fragments is more complicated. Woollen checks had to be carefully planned during the warping of the loom, with a set number of threads of each colour in each stripe. The weaver followed the same plan in shooting the weft, so that the stripes corresponded.

[1] Crowfoot & Griffiths (1939), 40 ff. S-spun yarns; cf. Crowfoot (1962), 54, no. 2, fig. 14, from Cave of Murabba'at (undated). Crimea: C-R. Comm. Imp. (1877–9), 136 f.; Atlas (1878), Taf. v, 5. Weft here three-ply in black, dark-brown and yellow yarns.   [2] BJb, 77 (1884), 240 f.; 78 (1884), 170 f.

[3] Pfister (1937), 35 ff.; idem (1940), 75 ff.; The Art Bulletin, xxv (1943), 358 ff.

[4] Diodorus, v. 30. 1; Pliny, N.H. VIII. 196; cf. Wild (1964) for the literary evidence. Pliny's phrase (sc. vestes) scutulis dividere, which is verbally very close to Diodorus' πλινθίοις . . . διειλημμένους, can be more easily understood as a reference to tartans than to tablet-weaving, as I once took it. Woollen tartans were called scutulata in Latin, a word which in other contexts covered check silk damasks too.

Margrethe Hald records many tartans among the Danish bog-finds, dated both to the pre-Roman and Roman Iron Ages.[1] The North-German bog-finds contained others.[2] Check effects achieved by alternating S- with Z-spun yarns without a colour change are common among prehistoric finds, but are as yet without parallel in the Roman provinces.[3] The multitude of *scutulata* from the North contrasts markedly with their rarity in the East and confirms Pliny's statement that tartans are a peculiarly northern form of decoration.[4]

Garments decorated with woven bands were known both to the Gauls and to the Mediterranean peoples. There were, however, some technical differences in their treatment. While the Gauls simply used weft (or warp) of a different colour, without changing the thread-count, weavers of the Mediterranean area packed the coloured weft tight to cover the warp—a simple form of tapestry-weaving. Two pieces of banded woollen cloths (light-coloured bands on a darker ground) were found in the Walbrook in London (table A, 7–8) and one came from a similar context in Mainz (table B, 5). The linen from one of the gypsum burials at York appears to have had a (purple ?) band attached to, or woven into it (table A, 39 (4)).

The Walbrook fragments are important as the earliest tapestry-woven ornament in the western provinces. In a cosmopolitan city such as London they may well of course be imports. If home-produced, they are the first undisputed evidence of a Roman (or more properly an East-Mediterranean) technique being practised in the North.

Self-bands, decorative stripes formed by extra thick weft-threads, were popular for linen towelling (table A, 39, from York). An idiosyncrasy of linen weavers was to leave a band across the width of their products quite free of weft; and to accomplish this, they inserted a flat ferule into the shed and left it there while they wove another strip of the cloth (table B, 49; fig. 34, from Trier). This practice may have been learnt from workers in the East. It is unparalleled in prehistoric Europe[5].

While the prehistoric peoples of Europe were satisfied with strictly planned colour effects in warp and weft, the art of weaving intricate designs in Gobelin

[1] Hald (1950), 40, fig. 27; 43, fig. 29; 45, fig. 31; 93, fig. 82.

[2] Hahne (1915), Taf. xxxvIII, Abb. 5, 6; Hougen (1935), 65, fig. 15, Taf. xII, 2; Schlabow (1951), 176 ff., Abb. 6.

[3] Hundt (1959), 78, Nr. 16, Taf. 22; Potratz (1942), 18, Taf. 9, 10.

[4] The only checks I know from the East are: from Palmyra in cotton (Pfister (1937), 16, T 69, pl. IV, c; not a closed find, but probably third century A.D.); from Halabiyeh (before A.D. 610), one in wool (Pfister (1951), 31, no. 79, pl. xxI) and two in linen (*ibid.* 28, nos. 62, 63, pl. xxI). Certain types of simple blue-and-white checks, not unlike the Halabiyeh pieces, are found in Coptic Egypt and N. Africa in the Early Islamic period.

[5] *BCAC*, LXV (1937), 77 ff.

tapestry technique was already flourishing in Dynastic Egypt.[1] The patterns were worked in weft of various colours darned free-hand over the warp (see p. 71). Roman writers regarded it as an Egyptian invention. There is good evidence for tapestry in classical Greece.[2] In late antiquity the technique was widely practised in Syria and the other eastern provinces.[3] Most collections of Coptic textiles consist of up to 90 % of tapestry ornament of this kind.

Gobelin tapestry-weaving is a complex free-hand technique. Its products were probably called *vestes polymitae*. But the Walbrook textiles mentioned above might also have fallen into this category in Roman eyes, although they are woven mechanically, not free-hand. The famous *testamentum Lingonum* from Langres records *vestes polymitae* among the possessions of the dead man.[4] It is hard to say if these were figured tapestry designs or less sophisticated woven bands.

The only remains of free-hand tapestry from the northern provinces are a woollen band and a roundel from a late-Roman burial at Conthey (Kt. Wallis) (table B, 90; fig. 47). Both were woven separately and afterwards sewn upon the silk tunic (Sylwan Class C; see p. 71). The fine Z-spun weft of the roundel suggests a Syrian rather than an Egyptian workshop. A recent find from Xanten of a closely similar burial dated to the early fifth century is as yet unpublished.[5]

The speckled effect which can be created with warp and weft of different colours without a special pattern-weave was not exploited in the northern provinces. There is indeed only one example of it[6] (table B, 7). Others may perhaps have been spoiled by the peat-acids. Blended yarns of wool of different shades, which had been dyed in the fleece, are attested only once (table B, 72). There are no textiles in the North with painted or block-printed decoration (see p. 80).

5. BORDERS

Facts about weaving methods can often be gleaned from an examination of the borders of textiles, even if they are poorly preserved.

Diagnostic of the warp-weighted loom is the so-called starting-border (p. 63),[7]

[1] See Carter & Newberry (1904), 143–4 (fifteenth century B.C.); Dimand (1924), Taf. v, Abb. 9; Wild (1967 b).

[2] Gobelin ducks from the Crimea (fourth century B.C.): *C-R.Comm. Imp.* (1877–9), 133; *Atlas* (1878), Taf. v. 2.

[3] *Dura* (1945), *passim*; Pfister (1934), (1937), (1940), *passim*.

[4] *CIL*, XIII. 5708; see J.-J. Hatt, *La Tombe Gallo-Romaine* (1951), 66 ff. It is probably to be dated to the late first or early second century. See Wild (1967 b).

[5] From Xanten, Memoria II K. I am grateful for this information to Dr Ullemeyer and Dr H. Borger, the excavator.

[6] See *Viking*, x (1946), 177, pl. XI, for a diamond twill (*c.* A.D. 400) in contrasting colours. I am grateful to Dr Hoffmann for drawing my attention to this.   [7] For full account see Hoffmann (1964), 154 ff.

a separate band which is woven in a preliminary operation on a small band-loom. It provides firm anchorage for the main warp, which is woven into it (plate IX a). The band is sewn to the upper beam of the main loom and the unworked warp hangs down from it. Only one example has been discovered so far as I know in the western Empire, that at Verulamium (table A, 49). It is in plain-weave, attached to a diamond twill, and both its warp and weft are paired (fig. 28).

Unfortunately no selvedges survive on the cloth, so that the purpose of the border might be questioned. Several close parallels to it in structure can be quoted from Scandinavia;[1] and these are certainly starting-borders. On the other hand, there is at least one example from the salt-mines which is equally clearly an ornamental selvedge; it is in plain-weave on 2-over-2 weft-chevron twill.[2] System (1) of the Verulamium cloth is Z-spun, and so is the fringe, while system (2) is S-spun. The spin and the fringe together suggest, on analogy with other northern fabrics,[3] that system (1) is the warp. The border will then be a starting-border.

The following types of selvedge were woven in the Roman West:

(1) Plain selvedge with no special strengthening[4] (fig. 30).

(2) Tablet-woven selvedge over two extra warp-threads (fig. 32).

(3) Hollow selvedge over a tube of eight single warp-threads (tablet-woven ?). This gives a particularly strong edge to the cloth and was regularly used on pre-historic textiles[5] (table B, 59, 60; figs. 36, 37).

Tablet-woven selvedges do not appear to be known in the eastern Roman provinces (see p. 73).

Two methods of treating the loose ends of warp left after weaving deserve mention. The first and simplest is the fringe (table A, 49; B, 49), where groups of warp-threads are twisted together into a series of strands, which prevent the weft from fraying. A painstaking refinement on the fringe is the cordeline (table A, 44; fig. 49), where the already plied strands of the fringe were further twisted together in one direction parallel to the edge of the cloth. Work began at one corner of the web and proceeded steadily along the edge until all the loose strands were drawn into the cord and their ends tucked in.[6]

[1] E.g. Hald (1950), 164, fig. 166.

[2] Hundt (1960), 132, Nr. 29, Abb. 2.

[3] In textiles with a Z-spun and a S-spun system, the Z-spun is usually the warp in the North; cf. Hald (1950), 142. The fringe may be the lower edge of the cloth.

[4] See Yadin (1963), 200, fig. 67.

[5] Early Iron Age: Hundt (1960), 134, Nr. 31, Abb. 4; Roman Iron Age: Hahne (1915), Taf. XXXXI, Abb. 4; *Offa*, 3 (1938), 119 (no details given); Hald (1950), 156, fig. 150.

[6] See Audollent (1922), 61, with fig. (Les-Martres-de-Veyre); Yadin (1963), 202, fig. 68 (Cave of Letters).

6. SEWING TECHNIQUES AND EMBROIDERY

In contrast to the range of stitches applied to the textiles of prehistoric Denmark,[1] what is known of the provincial-Roman repertoire is somewhat limited. It can at least be said that sewing-thread was usually S-spun or S-plied in contrast to the Z-spun yarns in the cloth.

Plain running stitches were used to join two straight lines together on the wrong side (table A, 49; B, 37).[2] Simple overcast-stitches, found only once (table B, 34), are a normal feature of Iron-Age textiles.[3]

Two Roman edging-stitches have no precedents or parallels in antiquity so far as I can discover, and they are purely ornamental. The first example, from Mainz (table B, 18), is an elaborate form of couching, securing a thick thread against the cut edge of the cloth (fig. 31). The stitches on the surface of the fabric form a series of neat figures-of-eight (in running stitch), clearly to be viewed from one side only. The second example, from Verulamium (table A, 49; fig. 27) is a curious form of decorative overcast-stitching. The simple overcast-stitches themselves serve as 'warp' for six 'weft-threads' darned over them 1-over-1. A Coptic compound cloth of uncertain date and provenance in the Ashmolean Museum, Oxford, has precisely the same form of stitching; the overcast-stitches are in red, the 'weft' in alternate red and green thread.[4] The implication is that the Roman overcast-stitching was in colour too.

Decoration by brocading—a technique which is part weaving, part sewing—was well known in the Islamic period. I do not know of any Roman example, but it would be unwise to state that it was not a Roman technique.

The tradition of embroidery in western Europe before the Roman conquest was vigorous, but perhaps restricted in scope in comparison with the Hellenistic and Scythian work discovered in the Crimea and the Far East.[5] It is disappointing that the only provincial Roman embroidery (table B, 92 from Mainz) is a fragmentary zig-zag line in tent-stitch. The funerary inscription from Lingonian territory records *vestes plumariae*,[6] which there is good reason to believe were embroidered stuffs.[7]

---

[1] Hald (1950), 284 ff.   [2] *Ibid.* 285, fig. 287.   [3] *Ibid.* 285, fig. 284.

[4] Ashmolean Museum, Oxford, Inv. no. 1891.287 from Upper Egypt.

[5] Swiss neolithic embroidery: Vogt (1937), 76 ff.; of Hallstatt date from the Hohmichele: Riek & Hundt (1962), 206 f., Taf. 37; brocade from the Hallstatt saltmines: *Mit. Anthr. Ges.* LVI (1926), 346 ff., Abb. 1; Hellenistic embroidery from the Crimea: *C-R. Comm. Imp.* (1877–9), 113; *Atlas* (1878), Taf. III, 1–3; from Mongolia: *AJA*, XLVII (1943), 266 ff., figs. 1–4; from Greece: *ILN*, 23 January 1954, 114.

[6] See n. 4, p. 55.

[7] Mommsen & Blümner (1893), 156 f.; Blümner (1912), 218 f.

Needles of all classes and sizes in bone and bronze are found in profusion in the Roman provinces. The Corinium Museum, Cirencester, for example, has a representative selection from the Roman town, which I have examined.[1] Only one type, the small bronze needles (4–5 cm. long) with one or two eyelets close together, is likely to have been employed for the work described in the foregoing paragraphs. The bone needles would in most cases have been too large and clumsy. Thimbles in bronze precisely similar to their modern counterparts have turned up on several Roman sites (table I). Unfortunately none is stratified and none yet beyond doubt Roman, although this is highly likely. Literary evidence also fails us here.

[1] I am grateful to Mr John Rial of the Corinium Museum, Cirencester, for his kindness in showing me his material. If a representative selection of Roman needles could be compared with needles in use in modern primitive communities, more information by analogy might be forthcoming to assign the different types to their correct function(s).

VI

NON-WOVEN FABRICS

A number of fabrics which might broadly be classed as textiles, although they are not woven in the conventional way with warp and weft, deserve a chapter to themselves. On a theoretical basis they may be considered as the forerunners of woven cloth.[1]

1. KNITTING AND PLAITING

The best documented of the ancient techniques for the production of open- or close-work interlaced fabrics is called Sprang. The use of a Scandinavian loan-word to describe the technique is both a tribute to the work of the Scandinavian archaeologists and a reminder that it is still practised among the popular crafts of the North. I have adopted Margrethe Hald's description of the words and her diagrams[2] (fig. 51).

A fairly simple piece of Sprang was found in the rubbish-dump at Vindonissa (table B, 93; plate IX *b*). It would not be surprising to discover in the future that the craft was widely practised in the Roman provinces; for it is attested in many complicated forms in the pre-Roman Iron Age. It reached Egypt in the late-Roman period.[3]

The warp is spanned between two fixed rods on a framework. The loom may have been like the small loom from Oseberg, which I shall discuss in connection with tapestry-weaving (p. 72). Two rods (fig. 51, I and II) are inserted top and bottom to bring the rear system forward (fig. 51 *b*). With the aid of a stout pin, the weaver makes adjacent threads at the centre of the warp interlace and lock round their opposite numbers in the neighbouring pair. As soon as the threads have been twined together, two more rods (III and IV) are inserted to lock the crosses. The weaver then pushes each rod to its end of the frame and in so doing moves the points of the interlacing apart (fig. 51 *c*) to opposite ends of the warp. Top and bottom are in fact mirror-images of each other. When the next row is interlaced, the outer rods (I and II) can be removed and used again (fig. 51 *d*). The Vindonissa Sprang was twined on this principle, but each thread was wound thrice instead of once round its neighbours. The final crosses in the centre of the work have to be sewn into position to prevent the whole web from unravelling.

---

[1] La Baume (1955), 11 ff.   [2] Hald (1950), 249 ff., fig. 258.   [3] *Ibid.* 262 ff., figs. 263, 264, 269.

A curious plaited cord from a late-second-century female burial at Esch ('s-Herto-genbosch) in Holland has been interpreted as a piece of 'bobbin-work' by the exca-vators (table B, 95; fig. 50). (Bobbin-work is still done by children at the present day, using a cotton reel with four nails in the end.) The diagrams and photographs, on the other hand, do not bear this out, and a simpler technique, the interlacing of four threads by hand, may in fact be the solution. Bobbin-work as I understand it is based on only one thread. Margrethe Hald has published and explained a number of hand-plaited cords which, superficially at any rate, bear a close resemblance to the cord from Esch.[1]

The same tomb yielded a pair of bronze knitting needles in a wooden case. They are pointed at one end, blunt at the other, and measured originally about 20 cm. in length.[2] Their shape and context suggest that knitting was their purpose, but so far no knitting has been found in the northern provinces. The only Roman knitting I know was unearthed at Dura-Europos.[3]

2. FELT

Felt consists of a sheet of compressed woollen or other fibres, not spun, but held together by the surface irregularities of the fibre alone.[4] Wool with its elaborate scale structure is ideal for the purpose.

Felt linings for helmets (table A, 53 from Newstead) and for shoes (table B, 97 from the Petersberg, Basel, of hares' wool) must have been very common in the northern provinces. Felt-making, although known, is not described in detail by Roman writers, but there is plenty of evidence for its existence in Italy and Greece.[5] The wall-paintings from the workshop of Verecundus in Pompeii depict *coactiliarii* at work (fig. 52).[6] Two men stand on either side of a small boiler containing a heated liquid. Each pair has between them a draining-board supported on a trestle which leads back surplus moisture into the boiler. They appear to be kneading a mass of light-coloured fibres with their hands. All four factors to be expected in felt-making—pressure, friction, heat and moisture—are shown here.

[1] Hald (1950), 245, figs. 240–2.
[2] Information from Mr van den Hurk, who is shortly to publish the finds. Other finds of knitting-needles are somewhat dubious: see Fremersdorf (1950), 44 (from Köln).
[3] *Dura* (1945), 54 ff., no. 265, pl. XXVI. I find it hard to believe in the fragment of knitting in stocking-stitch exhibited in the Museo Nazionale, Naples, and assigned to Pompeii.
[4] *CIBA-Review*, 129 (1958), *passim*.
[5] See Forbes (1956), 89 ff. For felt-backing of a La-Tène shield from Egypt: *Germ.* 24 (1940), 109 (felt identified by von Stokar).
[6] Spinazzola (1953), I, 194 f., Tav. d'agg. 2; details of this wall-painting are now weathered beyond recogni-tion. For *lanarii coactores* see *CIL*, v. 4504, 4505, from Brescia.

VII

LOOMS

Until comparatively recently scholars were limited to two main sources of evidence for the looms and weaving methods of classical antiquity.[1] These comprised brief descriptive passages in ancient literature and a number of representations of looms, notably in Greek vase paintings. The sources were often misinterpreted since little was known about primitive looms from any period or area. Gradually, however, thanks to the efforts of a number of prehistorians and textile-students, more was learnt about the character and modes of operation of the most primitive looms and implements. The most recent outstanding contribution is that of Marta Hoffman, of the Norsk Folkemuseum, Oslo, who has collected the evidence relating to the modern warp-weighted looms of Scandinavia. The most valuable part of her work has been to record the methods of the weavers who still use these implements, following in a tradition from prehistoric times. I have made liberal use of her results, for they are the key to the understanding of the Roman loom.

1. WARP-WEIGHTED VERTICAL LOOM

The archaeological sources indicate that in Britain and the Rhineland before the Roman conquest the warp-weighted loom was more widely used than any other type.[1] The evidence for the Roman period is meagre. The characteristic features of the warp-weighted loom outlined below are listed by Seneca (writing c. A.D. 63, but probably paraphrasing Poseidonius (*ob. c.* 50 B.C.)) and mentioned in passing by other writers.[2] Sufficient facts are available from these sources to make it highly probable that Marta Hoffmann's descriptions of the looms of Scandinavia could almost be taken word for word to apply to Roman looms.

The Roman warp-weighted loom (fig. 53) was made up of two wooden uprights (i), 2 metres high or more, joined across the top by a cloth-beam (ii), which could probably revolve in crochets or holes in the uprights. It might be as much as 3 metres

[1] For special studies of Greek and Roman weaving see Blümner (1912), Johl (1917), Ling Roth (1951), Crowfoot (1936–7). Hoffmann (1964), 297 ff., is basic. I have rarely referred to secondary accounts in this chapter; they are quoted at some length in Hoffmann (1964). For prehistoric looms see La Baume (1955).

[2] Seneca, *Ep.* XC. 20 f.; Plutarch, *Conviv. Sept. Sap.* 156 B (c. A.D. 100); Pollux, *Onom.* VII. 36 (late Antonine); Hoffmann (1964), 39 ff., 63 ff., 81 ff., 109 f.

long.[1] From each upright at about breast height there projected a short bracket (iii), the end of which was usually forked to support one end of the heddle-rod (iv).[2] The brackets were set in holes in the uprights and could be adjusted for height. The heddle-rod itself was usually of wood, but may sometimes have been a stout reed.[3] (A single heddle-rod was all that was needed for plain-weaving; but two more would be added for 2-over-2 twill.)

Lower down the frame of the loom a shed-rod (v) spanned the gap between the uprights. The latter did not stand vertically, but were made to lean against a beam or a wall at a slight angle. All the odd numbered warp-threads (A) (or even-numbered as the case may be) hung down perpendicularly behind, but free of, the fixed shed-rod. Groups of them were fastened to each loom-weight. The leashes (that is, adjacent loops made out of a single length of twine) bound each of these odd-numbered warp-threads individually to the heddle-rod, which lay in the angle between the brackets and the uprights. The even-numbered warp-threads, on the other hand, were tied to a corresponding but separate row of loom-weights, and hung over the front of the shed-rod, parallel to the tilted uprights.[4] In this position (fig. 53 a) the so-called 'natural' shed (X) is open. To change it, the heddle-rod is placed in the forks of its supports and the back row of (odd numbered) warp-threads is thus drawn to the front of the even-numbered (fig. 53 b). This creates the artificial shed (Y). Two spacing-cords (vi), one for each system, were stitched in and out of the warp-threads to hold them apart correctly. The ends of the cords were tied to the uprights.

The archaeological evidence for Roman looms is limited. Several houses in Herculaneum (before A.D. 79) had looms set up in the courtyard.[5] All that remains of them is a row (or perhaps two rows) of baked clay loom-weights. The Greek vase paintings are another indirect source of information, but no Roman representations or warp-weighted looms exist.[6] I know of no actual remains of looms in the western provinces.

Under these circumstances the loom-weights which survive are important. Identification of them is difficult, unless they are found in groups. Isolated finds of

[1] Figures in Hoffmann (1964), 314, 388, note 35.

[2] Hoffmann (1964), 309 f.

[3] (H)arundo, 'reed', separates the warp according to Ovid, Met. VI. 55; cf. κάλαμοι, which appear to be heddle-rods in Joh. Chrysostomus, Homilia. XII (ed. Migne, 62. 92), and P. Teb. 414. 12 (second century A.D.). This is a reed in a botanical sense, not the 'reed' or batten on a modern handloom.

[4] Where the loom has been burnt in situ, two rows of loom-weights may be found (Hoffmann (1964), 311 ff.). No record has yet been published of an instance of this at Pompeii.

[5] Maiuri (1958), 430.   [6] Hoffmann (1964), 297 ff.

weights, especially if they are marked with their value, must be treated with care.[1] Provincial-Roman loom-weights are pyramidal, with a single hole at the vertex (see table M; fig. 16). They can be easily distinguished from the triangular loom weights of the British Iron Age and the circular weights of the Anglo-Saxons and tribes of free Germany. Pyramidal weights are, however, found in both pre- and post-Roman contexts. The list of Roman loom-weights is relatively short, but this need not indicate that the warp-weighted loom was rare too. Weights in sun-dried clay would rapidly disintegrate.

WARPING AND DRESSING THE WARP-WEIGHTED LOOM

The framework of the warp-weighted loom which I have described above and the principles of weaving plain cloth with one heddle-rod are relatively easy to grasp from the ancient written sources and modern parallels. The essential details of how the loom was warped, how the heddles (leashes) were knitted and how the weft was shot can only be tentatively described, and that mainly by reference to modern Scandinavian practice (fig. 54; plate X). The starting-border from Verulamium (table A, 49) and the faults detected in certain textiles are the only clues as to Roman methods. Much more can be deduced from the rich prehistoric material in northern Europe; and to a large extent such deductions will also be valid for the western Roman provinces. As I have said elsewhere, in this area the Roman invasion brings no immediate changes in textile methods; and it would be virtually impossible to distinguish Iron-Age from Roman cloth on technical grounds alone.

The warp of the warp-weighted loom was attached to the clothbeam by means of a starting-border in plain-weave, which was woven in a preliminary operation on a small band-loom[2] (see below, p. 72 and plate X c). The warp-threads of the band (six pairs in the Verulamium textile) are A–A in my diagram (fig. 55). The ball of weft (B) remains always on the same side of the band and the weaver pulls a loop of weft (C) through the open shed with her crooked finger. She draws the loop round two pegs (D and E) and finally slips it over the top of peg D. (It is characteristic of starting-borders to find two weft-threads in each shed.) When about twenty loops have been woven, she removes them from the pegs. Inserting her hand through the loops, she makes a cross and divides the odd and even threads, so that they can be rolled into separate balls. She works in this fashion until she reaches the end of the band.[3]

[1] They may be simple weights; but since the weight of the loom-weights is important in balancing the warp-systems (Hoffmann (1964), 42), some may have been deliberately marked.

[2] For details see Hoffmann (1964), 63 ff., figs. 24–7, 151 ff.

[3] A starting-border in this state (of Roman Iron Age date) was found at Tegle in Norway and has been republished recently by Hoffmann & Traetteberg (1959).

The starting-border with its hanging bundles is sewn to a perforated strip of wood attached to the cloth-beam of the main loom.[1] Each bundle containing a group of odd numbered warp-threads is loosened and tied to a single loom-weight; the warp then hangs vertically from the beam behind the fixed shed-rod. The even numbered warp-threads are treated similarly, but hang over the front of the shed-rod[2] (plate X *b*). A spacing-cord is then tied like a chain around the warp-threads of both systems to space them evenly and pushed down to within a short distance of the loom-weights.

The heddle-rod (lying on its brackets) is then connected ('knitted') by a separate loop or leash to each of the warp-threads of the rear system. Each leash passes between two threads of the front system. For weaving 2-over-2 twill, the knitting of the heddles (there are three heddle-rods and a shed-rod) is more complicated; each leash on the upper and lower rod holds one thread from the front system and one (adjacent) thread from the rear system (fig. 54). The method of warping with alternate threads in front and rear systems may often have been adjusted to put alternate *pairs* in front and rear.[3] The northern weavers no longer weave twill in the old way, but Marta Hoffmann has established how their heddles were knitted from Icelandic written accounts.[4] It is clear from these that a single heddle-rod governs a single shed, in contrast to modern hand-loom weaving, where two (linked) shafts are moved to open each shed (fig. 54).

The faults in Roman textiles which might be thought to throw some light on how the heddles were knitted are unfortunately ambiguous. We rarely know which is the warp or which is the front face of the cloth. Some mistakes were probably caused by faulty knitting of the heddles (e.g. two threads in the same leash instead of one) or the breaking of a leash. Others may equally well be weft-faults caused by the weavers forgetting to change the shed between shots.

The weaver of the Huntcliff twill (table A, 43), which has paired warp-threads, was clearly in some difficulty. Some of her shots are 1-over-3. The theoretical explanations of this are not entirely satisfactory (fig. 25).

By the Icelandic method, where each heddle-rod opens a complete shed, each leash should hold two warps, or in this case, two paired warps, four threads in all (figs. 54, 56). On this showing each leash on the Huntcliff loom held one (paired) warp instead of two; and another string of leashes bound to the same rod took up

[1] Hoffmann (1964), 64, 109 ff.
[2] The end of the warp may trail on the floor, while the weights are tied so as to hang just above the floor and can be adjusted as the web is rolled up on the cloth-beam.
[3] See Hald (1950), 164, 168, fig. 173.   [4] Hoffmann (1964), 131 ff., figs. 59, 91.

the relevant adjacent (paired) warps to make up the 2-over 2-under weft-passage. Withdrawal of one of these strings (the fault) would leave 1-over 3-under. It is hard to see how this could have happened all at once. An alternative theory on modern lines would be to assume that the weaver raised two heddle-rods for each shed (fig. 56) and occasionally forgot to raise the second rod of the pair. But the effort involved for her in lifting two rods instead of one heavier rod would slow the work down, unless there were some good reason for her to divide the weight of the heddles between two rods.

In Scandinavia the weft is normally introduced into the open shed in the form of a dolly, a skein of yarn with a hard 'head'[1] (fig. 58). The shuttle (med. Lat. *navicula*) was unknown to the Romans,[2] and the Greek stick-spool (πηνίον) is hardly mentioned in the Roman period. It is natural to suppose, therefore, that a dolly was used and that Nonius' gloss 'roll of weft' (*tramae involucrum*)[3] with reference to *panus* is evidence of this.

The shed is wide enough (*c.* 20 cm., 8 in.) for the Lappish weavers to throw the dolly half-way through, and carry it by hand for the rest of the way.[4] It is clear from Margrethe Hald's analysis of complete Iron-Age textiles[5] that two or more weavers were often employed on the same web. Each would have her dolly and walk to and fro in front of the loom as it was passed through the shed. Roman writers often mention weavers walking about or standing at their looms.[6] When the shed was changed between each shot, if two women were weaving, each would take one end of the relevant heddle-rod; for it would be too heavy for one person to lift in a single action.[7] If the fabric was fairly coarse, the weft could be beaten up after every few shots with the fingers alone.[8] When a certain amount of cloth had been woven, it could be wound up on the beam and the loom-weights tied lower down the warp, as is shown in the Greek vase paintings.

IMPLEMENTS FOR BEATING-UP

A number of special tools were associated with the action of beating-up in antiquity. Characteristic of the cultural assemblage of the Early Iron Age in south-western Britain is a series of bone tools which have been claimed as textile implements.

---

[1] Hoffmann (1964), 55, fig. 19.

[2] For perhaps the earliest illustration of a shuttle see Singer & Holmyard (1956), II, 212, fig. 181 (MS 0.9.34 fo. 32b in Trinity College Library, Cambridge; *c.* A.D. 1250).

[3] *Panus* (Greek πήνη) glossed by Nonius (149. 17), who quotes Lucilius.

[4] Hoffmann (1964), 67, 89 f.   [5] Hald (1950), 152 f., figs. 139–40.

[6] Artemidorus, *Onir.* III. 36; Servius, *ad Aen.* VII. 14.

[7] Hoffmann (1964), 67, 110.   [8] Hoffmann (1964), 67, 71, fig. 31.

They are found in large numbers in the lake-villages of Glastonbury and Meare in Somerset and also in the brochs and dwellings of northern Scotland.[1] They include bobbins (which have been described above, p. 34), pin-beaters and weaving-combs.

The pin-beaters (famous as 'bone gouges'[2]) are cut from the tibia or metatarsal of the sheep or goat; the shaft is cut diagonally to give a point and the butt-end may be roughly trimmed.[3] The point would be inserted instead of the finger directly through the warp to push up the loose weft. This type is rare in the Roman period, and occurs rarely outside Britain (table J).[4] The implement may well have been used for purposes other than weaving in other contexts. It occurs, for example, in suspiciously large numbers at Maiden Castle when set against the small number of weaving combs recorded here.[5]

A more sophisticated version of the same tool is found after the Roman conquest (table K). Both Romans and Saxons were familiar with it. Shaped like a cigar, about 10 cm. long, it is sharp at both ends, polished and round in section (fig. 16). In Scandinavia an identical object was used for pushing home the weft and rearranging the warp-threads when they became displaced.[6] It was either thrust directly into the warp from the front beneath the loose weft or drawn lightly across the face of the warp, as if the latter were the strings of a musical instrument.

Only pin-beaters of bone have been found, but if the equation of the pin-beater with the *radius* of literature is correct,[7] they may often have been of wood as well. The same implement was also used as the *broche* or spool in tapestry-weaving.

A bone or antler weaving-comb was an everyday part of the equipment of the weaver in the Iron Age in Britain. Its function was once disputed; but identical tools are used by weavers in Central America today. Plano-convex in section, it has a long handle (10–20 cm.) and about ten short teeth (fig. 16). The handle is often decorated and the teeth sometimes show signs of wear.[8] It was used in the same way as the pin-beater to beat up the weft from the front, but may only have been used on fairly coarse woollen cloth. Both tools could have been brought into play on the same web.

[1] Childe (1935), 239, 257-8.

[2] Identified by Mrs Grace Crowfoot in *Antiquity*, XIX (1945), 157-8.

[3] Wheeler (1943), 303 ff., with literature.

[4] Examples of uncertain date are found in the Frisian terps, perhaps imported from Britain: Roes (1963), 34 ff., pl. XXXVII.

[5] 75 against 25 (Wheeler (1943), 297, 303).

[6] Hoffmann (1964), 126 f., 135 ff., fig. 61, 279 ff. For Anglo-Saxon examples see *Med. Arch.* VIII (1964), 61, 64, fig. 16, nos. 21-2.

[7] Wild (1967 *b*).

[8] Against identification: Ling Roth (1951); comb from America in Museum of Archaeology and Ethnology, Cambridge, Inv. no. 24.1216. British combs: Bulleid & Gray (1911), I, 266 ff.; Henshall (1950), 160.

If the weft were caught up, the teeth of the comb might break and the pin-beater could have been taken instead.

Bone weaving-combs of Iron-Age type are relatively common on Roman sites in North Britain (table L), but absent from the Rhineland and most of lowland Britain.[1] Literary evidence for the weaving comb (*pecten*) does not connect it with the warp-weighted loom; but if bone combs were associated with it (as the Iron-Age contexts suggest), then wooden *pectines* may have been known in the North too.[2]

The third implement for beating-up is the weaving-sword (*spatha*). As its name implies, it was a long, flat blade (c. 50 cm. in length) which was thrust into the shed to push up the weft (plate X *a*). The weaver held the handle in both hands in order to do this. The Germanic people used iron weaving-swords from the Early Iron Age until the Migration Period and they are still in use in Scandinavia.[3] I have found no extant Roman weaving-swords, but the literary evidence, both Greek and Roman, leaves no room for doubt that they were used with the warp-weighted loom.[4]

DISTRIBUTION AND DATING OF THE WARP-WEIGHTED LOOM

Both Seneca (the passage was written c. A.D. 63)[4] and Julius Pollux (writing c. A.D. 180–192)[5] hint or state that in their own time the warp-weighted loom was being rapidly displaced by the two-beam loom in Italy and the Mediterranean provinces. What the situation was in the northern provinces is unknown. The loom-weights and the starting-border imply that the warp-weighted loom was used in the area until at least the third century. I have tried to show that the weaves and some of the tools associated with the warp-weighted loom in the Iron Age continued in everyday use into the Roman period in the provinces and the same may be true of the warp-weighted loom itself. It is noteworthy, however, that Roman loom-weights are found in greater numbers on the least Romanised dwelling-sites in the provinces (table M).

For the weaving of certain classes of fabric the warp-weighted loom may have held its own, even if it was displaced in most fields by new types of loom. The situation in late antiquity, where there is both written and material evidence, is instructive.

---

[1] For weaving-combs from the terps: Roes (1963), 26 f., pl. XXXIII, 1, 2. Voconia Nigrina on a gravestone from Chester is said to be holding a weaving-comb (*Cat. Chester* (1950), pl. XXV), but I cannot see it on the stone. For North British combs see Henshall (1950), 147, fig. 5; Richmond (1958), 26 f.

[2] *Edictum Diocletiani*, XIII. 4, where it is as cheap as a pin-beater (*radius*) and a spindle, and must have been smaller than the Egyptian tapestry-combs.

[3] Hoffmann (1964), 279 ff., for full account of weaving-swords at all periods; for an oak *spatha* of Roman Iron Age date from Holland: *Palaeohistoria*, XI (1967), fig. 65, 1, pl. 16, 3.

[4] Seneca, *Ep.* XC. 20; Pollux, *Onom.* X. 125; cf. Hesychius *s.v.* σπαθατόν. [5] Pollux, *Onom.* VII. 36.

Festus (in the late-second century)[1] states that the *tunica recta*, a special garment worn by boys and brides, was woven on a loom at which the weavers stood and beat the weft up (*a stantibus et in altitudinem*)—that is, on the warp-weighted loom. In the fourth century Servius[2] explains a Vergilian phrase with the words: 'because they used to weave standing in former times, as we see the linen weavers (*linteones*) doing today'. The *tunica recta* was probably of linen (Festus' *ominis causa* may imply that it was a symbol of purity), so that the two passages of the grammarians can be taken to refer to the same type of linen garment woven on the warp-weighted loom.

The practice persisted until the eleventh century at least in some parts of the Roman world. Theophylact, once a tutor at the Byzantine court,[3] says that the warp-weighted loom was still in use in Palestine in his own day. He thinks that the seamless (ἄρραφος) robe of Christ was woven in one piece on this type of loom. Coptic cruciform tunics, which are of the same shape and size as the Gallic coat, possess in some cases a starting-border or a heading-cord.[4] They may have been woven on the warp-weighted loom and may be examples of what earlier writers called the *tunica recta*.

If my interpretation so far is correct, the warp-weighted loom had some marked advantages over other types of loom which ensured its survival. The unusual width of the cloth which can be woven on it (webs over 2 metres wide) may be one important factor. The northern two-beam loom was probably somewhat narrower.[5] The shed which can be opened on the warp-weighted loom is exceptionally wide and allows the dolly to be thrown or passed by hand over a long distance. The narrower shed on the two-beam loom where the warp is less flexible may not permit such a long shot of weft, nor has the seated weaver so long a reach.[6]

All the late references quoted above apply to linen weaving and may not seem relevant to the northern provinces. They do, however, show the value of the 'old weaving method', as Pollux calls it,[7] in an area where competition from other types of loom was particularly strong.

---

[1] Festus, 380 (p. 342); 403 (p. 364).

[2] Servius, *ad Aen.* VII. 14; Johl (1917), 67 ff., rejects both passages as mistaken, but he has an axe to grind.

[3] Theophylactus, *ad Johannem.* XIX. 23 (Migne, 124. 276).

[4] Hald (1946), 57 f., fig. 5 (linen strip); Hald's tunics are 2.30 m. (p. 67 f., fig. 16) and *c.* 2.60 m. (p. 70 f., figs. 18–19) wide; cf. Hoffmann (1964), 392. Gallic coat: *BJb*, 168 (1968), 168 f.

[5] The Huldremose skirt is 1.68 m. wide (Hald (1950), 49).

[6] Hald (1946), 57 f., fig. 5, with *eadem* (1950), 183, figs. 202–3. It is interesting to note that the size of the web woven on the warp-weighted loom in the Middle Ages was a factor in its survival: Endrei (1961), 130.

[7] Pollux, *Onom.* VII. 36.

2. TWO-BEAM VERTICAL LOOM

Seneca regarded the two-beam loom as a more refined instrument than the warp-weighted loom.[1] When it was introduced into Italy is unknown, but it was established there before the beginning of our era. It was known at an earlier date in both Egypt and Scandinavia.[2]

Four representations of the loom in the Roman period give some valuable facts about its structure.

A frieze from the Forum of Nerva in Rome (finished under Trajan) portrays the story of the tapestry-weaving contest between Arachne and Minerva[3] (fig. 59; plate XI a). Three identical looms are shown. They each have (wooden) uprights about 2 metres high, to judge by the size of the figures. They are square or perhaps rectangular in section and stand free on blocks. One feels that the dimensions of the timbers may be exaggerated. The upper and lower beams appear to be flat and were probably pegged to the front of the uprights. In two closely related, but damaged, scenes a standing and a seated female figure are between them setting up the warp on the loom. The bundle of warp-threads can be seen in their hands. In another scene Minerva is striking the seated Arachne, but the loom behind them in very low relief shows no trace of the presumably finished tapestry. The looms are set up out of doors.

A sketched outline of a similar loom formed part of the scene on a third-century tombstone.[4]

More details survive on a wall-painting of the first half of the third century in the *hypogeum* of the Aurelii in Rome[5] (plate XI b). The theme is Odysseus' arrival on Circe's isle. The free-standing uprights of the slender loom are supported on square blocks of wood. The two beams and the warp can be clearly seen. The weaver stands behind the loom, seen from the point of view of those looking at the wall-painting. Consequently the single heddle-rod (?), set at about breast height, runs on the far side of the uprights and the ends of its brackets (?), pegged through the uprights, are visible. There appears to be a short shed-rod some distance above the

---

[1] *Ep.* XC. 20: *subtilius genus.* He was writing in the mid-first century A.D.

[2] Singer & Holmyard (1954), I, 438 ff.; Hald (1950), 211 ff.

[3] Von Blanckenhagen (1940), 124, Taf. 40–2. I cannot accept Mme. Picard-Schmitter's forcefully presented, but totally unproven, thesis that these are horizontal draw-looms (*Latomus*, XXIV (1965), 296 ff.); see Wild (1967 b).

[4] Johl (1917), 48, Abb. 32. I am grateful to Dr Hoffmann for supplying me with a photocopy of this figure.

[5] *Art and Archaeology*, XI (1921), 169 ff., pl., fig. 1; Carcopino (1956), pl. XIV (lower fig.); Wilson (1938), 22, pl. X, fig. 11.

heddle-rod. There are peg-holes to the top of the uprights which would allow the upper beam to be adjusted. The web which has so far been woven carries a coloured band. To judge by the position of the web and on analogy with the looms in the Forum of Nerva, the weaver must have worked seated. Again, it is an outdoor scene.

The famous early fifth-century *Codex Vaticanus*, 3225, illustrates the story in Vergil's *Aeneid*, VII. 5–9, with a picture of Circe at her loom[1] (fig. 60). The loom is strikingly similar to that in the *hypogeum* just described and presumably stems from the same traditional copy-book. This loom is provided with more peg-holes in the uprights.

There is no direct evidence for the presence of the two-beam vertical loom in Gaul or Britain. On the other hand a group of Danish textiles published and discussed by Margrethe Hald[2] point to knowledge of it in Scandinavia during the pre-Roman Iron Age. The 2-over-1 twills from Bastheim, Mainz and Corbridge (p. 49) may have been woven on this type of loom.

The loom was probably warped directly with one or two balls of yarn. Margrethe Hald's analysis of certain 'tubular-woven' fabrics, particularly the Huldremose skirt (which retains the cylindrical shape which it had on the loom), reveals several ways in which this was done in the Iron Age.[3] A rod set across the front of the loom in the position of a shed-rod is the focal point of the operation (fig. 57). While the yarn spans the whole of the space between the two beams at the back of the loom, it reverses round the rod at the front and returns to the back again. This arrangement is immediately suitable for plain-weave.[4] If the loops round the rod are readjusted after warping, they can be paired and so form the basis for 2-over-2 twills[5] (fig. 61).

Marta Hoffmann has expressed the opinion that 2-over-1 twill, which cannot make such good use of the natural division of the warp into two halves on the warp-weighted loom as 2-over-2 twill does, is more suited to the two-beam than to the warp-weighted loom.[6] The natural division makes knitting the heddles for 2-over-2 twill easier; without it the threads for all four sheds (not just for three) would have to be separately counted out for the heddle-rods and shed-rods. This is less of a problem where only three sheds are involved. The suggestion is theoretically attractive, but cannot as yet be shown to be true from archaeological material.

[1] *Cod. Vat. Lat.* 3225. Pict. 39; De Wit (1959), 151 ff., 205 ff., Taf. 22, 2 (with discussion of dating).
[2] Hald (1950), 167 ff., 211 ff. A further account of these looms is promised by Dr Hald.
[3] Hald (1950), 167 ff.   [4] Hald (1950), 169, fig. 175.
[5] Hald (1950), 168, figs. 173–4.   [6] Hoffmann (1964), 251 ff.

Two types of fabric could be woven on the two-beam loom. On the one hand, plain cloth or twill could be woven with the aid of a number of heddle-rods and a shed-rod, just as it was on the warp-weighted loom. On the other hand, the two-beam loom could be used as a tapestry frame for decoration in Gobelin and allied techniques, where a single heddle-rod and a shed-rod opened the shed for the plain ground-weave and the weaver herself opened the sheds for the free-hand tapestry. The pictures of looms mentioned above all show tapestry-weaving in progress.

Details of how plain cloth or twill was woven are not available.[1] The shooting of the weft and the manipulation of the heddle-rods would in principle be the same as for the warp-weighted loom. Writers emphasise that the weavers sat down at the two-beam loom, beating the weft downwards, but stood and walked to and fro before the warp-weighted loom.[2] As the fell of the cloth advanced, the warp could be made to slide round the beams to bring the edge back to within easy reach of the weaver. Johannes Chrysostomus (late fourth century) says that a comb (κτήν) was used to beat up the weft.[3]

Ovid provides the classic description of the tapestry-weaving contest between Arachne and Minerva, which is represented on the frieze in the Forum of Nerva.[4] The shed is opened by a shed- or heddle-rod (*harundo*) for the ground-weave. The brightly coloured weft is introduced on a series of pointed spools (*radii, broches*) into sheds opened with the fingers (? *quod digiti expediunt*). The web is beaten up with a weaving-comb (*pecten*). The poet gives a glowing account of the colours, the complexity of the designs and the shaded bands (*parvi discriminis umbrae*). He is quite clearly drawing on his own experience and is anxious to prove himself *doctus*— well-informed.

Egyptian tapestry of the Coptic period allows a technical insight into certain weavers' methods. The plain-weave linen ground was woven with rods, but there were various ways in which the coloured woollen weft of the Gobelin decoration was introduced. Vivi Sylwan has put them into three categories.[5]

In Class A the weft of the ground-weave turned back at the point where the weaver planned a roundel or figure. She grouped the free warp-threads by hand into bundles (sometimes leaving some warp out) and inserted the weft round them in plain-weave (so-called 'tapestry over x warps'). The shed was always picked up by hand. The space available was filled as if with mosaic-work and the weft was not

---

[1] For the use of modern Syrian looms of this type: Hald (1963), 98 ff.

[2] Artemidorus, *Onir.* III. 36.

[3] *Homilia.* XII (Migne. 62. 92). The κάλαμοι (heddle-rods?) imply that he is not talking of pure tapestry-weaving.

[4] *Met.* VI. 55 ff.   [5] Dimand (1924), 22 f.

always at right-angles to the warp. She would beat up with the point of a spool (*radius*), using it as a pin-beater. When the space was full, she continued with the ground-weave.

For Class B tapestry the weft of the ground-weave was cut away and the woollen weft inserted in its place. Class C tapestry was woven separately on a different loom (perhaps like the loom discussed below), and sewn afterwards to the garment or hanging. The roundel from Conthey (fig. 47; table B, 90) was of this type.

The weaving-comb (*pecten*), which is mentioned as the characteristic tool of the tapestry weaver, was of wood.[1] The Coptic combs from Egypt, a number of which have reached European museum collections, have a very wide head and many short teeth (fig. 16). With a narrow comb of the British Iron-Age type it would not be easy to bring the various sections of the weft into line.[2]

An unusually small two-beam loom, probably for weaving tapestry, is mentioned in a mid-first century document from Oxyrhynchus.[3] Its height is three weavers' cubits minus two palms (that is, about 90 cm. or 3 ft.), and it comprises two up-rights (ἱστόποδες) and two beams (ἀντία). Slightly larger is a finely finished minia-ture wooden loom from the Oseberg ship-burial in Denmark, which formed a small item in this extraordinarily rich Viking grave.[4] Its uprights are 119 cm. high (3 ft. 8 in.) and the maximum breadth at the base is 75 cm. The beams are carefully shaped to take a web about 33–34 cm. wide, the length of which could be adjusted (fig. 68). Although it is far removed in time and place from the Oxyrhynchus loom, the cultural connections of the Viking find point to the Mediterranean world.[5] The loom may have been used for tapestry-weaving or for Sprang (see p. 59).

3. BAND LOOMS

Knowledge of Roman band looms is restricted to what can be deduced from the textiles themselves. They existed, but beyond this bare fact there is no information. Bands can be woven from warp stretched between the weaver's belt and a convenient fixed point, in which case there is no loom-frame.[6] On the other hand, the starting-border may have required some sort of rigid framework; for its weft had to be carefully measured out.

---

[1] Ovid, *Met.* VI. 60; Martial, XIV. 150.
[2] Norwegian weavers used a similar instrument: Hoffmann (1958), 65 ff.
[3] *P. Ox.* 264. 3–5 (A.D. 54). For a horizontal tapestry-frame (?) from Herculaneum see p. 75 below.
[4] *Oseberg*, II, pl. XIV; cf. Hoffmann (1964), 330 f., fig. 137.
[5] For cultural connections see *Oseberg*, III, 410 ff., 418 ff.
[6] *CIBA-Review*, 117 (1956), 4 ff.

There are three methods by which the sheds of the bands were, or may have been, opened. They are: with tablets, with a rigid heddle-frame, or with heddles of string.

Tablet-weaving (*Brettchenweberei*) has over the past sixty years claimed almost more than its fair share of attention. As a popular craft it is practised all over the world; and the evidence for it among prehistoric finds has naturally aroused great interest. I do not propose to describe the technique in detail here, since many full accounts of it in all the major European languages are available.[1]

Roman tablets are of thin bone or bronze, usually about 4 cm. square with a hole at each corner[2] (fig. 64). A variant form of triangular shape is sometimes found (fig. 63), but too few firmly dated examples are known for it to be possible to use the shape as a guide to the date (table O). The pattern of evidence is one of sporadic finds of individual, or pairs of, tablets, but their identification is assured by the peculiar nature of the wear round the holes. Nothing like the magnificent pack of fifty-two wooden tablets from the Oseberg ship has yet been found that can be assigned to an earlier date.[3] There are no recorded tablets outside the northern provinces and Coptic Egypt, so that it is impossible to say whether the technique was a familiar one in Italy and Greece.

Each tablet governs the four (or three) warp-threads which are threaded through its holes[4] (fig. 66); and the pack of tablets is held in the hand like a pack of cards, parallel to the warp. By turning the tablets either backwards or forwards consistently, the shed which lies between the upper and lower pair of threads on each tablet is changed and the groups of warp-threads are twisted into a cord. The weft, which is invisible, merely serves to hold the cords together. By varying the colours of the warp-threads and turning individual or groups of tablets in different directions, complicated figured patterns can be achieved in the warp.

Primitive weavers favour a kind of forked shuttle for bandweaving which could be used equally well for tablet-weaving.[5] It bears a striking resemblance to the so-called 'netting-needles' found in abundance on many Roman sites (table N). The weft is wound parallel to the shaft of the 'needle' between the two sets of prongs (fig. 65). While it would be inadmissible to argue from the lack of actual netting surviving in the Roman West that netting-needles were not used for netting, there is a strong presumption that they were used for band-weaving.

[1] Pralle (1921); Hald (1934); Schlabow (1957); *CIBA-Review*, 117 (1956), 1 ff.
[2] Behrens (1925).   [3] *CIBA-Review*, 117 (1956), 1 ff.
[4] Schlabow (1957), 10 ff., Abb. 3–7.
[5] A selection is on exhibition in the Bankfield Museum, Halifax, Yorkshire.

Three provincial-Roman textiles from Mainz (table B, 8, 59, 60) have tablet-woven selvedges. The selvedges in question were probably woven on one of the larger looms at the same time as was the main body of the web. Only two holes of the tablets were required, and the weft of the main web is also the weft of the selvedge. One of the selvedges is very simple (table B, 8) and could have been made with a single tablet (fig. 32). The other two are tubular (see p. 56) (fig. 37) and would have needed perhaps four tablets. Some very elaborate textiles with tablet-woven borders have been found in Free Germany.[1] Some of the plain-woven bands from Mainz may have been woven on tablets with two holes, but there is no way of proving this.

Tablet-weaving was regularly used for the starting-borders of Iron-Age textiles and this seems to have been its primary function. The corded structure of the band affords particularly strong anchorage for the main warp. In the later Iron Age (Migration and Viking periods) the full potentiality of tablet-weaving was realised and the bands became works of art. They were woven specially on a separate loom and required a weaver skilled in the manipulation of the tablets to get the maximum effect from the multicoloured warp-threads. The bands were sewn to the edges of the garments afterwards.[2]

It is difficult to judge whether tablet-weaving was peculiar to the northern provinces, but at the moment it appears to be so. A recent find of classical Greek date from the Kerameikos in Athens may possess a tablet-woven selvedge. The earliest tablets unearthed in Egypt are Coptic.[3]

A second implement in use in Scandinavia for opening the shed in band-weaving is the rigid heddle or heddle-frame. I know of only one (incomplete) example in the northern Roman provinces.[4] It was found in the 'Lawe' on the site of the Roman supply-base at South Shields, but its exact find-spot was not recorded[5] (plate IX *a*).

[1] Schlabow (1951); La Baume (1955), 144, Abb. 114.

[2] Hald (1950), 229 ff.; *Birka*, III. 76 ff.

[3] Information from Professor H.-J. Hundt of the Römisch-Germanisches Zentralmuseum, Mainz. For Egypt: Singer & Holmyard (1954), I, 441, with literature. A set of sycamore-wood tablets was found in a (Coptic) grave at Antinoë: *Liverpool Annals*, x (1923), 8.

[4] I know of the existence of two others: (1) Pompeii; flat, bone, *c.* 6 by *c.* 2 cm., 10 slits, 11 slats; in Antiquarium, Pompeii; (2) Pilismarót (Pannonia) (late fourth century); bronze, 8.8 by 6 cm., 5 slits, 6 slats; *Folia Archaeologica*, XII (1960), 113, Abb. 30, Nr. 10, 129 ff., Taf. XXIII, Nr. 5. For Scandinavia: Hoffmann (1964), 106 ff.

[5] The slats are 0.5–0.7 cm. wide, *c.* 1 mm. apart. The maximum width is now 4.5 cm., height 7.7 cm. (Museum of Antiquities, Newcastle-upon-Tyne, Acc. no. 1956.226 A; *AA*³, XVI (1919), 227 (fig.); *AA*⁴, XXVI (1948), 89).

The frame of this piece consists of a series of slats of bone, each with a hole, set parallel to, but at a slight distance from one another. Three or four slats are carved from a single flat piece of bone and the whole framework is held together top and bottom by (silvered?) bronze sheathing, which is riveted through the bone. The incised patterns of circles (on the bone) and crosses (on the bronze) cannot be used for dating purposes since they are found both in the Roman period and much later. A Lappish heddle-frame illustrated by Dr Hoffmann bears a very strong resemblance to it in design and construction.[1]

The rigid heddle was a convenient way of opening either shed on a band. The threads of the one warp-system passed through the holes, those of the other through the spaces between the slats. By raising or depressing the frame two sheds were opened (fig. 67).

The most obvious way of weaving bands would be with a miniature warp-weighted loom, either vertical or horizontal, using a heddle-rod with leashes and the natural shed. This is probably the method by which the plain-woven bands from Mainz were woven, since it is the simplest.[2]

4. RAISED HORIZONTAL LOOM

One of the thorniest and at the same time most fascinating problems of Roman textile technology is the date of the introduction of the horizontal loom. Closely connected with this, and introduced either at the same time or as a later refinement, is the draw-cord device for weaving figured textiles. Most authorities on ancient textiles have ventured an opinion on this subject at some time, but none of their theories can conceal the lack of firm evidence.[3] Roman writers do not mention the loom and there are no pictorial representations of it earlier than the Middle Ages and no physical remains. The textiles themselves must form the basis of the discussion.

The excavators of Herculaneum found *in situ* the badly burnt remains of a loom, which was restored as a small four-legged horizontal frame for tapestry-weaving. There was a high stool in front of it, better preserved.[4] Unfortunately it is not clear on what evidence the reconstruction rests. There are four loom-weights which are assumed to have hung from each corner of the loom to keep the warp spanned. In

[1] Hoffmann (1964), 108, fig. 51.
[2] See La Baume (1955), 79, Abb. 61.
[3] For their opinions see Hoffmann (1964), 334 ff. No concrete evidence is cited in support of most theories. The evidence which Mme. Picard-Schmitter advances (*Latomus*, XXIV (1965), 296 ff.) for an early date cannot be accepted. The best account is Endrei (1961).
[4] Maiuri (1958), 463, fig. 420.

view of the uncertainty about its original shape and function, it cannot safely be used as a basis for discussion here.

The main advantage which the horizontal loom has over the two-beam vertical loom, theoretically considered, is the easier control of multiple heddle-rods; for the principle on primitive looms is that one rod should govern one complete shed.[1] When a large number of heddle-rods or the equivalent is involved, it is easier to keep them in place when they are not being used if the warp is set on a horizontal plane and the sheds are opened vertically. Hence, the more sheds need to be opened, the more likely it becomes that the loom was horizontal.

This tenuous line of argument in fact is the only way at present that it is possible to approach the problem of the horizontal loom. When textiles reach a certain degree of complexity, such as the silk damasks described below, then it is reasonable to wonder if they were woven with more sophisticated mechanical aids. But it is nevertheless worth remembering that one should always think in terms of the *simplest* device needed for the given result. Recent work on complicated textiles woven on very simple looms makes it clear that past researchers have regularly been inclined to visualise much more sophisticated looms than are really necessary.

The mediaeval horizontal loom when it is first illustrated in the thirteenth century is already a developed implement. It has a set of treadles, operated by the weaver's feet, which change the shed by simultaneously raising and lowering a heddle-rod (or 'harness') by means of pulleys. One shed is thus governed by two sets of leashes. There is no evidence for the use of treadles in any context in Europe before the Middle Ages, when they first appear on looms.[2] But it is reasonable to suppose that they were introduced at the same time as the horizontal loom (fig. 69).

Walter Endrei has recently opened a very profitable discussion on the simpler types of horizontal loom in the East.[3] The horizontal ground-loom of Ancient Egypt of course is well known, but, despite the fact that it was certainly still in existence in the Roman period—the Bedouin use it today—there is no indication that it was the direct forbear of the late-Roman horizontal loom. Rather, as Endrei suggests, knowledge of a horizontal loom without a frame, but with treadles set in a pit, may have been brought into the Roman world with the imported Han silks (p. 53). A horizontal loom with a frame, as is known in the Middle Ages, may have been developed from this; for a frame would guarantee more constant tension on the warp of silk fabrics. There is as yet no archaeological or literary evidence

[1] Hoffmann (1964), 133 ff.
[2] Singer & Holmyard (1956), II, 212, fig. 181; White (1962), 117.
[3] Endrei (1958, 1961). Egyptian looms: Singer & Holmyard (1954), I, 436 ff.

to support this line of argument, but it accords with the very few facts at our disposal.[1]

The weaving of figured textiles, especially damasks, requires a large number of different sheds. This raises a second problem. When was the draw-cord device first used and is there any simpler means to the same end?

The principle of the drawloom is as follows (fig. 70). Each warp-thread or group of warp-threads is attached to a draw-cord. By pulling a number of these cords a shed is opened. As many different sheds are possible as there are combinations of draw-cords. If the cords are numbered, each shed has its own code and can be reproduced when it is required.

It has, however, been pointed out that on certain types of mediaeval loom many successive sheds are kept open side by side by means of a series of shed-rods.[2] It was apparently a practical possibility to use as many as fifty of these. Clearly, this type of loom merits careful consideration before we accept that the Romans must have known the drawloom.

We can now turn to the known complex weaves of late antiquity and see what information they can give.

The silk from the coffin of St Paulinus in Trier (table B, 88) has a free curvilinear pattern of circles and crosses woven in 3-over-1 compound cloth (fig. 46). The number of sheds which are involved in its construction is very high, but no exact weaving pattern is yet available. If a loom with multiple rods is indicated here, then the *terminus ante quem* for its introduction is *c.* A.D. 395.

Next arises the question of how the simple silk *scutulata* in 2-over-2 and 3-over-1 twill from Syria were woven (p. 51). One of the provincial-Roman pieces was woven with sixteen sheds (table B, 86). It may in fact have been woven on sixteen heddle- or shed-rods.[3]

The closed loops on the border of one of the Coptic woollen four-shed compound cloths described by Mrs Crowfoot do not unfortunately add anything to our knowledge.[4] They resemble the loops of the tubular-woven textiles from Scandinavia, which were probably woven on a two-beam vertical loom.[5]

The elaborate early Byzantine silks from Swiss churches published recently by

---

[1] Textile experts have often cited the alleged treadle-pits in the sixth-century monastery at Thebes (Winlock & Crum (1926), I, 65–71), but to an archaeologist they seem hardly credible. Some of the textile terms recorded by Hesychius in the sixth century may refer to parts of a horizontal loom (*Latomus*, XXIV (1965), 296 ff.), but this is far from certain.

[2] I am grateful to Dr Endrei for putting this idea to me and discussing it.

[3] For its weaving on the basis of an advanced horizontal loom see *Germ.* 18 (1934), 203 f.

[4] Crowfoot & Griffiths (1939), 41 f., fig. 2.   [5] Hald (1950), 174 fig. 181; 175, figs. 182–3.

Emil Vogt are fairly certainly the products of a horizontal loom.[1] They are compound twills. Both the weave and the spin of the yarns (Z-spun warp, unspun weft) point to the same Syrian milieu as that which produced the Holborough damask (p. 52). The pattern in these silks is formed by the weft, in contrast to the warp-pattern of the Han silks found at Palmyra.[2] The Syrian horizontal loom is unlikely therefore to have been copied directly from the Chinese loom.

[1] *ZAK*, xIII (1952), 1 ff.   [2] Pfister (1940), pl. xv e, f.

VIII

DYEING AND FINISHING

The two activities of dyeing and finishing cloth, which in the Roman period were in the hands of specialists with their own industrial plant, have left surprisingly few traces in the northern Roman provinces. Several attempts have been made to explain vats and troughs on Roman sites in terms of fulling or dyeing (see below), but remains unequivocally connected with either industry are yet to be found.

Professor Forbes in his volumes on ancient technology[1] cites a mass of written and material evidence relevant to dyeing and finishing in Italy and the Mediterranean. Against the background of his work I have concentrated on evaluating the sources which are immediately relevant to Gaul and Britain. It is a fair assumption that Roman industrial methods and equipment, which represented in this field a considerable advance over the techniques of the Iron Age, were adopted and adapted in the northern provinces. But until archaeological discoveries can reveal how far provincial dyeing and fulling were industrialised and refined by the Romans, a full account of their achievement cannot be offered.

1. DYEING

The salt-mines of the Hallstatt period and area of Austria and the deserts of the Near East are the only lodging-places of ancient textiles which allow them to retain their original colours. The peat-acids either dissolve or conceal the dyestuffs, so that they are no longer susceptible to the type of chemical analysis which Pfister was able to use with success on the textiles from Palmyra and Egypt. Consequently, only the green felt of hares' fibre from the Petersberg at Basel (table B, 97) shows traces of its dye. The colours of the textiles found in bogs in Northern Europe have suffered likewise.

Dyestuffs can be divided into substantive and adjective dyes. The former class includes direct dyes, which can be applied to the cloth or fibres without any intermediary (e.g. smeared on), and vat dyes, in the case of which the cloth is dipped into a heated tub of liquid containing the dyestuff in solution. The second class (adjective

---

[1] For full account see Forbes (1956), 98 ff. Dyers' shops at Pompeii: House of the Ephebe (Reg. IX, Ins. 7, no. 19): Maiuri (1960), fig. 98; *idem* (1956), 75; House of Ubonius (Reg. IX, Ins. 3, no. 2): Maiuri (1960), 126; *idem* (1956), 56.

dyes) cannot get a purchase on the fibres unless they have been pre-treated with a mordant (literally, a 'biting-agent').

The equipment of a dyer's workshop, as the finds at Pompeii demonstrate,[1] comprised a number of boilers, stone or metal vats, which were set over a small furnace. Several of them were needed in the same shop, since the various stages leading up to the final dipping of the cloth or fibres required their own containers if the workshop was to keep up a steady output of goods.

Ancient writers seem to assume as a matter of course that wool is dyed in the fleece, and not after spinning. There is no direct statement of this, but indirect references abound.[2] Flax fibres take dye less readily than does wool, and are therefore rarely mentioned in the extant dyeing-recipes. Resist-dyeing, mentioned by Pliny,[3] and printed textiles[4] indicate a certain amount of piece-dyeing, but perhaps only for special effects.

Each dye requires a different treatment and it would be both laborious and unnecessary to describe every treatment in full here. It is sufficient to say that woollen fibres in every case had to be scoured with some variety of detergent (decayed urine or fullers' earth) before dyeing. If adjective dyes were to be applied, the fibres were heated in a vat containing the mordant in water or urine. While this was going on, the actual dyestuff (either in a dried form or as chopped leaves and flowers) was fermented and dissolved in another vat. It was into this solution that the mordanted fibres were dipped and boiled.

The above account is an oversimplification of the processes, but gives some idea of their complexity. The amount of mordant can affect the final shade and colour and several dyes can be combined for effect. Several dyers' recipes are extant, giving exact details of the techniques to be adopted for each colour.[5] They are best appreciated by a chemist.

Direct information on dyeing and dyers in the North is limited. The bases of a number of circular boilers with firing chambers and flues under them were uncovered at Silchester and interpreted by the excavators as dye-vats. George Boon has pointed out that several trades, such as brewing, need vats of this kind; and without further excavation their purpose cannot be decided.[6] So far as I know, no physical remains

---

[1] See n. 1, p. 79.

[2] See *Papyrus Graecus Holmiensis* (ed. Lagercrantz (1913)); further references in Blümner (1912), 225 ff. Linen was dyed in the hank: Wipszycka (1965), 145. [3] *N.H.* xxxv. 150.

[4] At Achmîm-Panopolis in the late Roman period; see Forrer (1898) and the items from his collection in the Victoria and Albert Museum, London.

[5] *Papyrus Graecus Holmiensis*, p. 26 ff.

[6] *Archaeologia*, LIV (1904), 459 ff., pl. XLVII, 2; Boon (1957), 193 f.

of a dye-works have been found anywhere within the northern provinces. This is odd; for boilers can hardly have been made of perishable materials, if they came into contact with fire.

Two scenes on a funerary monument from Arlon[1] may represent dyeing. On one of them three men in short-sleeved tunics are stirring the contents of a vat. On the other, only one man is shown (fig. 71). The inscriptional evidence for dyers is slight. A certain *Publius offector* (*sic*) is solemnly cursed on a leaden tablet from Kreuznach:[2] the form of the name is odd, but the reading appears to be accurate.

Pliny states that Gaul produced many dyestuffs,[3] but there is little external evidence to support him. Prehistoric textiles seem to have relied heavily on varied spin-direction and undyed yarns in various shades for their colour-effects.[4] What little is known about Gallic and British dyestuffs is set out in Table P. Most of them are vegetable dyes. The range of plants in Roman Britain which the present-day dyer of home-spuns could make use of is extensive and more plants may have been used for this purpose than the sources now indicate.

The notorious British woad contains a similar colour-constituent to the rarer indigo. The Thorsberg mantle[5] and some mummy-wrappings from Aquincum-Budapest,[6] said to be indigo-dyed, may in fact have been boiled with woad. Wool which has been dyed in a vat prepared with pulped and fermented woad comes out greenish, but oxydises to blue in the air.

Shades in the red-purple range were achieved by a substantive dye drawn from a type of whelk which lived on the Atlantic coast of Gaul. This mollusc was related to the *Murex brandaris* of the eastern Mediterranean which yielded the prized 'true purple'. Lichen gave a red-purple dye (archil) which needed no mordant. Among the adjective dyes madder may have grown in Gaul, for Pliny says that all the provinces abound with it. Fibres mordanted with alum and then dyed with madder take on a reddish shade; those mordanted with iron-salts become purple-brown.

The mordants in which the fibres were prepared tended to be either a type of natural alum[7] or iron-salts. Both were obtainable in Gaul. The textiles from the Caves of Bar Kokhba[8] had been dyed yellow with saffron, red with madder and blue with indigo. Purple was won from a combination of indigo and kermes. The mordants present, which had been varied in amount according to the shade required, were alum and iron.

---

[1] Esp. 4125, 4136. [2] *CIL*, XIII. 7553. 18. [3] *N.H.* XXII. 2.
[4] For prehistoric dyeing: *CIBA-Review*, 54 (1947), 1967.
[5] Schlabow (1951), 176 ff. [6] *Arch. Ért.* 91 (1964), 193.
[7] *N.H.* XXXV. 183–8. [8] Yadin (1963), 173.

The green dye of the felt insole from Basel may be a copper lactate; in other words, it was dyed in sour milk which had been left to stand in a copper vessel.[1] Professor Hundt has suggested that the olive-green cloth from Hallstatt was boiled first with ling to a yellow shade, then in a cast-iron pot until it became green.[2] The iron pot takes the place of a mordant, in this case applied after the dye.

2. FINISHING

The craft of fulling was one of the largest and best organised industrial activities in Italy. Digging at Pompeii has revealed workshops complete with wall-paintings and inscriptions (fig. 72). The plant and tools of the trade were expensive to build, buy and maintain; and the series of special operations which took place in the fullery could hardly have been carried out by one man. Only the wealthy could afford to run a private *fullonica*, so that most of the cloth which was woven at home or bought had to pass through the professional fuller's establishment. He acted as the finisher of cloth in loom-state (*de tela*) and as the launderer of soiled garments.

Iulius Verinus, who died in Köln, probably in the third century, was a *fulloniae artis magister*, master-fuller. He must have been in charge of a large establishment, for he held the leading position in the Köln guild of fullers.[3] An inscription from Alzey (Upper Germany) was set up by the fuller Vitalinius Secundinus to the patroness of fullers, Minerva.[4] These two men show that Roman methods of fulling on a big scale were well established in the northern provinces, at least in the large towns. Virtually nothing is known about fulling before the Roman conquest, except that it existed; its equipment must have been rudimentary in comparison with that in Italy.

A relief from Sens[5] (fig. 73) shows a fuller standing in a square (wooden?) tub of water, gripping the handrails while he treads the cloth underfoot. This is the first and most important stage in fulling, and if my derivation of the word *mantos*, mantle, is correct,[6] it was practised in the earliest times. Treading loosens the dirt, allows the cleansing agents to penetrate the fabric, and encourages shrinkage and felting. During the equivalent modern process (milling) there may be as much as a 35% shrinkage of woollen cloth. It is not clear from an examination of the textiles

---

[1] *ZAK*, 2 (1940), 22, Taf. 5, 5. [2] Hundt (1959), 85.

[3] *CIL*, XIII. 8345; cf. *magister* in *R-E*, IV. I. 420. The sarcophagus can hardly be earlier than the Antonine period, and the lettering and form of the name are unlikely to be of fourth-century date.

[4] *CIL*, XIII. 6264.

[5] Esp. 2768; see wall-painting from Pompeii (Reg. VI, Ins. 8, no. 20): Spinazzola (1953), 771, fig. 755; Schefold (1957), 106 f. [6] Wild (1966).

how often and to what degree cloth was fulled by treading in the Roman period. But it is unlikely that woollen checks (*scutulata*) containing dyed yarns were heavily fulled.

The cheapest of the cleansing agents was putrified human urine. Its ammonia content combined with the grease in the wool to form a soapy compound. Fullers in Rome put out pots in the street to collect the contributions of passers-by.[1] Probably Verinus and his colleagues did the same in Köln. The pounded stems and roots of the plant soapwort and various types of fullers' earth were another soap-substitute.[2] After treatment with substances of this kind, the cloth had to be rinsed well in clean water; and for this reason a steady water-supply was essential to the fuller.

The cloth was hung up to dry over wooden beams which are shown on two reliefs on a gravestone from Sens (fig. 73) and in Pompeian wall-paintings.[3] Linen would probably be left outside to bleach naturally. A scene from Pompeii shows the equipment used for sulphur-bleaching (fig. 74). It includes a semi-circular cage over which the cloth was laid and a pot, probably containing lump-sulphur, which burnt slowly inside the upturned cage.[4]

Peculiar to woollen cloth was the raising of the nap to give it a soft finish. The fabric, probably still damp, to judge from modern parallels, was slung over a horizontal beam and worked over with a special instrument (the *aena*) which is shown in two wall-paintings (fig. 74) and mentioned several times in literature.[5] It seems to be a flat wooden board (perhaps *c.* 20 cm. square (8 in.)), the face of which is covered with a layer of thistle heads[6] (fig. 75). The back has a strap or handle attached to it. By gently plucking up the surface fibres of the cloth, the fuller can raise a moderate nap. The advantage of using the thistle is that the spikes break off when they encounter a knot, instead of pulling out the thread.

The nap in this state might be somewhat uneven and was trimmed or cropped with a pair of cropping-shears. The only Roman example of which I know was found in an iron-worker's hoard at Great Chesterford near Cambridge[7] (plate XII *a*). It is

[1] Martial, VI. 93; XII. 48. 8; *CIBA-Review*, 56 (1947), 2034 f.

[2] *CIBA-Review*, 56 (1947), 2034; cf. Blümner (1912), 170 ff.

[3] Esp. 2768; Pompeii (Reg. VI, Ins. 8, no. 20): Spinazzola (1953), 774, fig. 759.

[4] Spinazzola (1953), 773, fig. 758; cf. Pliny, *N.H.* XXXV. 175.

[5] Spinazzola (1953), 773, fig. 758; Curtius (1929), 143 (Reg. VI, Ins. 15, 1, q). For *aena*: Wild (1968).

[6] *Spina fullonia*: Pliny, *N.H.* XXIV. 111; XXVII. 92. The fullers' teazle (*dipsacus fullonum*) was not used until late antiquity; it is not in Godwin's (1956) list of Romano-British plants. For teazle-growing see M. L. Ryder in *Folk Life* (forthcoming).

[7] In the Museum of Archaeology and Ethnology, Cambridge (*VCH Essex*, III, pl. IX A (top right)). For modern cloth-finishing see *Folk Life*, V (1967), 102–3; VI (1968), 18–67.

6-2

130 cm. (4 ft. 4 in.) long and has blades with cutting-edges 45 cm. (1 ft. 6 in.) long. The gravestone from Sens[1] shows how the Gallic shearmen used them (fig. 73). He tucked the handles under his right arm and, keeping the blades in the same plane as the free hanging cloth, trimmed off the shaggier parts of the nap.

While the bulk of woollen goods were finished by raising and cropping, certain fabrics appear to have been specially spun and woven with this style of finishing in mind.[2] They are referred to as *vestis pexa* and seem to have been popular for under-clothes. The phrase *tunica pexa* was current in Roman Britain in the abbreviated form *pexa*, for it was introduced as a Latin loan-word into Old Welsh.[3] Soft-finished fabrics were popular in Roman Britain, but may have been unknown before the conquest. Since the Greek text of Diocletian's Edict adopts the Latin term,[4] the technique may have been particularly highly developed in Italy.

The weft for *vestis pexa* was probably loosely spun out of particularly fine wool, so that the nap of the cloth could be raised easily. British and Rhenish fine wools would be ideal for the purpose (p. 8). Special care had to be exercised in the weaving, because the yarn would be liable to break. Spinners and weavers of *vestis pexa* earned high wages in the late-third century.[4]

The method which the shearman at Sens demonstrates, as he attempts to crop the nap of a textile hanging free from a beam, is patently inefficient. He could neither achieve a close nor an even nap without a firm support for the cloth. Like the mediaeval shearmen, the Roman fullers may in special cases have laid their cloth over a gently curved bench so that it had a firm base.[5] The mediaeval shears, although in principle identical with those from Great Chesterford, were designed with greater precision (plate XII *a–b*).

The Verulamium diamond twill has a definite nap which obscured the weave and must have been soft to touch (table A, 49). There is no sign that the weft was specially spun.

The warm handle of woollen cloth was enhanced by raising and cropping, but the qualities of linen were brought out by different means. Linen after scouring (and perhaps also after bleaching) was polished to a smooth, hard finish. The polishing implement was in the form of a flattened glass ball ('linen rubber'), which was

[1] Eydoux (1962), 199, pl. 222.
[2] Wild (1967 *a*).
[3] I have argued in a forthcoming note that loan-words regularly imply that the object which they describe has also been borrowed.
[4] *Edictum Diocletiani*, XXIV. 16; XX. 12; XXII. 6. 7. The cloth described in Linear B at Knossos as *pe-ko-to* (Chadwick (1964), 107) may be the same.
[5] See *Med. Arch.* I (1957), 104 ff., pl. XIII–XVI.

rubbed vigorously over the surface of the cloth as it lay on some suitable flat surface[1] (fig. 76). It has the same effect as a smoothing iron.

A linen rubber of dark glass (7.4 cm. in diameter, 3.4 cm. in height) came from an early-third-century grave at Hees near Nijmegen in Lower Germany[2] and another (3.8 cm. in diameter) was found with a third-century mortarium at South Shields[3] (plate XII *d*). Both show signs of wear on the undersurface. They are formed from a single droplet of glass. Similar implements are often found in Viking graves in Scandinavia and were until recently still used for linen glazing.[4]

References to clothes presses, one of which is depicted on the walls of a Pompeian *fullonica*[5] (fig. 77), are frequent, but the article must have been an expensive item.[6] An actual press from Pompeii,[5] the metal fittings of which survive, was of wood with two iron screw-cases. Perhaps the more prosperous fullers, such as Verinus, could have afforded one, but they may not have been very common.

In describing the finishing processes in which the fuller is concerned, I have tried to show at each stage what evidence is available from the northern provinces. I have quoted epigraphic and philological sources, the tools and the textiles themselves; but buildings and plant, tanks, vats, tubs and the like, which one would reasonably expect to find associated with the work of a fuller in the northern provinces, are most elusive.

In 1905 George Fox in an oft-quoted paper made out a case for commercial and private *fullonicae* at the villas of Chedworth in Gloucestershire, Titsey in Surrey and Darenth in Kent.[7] Recent excavation at Chedworth has demonstrated that the presumed fulling-tanks there are in fact part of a *laconicum*—bathing facilities with dry heat.[8] The complex of bath-buildings at Titsey and Darenth contain many structural alterations, the meaning of which was not recorded or appreciated by the excavators of those days. At neither site were alcoves discovered containing the

[1] *Sussex AC*, 101 (1963), 164 f.

[2] Brunsting (1937), 184, Vondst. 25, Nr. 7, now in Rijksmuseum G. M. Kam, Nijmegen, Inv. Nr. B.C.I. 121. Other examples in the Rijksmuseum Kam without certain provenance may also be Roman. I am grateful to Miss M. den Boesterd for showing me this material.

[3] Examined by courtesy of Dr D. J. Smith in the Museum of Antiquities, Newcastle-upon-Tyne (*PSAN*[4], 6 (1934), 355–7). The associated mortarium was dated by Mr. J. P. Gillam to the late second or early third century.

[4] Vistrand (1899–1900), 13 ff.; *Birka*, II. Taf. 153. 1–4.

[5] Mau (1908), fig. 244 (Reg. VI, Ins. 8, no. 20); Spinazzola (1953), figs. 764–6.

[6] For references see Blümner (1912), 182, 188.

[7] *Archaeologia*, LIX (1905), 210 ff. Fullonicae at Pompeii: Maiuri (1963), figs. 96–7; Spinazzola (1953), 765 ff. Ostia also contains some well-preserved examples.

[8] *Trans. BG*, LXXVIII (1959), 5 ff., 17 f.

tubs in which the cloth was trodden—perhaps the only features diagnostic of a *fullonica* (fig. 72), since vats and tanks alone can have any number of purposes. In view of the difficulty in understanding the structural changes at Titsey and Darenth and the lack of any features which clearly point to fulling, one would do well to be sceptical at present over Fox's thesis. Perhaps further excavation might corroborate it.

A Roman villa at Fordingbridge in Hampshire is said to have a fullery attached to it, but the evidence is not yet published. For the two Germanies and Gallia Belgica, I know of no remains which can be recognised as those of a fullery.

TABLES
BIBLIOGRAPHY
GLOSSARY
FIGURES

NOTES ON THE TABLES

Textile fragments are listed here according to weave (plain, 2-over-2 twill, 2-over-1 twill, fancy weaves, netting and plaiting, felt). Within the weaves they are classified according to fibre (animal, vegetable and textile impressions).

I have appended to the descriptions of a number of fragments the initials of the textile expert who first reported on the material, namely E. C. (Miss Elisabeth Crowfoot), G. M. C. (the late Mrs. Grace Crowfoot), A. S. H. (Miss Audrey Henshall) and E. V. (Professor Emil Vogt). Some of these I have examined again myself. Textiles without initials are published here in full for the first time. The literature cited indicates where they were first mentioned, sometimes with a brief description. I am grateful to Dr Ryder for his analysis of the wools.

All measurements in the tables are given in centimetres unless stated otherwise. The thread-count is given in the form 'x per cm.' The sign plus ($+$) after a measurement denotes that the original size was greater. Numbers following the name of a museum are inventory numbers in that collection. The term μ denotes 1 micron.

In the weaving-drafts the warp is shown running vertically, the weft horizontally. Black squares denote where the warp is uppermost on the surface of the cloth.

PLAIN-WEAVE

Animal fibres

1–4 CORBRIDGE (NORTHUMBERLAND)
The material is from an early Trajanic hoard of miscellaneous objects, mainly of iron, found under a floor near the *principia* during recent excavations. It is oxydised as a result of contact with the ironwork.

The yarn qualities are so varied that it is difficult to be sure how many distinct plain-weave textiles are involved. I have grouped the fragments according to spin-direction and count into four arbitrary categories, but some in fact may be from the same web. All appear under the microscope to be of wool.

Fuller details of the exact amount of textile surviving in each case will be found in my forthcoming report. The box numbers represent the temporary divisions of the material after its discovery.

1 *Textile (group 1)*
   System (1) *c.* 12 per cm., Z-spun.
   System (2) *c.* 12 per cm., Z-spun.
   Yarn: fairly fine, Z-spun.

A fragment from Box (21) has straight edge, probably cut. Remains of 2 running stitches and 5 holes for same, 0.6 cm. apart and 0.6 cm. from the edge. Thread: fine, Z-spun, S-plied, 2 strands.

2 *Textile (group 2)*
   System (1) *c.* 20 per cm., weak Z-spun.
   System (2) *c.* 16 per cm., strong Z-spun.

In Box 'A' a single stitch holds two very small fragments together. Thread: fine wool (?),

Z-spun, single strand. On another fragment there are two adjacent running stitches with holes set *c.* 0.5 cm. apart. Thread: very coarse, probably string, *c.* 0.25 cm. in diameter, perhaps a bast fibre; strands weak Z-spun, possibly S-plied.

3 *Textile (group 3)*
   System (1) 16–20 per cm., Z-spun.
   System (2) *c.* 8 per cm., Z-spun.

Despite a wide range of variation in count and strength of spin the fragments of this group are probably from the same textile.

Some doubles in both systems, probably accidental.

4 *Textile (group 4)*
   System (1) *c.* 10 per cm., weak Z-spun.
   System (2) *c.* 8 per cm., strong Z-spun.

Purpose of textiles in groups 1–4
Textiles of group 1 as represented in Box (59) and (63) and of group 2 as represented in Box (64) and (63) are covered with a layer of hair and feathers. It seems reasonable to suspect that they are the remains, perhaps the lining, of cushion-covers.

The association of a layer of 2-over-1 twill (see no. 50) with cloth of group 3 and 4 suggests that a lining-fabric may be represented here.

University Museum of Antiquities, Newcastle-upon-Tyne (*JRS*, LV (1965), 203; *AA*⁴, XLVI (1968), 115 ff.). I am grateful to Dr D. J. Smith for giving me access to this material.

5 ELVEDEN (SUFFOLK)

Stuffing in the mouth of a flask containing a hoard of denarii and antoniniani; TPQ A.D. 248, probably buried soon after.

System (1) warp ?, 11 per cm., strong Z-spun.

System (2) weft ?, doubles, 20 pairs per cm., both weak Z-spun.

Both yarns dark-brown; yarn (2) finer than (1) and of high quality. (A. S. H.)

Report of A. B. Wildman, Woollen Industries Research Association: Animal fibres, stained brown, but not naturally pigmented; a few fibres medullated with very slight indications of scales. Probably wool, but not certain.

Elveden Estate Museum in possession of Lord Iveagh (*Num. Chron.*⁶ XIV (1954), 204 ff.; *PSI*, XXVII (1956), 121 f.).

6 LIGHTWOOD (STOKE-ON-TRENT)

Wrapping of two silver bracelets in a pot containing a coin hoard; probably buried *c.* A.D. 278.

System (1) warp ?, doubles, 12–13 pairs per cm., Z-spun.

System (2) weft ?, singles, 10 per cm., Z-spun.

(2) a heavier yarn than (1), but both good quality, evenly spun. Small fragments only survive, largest *c.* 1.2 by 1.8 cm. in several layers. Thread in poor condition, now dark brown, stained green in places. (A. S. H.)

Report of Dr Appleyard, Woollen Industries Research Association: Fibres very friable, but of animal origin. Some medullated, few traces of scales, but not sufficient for identification.

City Museum, Hanley, Stoke-on-Trent (*N. Staffs. J.* 3 (1963), 17 f.).

7–8 LONDON (WALBROOK STREAM-BED)

A group of three textiles (see no. 44) from the bed of the Walbrook associated with coins of Vespasian and Titus and samian ware of the second century. The Walbrook had almost completely silted up by A.D. 160.

7 *Textile 1*

System (1) warp, singles, 14–15 per cm., strong Z-spun, max. length *c.* 11 cm., wide set threads.

System (2) weft, doubles, 11–14 pairs per cm., weak Z-spun, max. length *c.* 7 cm.

Both yarns are of moderately fine quality, evenly spun.

Six large and six small fragments of this cloth in half-basket weave survive, in all *c.* 150 sq.cm. It is peat-black in colour. A single tapestry-woven band in a lighter colour was inserted into the weft—yarn: singles, 30–32 per cm., S-spun, closely packed to cover warp; *c.* 1.9 cm. wide, *c.* 60 threads; max. length *c.* 4.5 cm. Occasional warp-threads are paired, but may represent damage.

Dr M. L. Ryder reports: The yarn (pigmented) has a diameter range 10–52μ with 1 hair 60μ (mean 24.3); it has a skewed to fine distribution and is generalised medium-fine wool. (The tapestry band was not examined.)

BM 1956.12.1.1 (D. D. Francis Greenway; to be published in *Festschrift H. Reichel* (forthcoming)).

8 *Textile 2*

System (1) warp, *c.* 10 per cm., Z-spun, coarse yarn, max. length *c.* 31 cm.

System (2) weft, *c.* 7 per cm., S-spun, max. length *c.* 22 cm.

It bears a lighter-coloured band in the weft—yarn: singles, 10 per cm., S-spun; *c.* 1 cm. wide, *c.* 15 threads. It covers the warp completely.

Dr M. L. Ryder reports: Yarn (*a*) (System (1)) (pigmented) has a diameter range 12–46μ (mean 24.3) including 2 hairs at 58μ; yarn (*b*) (System (2)) (pigmented) has a diameter range 14–52μ (mean 27.7) including 1 hair at 60μ; both yarns are skewed to fine on histogram and are generalised medium-fine wool.

BM 1956.12.1.2 (D. D. Francis Greenway; to be published in *Festschrift H. Reichel*).

9 NEWSTEAD (FIG. 19)

Half-basket-weave from Antonine pit (XXIII) in area of south annexe to fort.

System (1) doubles, 10 pairs per cm., Z-spun.
System (2) singles, 10–11 per cm., Z-spun.
Yarn (1) may be finer than (2).

Two fragments: 1. Max. length (1) *c.* 13 cm.
(2) *c.* 3 cm.
2. Max. length (1) *c.* 8 cm.
(2) *c.* 2.5 cm.

Faults in fragment 1: Three threads in same shed or leash instead of two; repeated once. Faults separated by six regular rows of pairs. Uncertain if warp or weft fault.

Dr M. L. Ryder reports (see *Nature*, 204 (1964), 562): Yarn (*a*) (System (2)) (pigmented) has fibres 12–36μ (mean 23.3) with 1 hair at 80μ; skewed to fine distribution, hairy medium-fine fleece-type.

NMA, FRA 1180 (Curle (1911), 289; *PPS*, N.S. XVI (1950), 136, 139; *PSAS*, LXXXVI (1951–2), 8 no. 5).

Vegetable fibres

10 CAERLEON (PLATE V*a*)

Attached to small piece of lead from the canister containing the pipe-burial (found across the Usk from the legionary fort); probably wrapping of cremated bones; TPQ *c.* A.D. 120.

System (1) warp ?, 12–13 per cm., Z-spun, max. length 16 cm.
System (2) weft ?, 14–15 per cm., Z-spun, max. length 11 cm.

The yarns are of very uneven quality; now a dirty pink colour due to corrosion products from the canister.

Mr J. E. Ford of the Shirley Institute reports that it is definitely flax in good condition; the flax appears to be of natural coloration (unpublished letter).

Legionary Museum, Caerleon (*Ant. J.* XXXIX (1959), 288–9, pl. XLV).

11–12 CAMBRIDGE (ARBURY ROAD)

Shroud (?) from late-Roman coffin.

11 *Fragment* 1 (*Fig. 22*)

System (1) warp ?, doubles, 8–9 pairs per cm., both Z-spun, max. length 2 cm.
System (2) weft ?, doubles, *c.* 12 pairs per cm., both Z-spun, max. length 4 cm.

Yarn (1) more widely spaced than (2), but same yarns. *c.* 40 very small fragments.

12 *Fragment* 2 Adhering in places to fragment 1.

System (1) singles, 12–15 per cm., weak Z-spun, max. length 2 cm.
System (2) singles, 18–20 per cm. (pulled out of shape), weak Z-spun, max. length 2 cm.

c. 11 fragments.

Woollen Industries Research Association report

states both to be of animal origin. Shirley Institute states that yarns weak-spun from fibre-bundles of vegetable origin, but not of flax or nettle; diameter range 4–16µ.

Museum of Archaeology & Ethnology, Cambridge, 52,445.C (*JRS*, XLIII (1953), 120; *Proc. CAS.* XLIX (1955), 19, pl. III *a*, *b*).

13   COLCHESTER (ST CLARE DRIVE)

Oxydised remains (?) of a 'fabric resembling linen' on back of thistle-brooch from a Claudian cremation-burial; probably the wrapping of the bronzes.

(*Ant. J*, XXII (1942), 60.)

14   GUILDEN MORDEN (CAMBRIDGESHIRE)

Small fragment of cloth adhering to the reverse of a bronze coin of Vespasian found in the mouth of a child in an inhumation-burial; perhaps late second century.

System (1) 12–14 per cm., weak S-spun, max. length *c.* 2 cm.

System (2) 18–20 per cm., very weak spun, apparently Z-spun, max. length *c.* 1.5 cm.

(1) Fairly widely spaced; yarn (2) is the finer, but unevenly spun yarns in both systems. They resemble superficially a bast fibre.

Museum of Archaeology & Ethnology, Cambridge, 37.67 (mentioned in Liversidge (1955), 55).

15   HOLBOROUGH, SNODLAND (KENT)

Fragment of lining of leather purse from child-burial in a barrow; TPQ *c.* A.D. 250. See silk, no. 51. Three fragments survive, certainly plain weave.

System (1) *c.* 20–22 per cm., fairly strong Z-spun, max. length 1 cm.

System (2) *c.* 20–22 per cm., weak Z-spun, max. length *c.* 1.5 cm.

(1) probably warp; finer yarn, better spun than (2).

The Linen Industry Research Association reported that it consists of seven layers of a fine fabric with a 'patterned weave': the fabric is probably linen.

Maidstone Museum and Art Gallery (*Arch. Cant.* LXVIII (1954), 56).

16   HUNTINGDON (THREE NUNS BRIDGE)

Small fragments of plain-weave linen (?) adhering to underside of a small ornamental bronze bucket in inhumation burial; associated with coin of Hadrian as TPQ.

Museum of Archaeology & Ethnology, Cambridge (*JRS*, LVIII (1968), 191). Miss J. E. A. Liversidge kindly drew my attention to this; it is to be published by Miss Elisabeth Crowfoot.

17   KINGSTON BUCI (SUSSEX)

Fragment of 'broadly woven cloth' from a Romano-British rubbish-pit associated with a stone building. No further details available. (*Sussex N. Q.* 1 (1926), 185 f.)

18   LONDON (SITE OF COOTS' BANK, LOMBARD STREET)

Cloth from a pit; second-century context.

System (1) 10 per cm., fairly strong Z-spun.

System (2) 9–10 per cm., weaker Z-spun.

Yarns of medium quality; in all *c.* 14 sq.cm. survive. Now black in colour (charred ?). Perhaps sacking, since the weave is open.

Report of Dr M. L. Ryder: It is flax.

Possession of Mr Peter Marsden, Guildhall Museum; Inv. No. A. 486.

19 MALTON (E. YORKS.)

Remains of the shroud of a woman buried in a gypsum-filled wooden coffin in the extra-mural cemetery; TPQ *c.* A.D. 340. Six small pieces.

System (1) *c.* 12 per cm., weak Z-spun (?)
System (2) *c.* 16 per cm., weak Z-spun (?)

Roman Malton Museum (*Ant. J*, XXVIII (1948), 177, pl. XXVI *g, h*).

20 OGOF-YR-ESGYRN CAVE (GLYNTAWE, BRECKNOCK)

Small fragment of linen (?) adhering to obverse of AE coin of Vespasian in association with coin of Hadrian (?).

System (1) singles, *c.* 10 per cm., Z-spun, max. length *c.* 2 cm.
System (2) singles, *c.* 25 per cm., Z-spun, max. length *c.* 2 cm.

National Museum of Wales, Cardiff; seen through the kindness of Mr G. C. Boon.

21 RADLEY (BERKS.)

Wrapping of a small coin hoard found in the grave of a young adult; buried about A.D. 330.

System (1) warp ?, 11–12 per cm., weak Z-spun, max. length *c.* 6 cm., loose.
System (2) weft ?, 11–12 per cm., weak Z-spun, max. length *c.* 7 cm.

The fabric appears to be linen.
Fault in (1); 3 threads in same leash (or shot).

Ashmolean Museum, Oxford, 1945.113 (*Ox.* XVII–XVIII (1952–3), 34, Grave 9).

22 RICHBOROUGH (KENT)

Oxydised remains of wrapping of wooden case containing iron shears and bone comb (barber's set ?); found in well of fort; Claudian.

Claimed by Bushe-Fox to be linen—that is, probably a plain-weave fabric.

(*Richborough*, II, 31, pl. XV, fig. 2).

23 RUGBY (CAVES INN)

From Roman well.

System (1) 21–22 per cm., Z-spun, max. length *c.* 5 cm.
System (2) 20 per cm., Z-spun, max. length *c.* 5 cm.

Irregular shaped fragment. Some variation of yarn fineness, but in general good quality. It appears to be linen.

(*Trans. BAS*, 80 (1962), 80–2).

24 SILCHESTER (PLATE VI *a*)

Remains adhering to bronze buckle found in tail of rampart; post-Boudiccan (A.D. 61–65) and possibly much later.

System (1) doubles, 14 pairs per cm., weak Z-spun, max. length *c.* 2 cm.
System (2) doubles, *c.* 14 pairs per cm., weak Z-spun, max. length *c.* 2.5 cm.

Yarns fairly evenly spun; appear to be linen.

Reading Museum (*Archaeologia*, 92 (1947), 147, pl. XXXVI *a, b*).

25 VERULAMIUM (ST ALBANS)

Fragment of cloth associated with the woollen textile in a child's coffin; TPQ A.D. 210. See twill, no. 49.

System (1) 22–23 per cm., very weak, probably Z-spun, max. length 2.5 cm.

System (2) 10–11 per cm., slightly stronger Z-spun, max. length 1.2 cm.

System (1) largely covers (2). The material resembles a bast fibre.

Verulamium Museum, St Albans.

26 WELSHPOOL (MONTGOMERY)

Wrapping of a series of bronze bowls; visible on discovery as an imprint, together with a few fibres, in the corrosion products encasing the handle of one bowl. It was a fine, plain-weave cloth, all traces of which have now disappeared. It is dated to the second half of the second century.

Dr H. A. Hyde of the National Museum of Wales reports that the fibres were of flax.

Bowls in National Museum of Wales, Cardiff (*Ant. J.*, XLI (1961), 17, 24).

27 WINTERBOURNE EARLS (WILTSHIRE)

Textile adhering to iron object found on chest of elderly woman; A.D. 375–400.

Fragments of two textiles, one in medium-fine half-basket-weave, the other in plain-weave, perhaps tapestry.

Fibre uncertain.

Kind information from Miss Elisabeth Crowfoot, who is to publish details.

28 YORK (REGION IV, AREA (*e*), BURIAL (ii), RAILWAY STATION)

Several layers of textile, the shroud in a gypsum burial; third or fourth century A.D. Probably linen.

System (1) 10–12 per cm., Z-spun, fine yarn.

System (2) 16–18 per cm., Z-spun, heavier closer set, yarn. (A.S.H.)

Yorkshire Museum, York (*Eburacum* (1962), 108).

29 YORK (CASTLE YARD)

Fragments of linen (?) cloth surrounding gypsum in lead sarcophagus; largest fragment 1.5 by 2.5 cm. Two layers.

System (1) 16 per cm., weak Z-spun.

System (2) 8–9 per cm., weak Z-spun.

Yorkshire Museum, York (*YAJ*, XXXIX (1958), 402, 412, pl. III A).

IMPRESSIONS IN PLAIN WEAVE

(N.B. Allow for 5% shrinkage in impressions on tile)

30 ASHTEAD (SURREY)

Negative impression on edge of flue-tile; first century A.D.

System (1) doubles, *c.* 8–9 pairs per cm., max. length *c.* 2 cm.

System (2) singles, *c.* 10–12 per cm., max. length *c.* 5 cm. (A.S.H.)

Information from A. W. G. Lowther, in whose possession the tile is (*cf. PPS*, N.S. XVI (1950), 136).

31 DEVIZES (SANDY LANE)

Impression of cloth on lead seal (?) found unstratified on Roman settlement site. (*Not* definitely Roman.)

System (1) warp ?, 10 per cm., spin uncertain, max. length 2.5 cm.

System (2) weft ?, 20 per cm., spin uncertain max. length 3 cm.

Devizes Museum, 282. I saw this through the kindness of Mr F. K. Annable.

32 KESTON (KENT)

Stuff impression of shroud in gypsum of late-Roman burial; appears to be a fine plain-weave linen.

London Museum (*Arch. Cant*, L (1939), 164–5, pl. II).

33 LULLINGSTONE (KENT)

Impression on tile from villa.

System (1) 7–8 per cm., spin direction uncertain.
System (2) 16–18 per cm., S-spun.
(2) heavier yarn and closer set than (1),

Impression under microscope appears to be of woollen cloth.

Unpublished information from Lt.-Col. G. W. Meates and Miss A. S. Henshall.

34 RADNAGE (BUCKS.)

'Markings on the rust of iron strappings' of a wooden casket of a late first-century cremation.

Casket presented to BM (*Ant. J*, III (1923), 335–7).

35 WROXETER

Shallow concave textile impression on hypocaust- or building-tile.

System (1) *c.* 6 per cm., Z-spun, max. length 5.5 cm., not close set.
System (2) *c.* 12 per cm., Z-spun, max. length 3.5 cm.

Yarn (1) is of even quality while (2) varies greatly. Near centre one warp- and one weft-thread is plucked up for a short length in each direction; probably damage rather than weaving fault.

By courtesy of Dr G. Webster; find no. WB (38), 20; (144).

36–42 YORK

36 *Site A. Region IV, Area (d), Burial (ix) from Railway excavations, new parcels office 1892*

Impression of:

(1) Fine plain cloth in gypsum within coffin.
System (1) *c.* 22 per cm.
System (2) *c.* 32 per cm.
(2). Coarser cloth from outer layer of wrappings.
System (1) *c.* 14 per cm.
System (2) *c.* 22 per cm.

37 *Site B. Region IV, Area (d), Burial (xi) Railway excavations. Gypsum impression.*
System (1) *c.* 16 per cm.
System (2) *c.* 14 per cm.

38 *Site C. Region IV, Area (d), Burial (xiii), South-East of Railway Station*
Impression of fairly coarsely woven cloth in gypsum.
System (1) *c.* 14 per cm.
System (2) *c.* 8–10 per cm.

39 *Site D. Region V (b), Clementhorpe; Burial (i) Bishopgate St.*
Impressions on gypsum in coffin containing mother and child.

(1) Fine cloth.
System (1), warp, 40–45 per cm.
System (2), weft, 20–22 per cm.
Some selvedge visible, but the form is uncertain.
(2) Medium cloth (impression, but minute fragments survive).
System (1) 32 per cm.
System (2) 16 per cm.
(3) Coarse cloth.
System (1) 28–30 per cm., warp; selvedge on baby's head.
System (2) weft, 11 per cm.

(4) Band of red-ribbed cloth (8.7–10 cm. wide).
System (1) warp, *c.* 56 per cm.
System (2) weft, *c.* 10 per cm.

Warp almost covers weft. Regular transverse ribs in weft—probably self-bands for decoration. There are traces of dark-red colour on the gypsum. Both (plain?) selvedges can be detected. The band seems to have been sewn as ornament on the fine cloth (no. 39, 1).

All four types of cloth (which may represent more than four actual webs) were used merely as wrapping for the bodies. Their original purpose, perhaps as towels or clothing, cannot now be established. (A. S. H.)

Yorkshire Museum, York (*Eburacum* (1962), 108–9).

PLAIN 2-OVER-2 TWILL

40 CAERWENT (FIG. 20)
Small fragment of woollen cloth, dark to russet brown in colour (dyed?), found in a cooking pot in House No. VII A in 1906; late fourth century in date.

System (1) 12 per cm., Z-spun.
System (2) 8 per cm., Z-spun.
(1) is finer yarn than (2).

(A. S. H.)

Mr J. E. Ford of the Shirley Institute notes that the fibres separated from the yarns were relatively smooth and featureless, although faintly striated on the surface and streaky in the interior. The diameters of the fibres range from 10 to 35µ. It is probably sheep's wool.

Museum and Art Gallery, Newport (*Archaeologia*, 60 (1907), 460; *BBCS*, XIX (1906–2), 344).

41 LLANGENNITH (BLUE POOL CAVE, GLAM.)
Heavily oxydised twill (probably 2-over-2) (*c.* 1 sq.cm.) on back of bronze figurine; an associated denarius of Marcus Aurelius, TPQ A.D. 169–170.
Both systems *c.* 8 per cm. No spin visible.

Ashmolean Museum, Oxford.

2-OVER-2 TWILL WEAVE WITH WEFT-CHEVRON PATTERN

42 FALKIRK (FIGS. 23, 48; PLATE VI *b*)
Fragment from the mouth of a pot containing a hoard of silver coins; TPQ A.D. 230, buried possibly *c.* A.D. 250.

System (1) warp (?), *c.* 6–7 per cm., strong Z-spun, max. length 6 cm.
  Contains 2 yarns: (1) light yellowish brown, (2) dark chocolate brown. The colour-change comes after 8 warp-threads.
System (2) weft (?), *c.* 6–7 per cm., strong Z-spun. Same two yarns; change in direction of slope of twill and colour come together after 9 shots of weft; max. length *c.* 7 cm.

(G. M. C.)

The yarns are both of uneven quality. There are remains of five colour-changes in the warp, six in the weft; both colours are found as natural pigments in the wool of the Soay sheep. The resulting check squares measure *c.* 1.5 cm. by 1.5 cm. There is no means of verifying which is warp, but the scheme adopted here is suggested by the Icelandic method of knitting heddles recorded by Marta Hoffmann (fig. 54).

Dr M. L. Ryder reports on three types of yarn from this piece:

(*a*) no pigment, 10–30μ diameters (mean 16.7); symmetrical distribution; classed as short or fine (white) wool.

(*b*) pigmented, 10–36μ diameters with 1 hair 80μ (mean 18.2); skewed to fine distribution; classed as hairy medium-fine wool.

(*c*) pigmented, 12–34μ diameters (mean 17.8); skewed to fine distribution; generalised medium-fine wool.

NMA, FR 483 (*PSAS*, LXVIII (1933–4), 32 ff.; LXXXII (1947–8), 227 ff., fig. 2; *PPS*, N.S. XVI (1950), 139; *CQ*, XIV (1964), 263 ff. with incorrect drawing).

43 HUNTCLIFF (SALTBURN, E.YORKS.) From well in late-Roman coastal signal station; TPQ *c.* A.D. 370.

System (1) warp ?, doubles, *c.* 8 pairs per cm., strong Z-spun.
System (2) weft ?, singles, *c.* 14 per cm., strong Z-spun.

The report in *JRS* (cited below) states incorrectly that there are 22 threads of System (2) in each stripe; the number varies, from 16 to 23, but is often 22 (Cardiff frag. 23/16/16/22; Oxford frag./18/22/22/22/ *c.* 20/22/ *c.* 22/). This suggests that it is a weft-chevron twill. There is full displacement in the direction of System (1). No selvedges survive.

The cloth was divided up by the excavators and presented to private individuals and museums. The surface area was probably at least 900 sq.cm. The yarns are somewhat unevenly spun.

Faults in the Oxford fragment.

Faults in System (2) weft (?) (fig. 25): (1) one weft-thread 3-over-1 for whole width of piece, never eliminated; (2)

same fault, three weft-threads further; not same shed; (1A) and (2A) between the above are 1-over-3.

Faults in System (1) warp (?): false displacement in direction parallel to (1); fault 5 cm. long (*c.* 75 weft-threads). Eliminated successfully at both ends.

Mr J. E. Ford of the Shirley Institute states that tests in hypochlorite showed that there is no admixture of bast fibres as the original report (1912) said (private communication of 8 Jan. 1962 to H. A. Hyde).

Dr M. L. Ryder reports: Yarn (*a*) (pigmented) has a diameter range of 8–40μ (mean 17.8) and a symmetrical diameter-distribution pattern; generalised medium or short wool. Yarn (*b*) (pigmented) has a diameter range of 8–56μ (mean 20.3) and a skewed to fine distribution; hairy medium wool.

One surface is now dark-brown, the other somewhat lighter. If it was dyed, the oxide of iron identified by Walter Gardner in *JRS* may be a mordant; or may have been merely absorbed from other material in the well. The natural colour would probably have been brown.

The largest portion (32 × 12 cm.) is now in the Ashmolean Museum, Oxford; pieces are also held by the Whitby Lit. and Phil. Soc. Museum, Keighley Museum, The National Museum of Wales, The Dorman Memorial Museum, Middlesbrough, and Chesters Museum (*JRS*, II (1912), 230 ff., pl. XVI; Kitson Clark (1935), 93; *PPS*, N.S. XVI (1950), 139).

44 LONDON (WALBROOK STREAM BED) Fragment of edged herringbone twill from context dated by samian ware and coins to the early second century. Light-brown, felted in places, possibly *pexus*. See nos. 7–8.

System (1) warp?, S-spun, 14–15 per cm., length 13 cm.

System (2) weft?, S-spun?, *c*. 12 per cm., length 2 cm.

The pattern is probably weft chevron; reverse in (2) after *c*. 22 threads/*c*. 36 threads/*c*. 14 threads. This suggests irregular reversal of sheds rather than unbalanced threading. Groups of threads in system (2) may perhaps be alternately S- and Z-spun, but this is not certain.

Edge (corded) (fig. 49). Groups of four and three adjacent weft (2) threads are twisted together (S-twined) to form an edge to the cloth. The damaged condition does not admit certain diagnosis; but this explanation appears to be correct.

BM 1956, 12.1.2 (to be published in *Festschrift Reichel*).

2-OVER-2 DIAMOND TWILL WEAVE

Wool

45 BALMACLELLAN (KIRKCUDBRIGHT) (FIG. 24)

Cloth found in a bog wrapping a small hoard of late-La-Tène bronzes; the latter may on stylistic grounds be of Flavian date, but could have been concealed much later.

System (1) warp ?, 14–16 per cm., Z-spun.
System (2) weft ?, 11–14 per cm., S-spun.
Yarn (2) is finer and better spun than (1).

There is no reliable way of determining the warp or weft, since no edges survive. The interpretation here adopted rests on Marta Hoffmann's observations on modern Icelandic methods of knitting the heddles. There is both warp- and weft-displacement; the direction changes after 10 warp-threads, 7 weft-threads. The three fragments amount to *c*. 35 sq.cm. Now light-brown in colour, they were probably affected by the bog acids.

Dr M. L. Ryder reports: Yarn (*a*) (System (2)) (no pigment) has a diameter range of 16–30μ (mean 20.6) and a skewed to fine distribution pattern; generalised medium-fine wool. Yarn (*b*) (System (1)) (no pigment) has a diameter range of 10–34μ (mean 21.1, with 2 hairs of 70μ) and a skewed to fine distribution pattern; hairy medium-fine wool.

NMA, FA 14 (*PSAS*, IV (1860–2), 294; LXXXII (1947–8), 225–7, fig. 1, pl. XLII *a, b*; *PPS*, N.S. XVI (1950), 139).

46–8 CORBRIDGE

Oxydised fragments from the Trajanic hoard; see nos. 1–4 above.

46 *Textile (group* 1)
System (1) 10 per cm., S-spun.
System (2) 8–9 per cm., S-spun.
Both yarns are of high quality.

Both systems so far as is visible have displacement; but the weaving pattern can nowhere be completely elucidated. The reverse in slope appears to come after 10 threads of System (2), after 14–16 of System (1).

47 *Textile (group* 2)
System (1) 10 per cm., Z-spun.
System (2) 8 per cm., S-spun.
Quality and fineness of yarn similar to that of Textile 1; fairly strongly spun yarns.

There is a reverse in slope after 10 or more threads of System (2), after 12 (or in another place 17–18) threads of System (1). Displacement in both systems.

48 Textile (group 3)

Three small fragments of badly crumpled cloth. Box (148).

System (1) 20 per cm., S-spun, max. length 1.5 cm.

System (2) 20 per cm., Z-spun, max. length 2 cm.

(1) predominates over (2). Yarn much finer than in Textiles 1 and 2.

Probably a diamond twill, but full pattern not recovered; reverse after at least 8 threads of System (2).

49 VERULAMIUM

Cloth from the lead coffin of an eighteen-month-old baby girl; it was rolled up to support her head. A coin in the mouth gives a TPQ, A.D. 210 (figs. 26–9).

System (1) warp, 19–20 per cm., Z-spun; threads set close, but not packed together.
System (2) weft, 19–20 per cm., weak S-spun.

The fabric is now a uniform dark-brown colour, stained by the corrosion products in the coffin. The presence of a group of lighter yarns in the border of fragment H suggests that it may originally have been in several shades. The yarns are fine and evenly spun, except for occasional coarser threads in the warp.

The weave is diamond twill, but the many root-holes and other damage prevent recovery of the weaving-pattern. There appears to be displacement in both systems; reverse after 8–10 threads of warp, and 8–10 of weft. One or both sides of the cloth had a thick nap. No weaving faults are visible. The probable starting-border on fragment H points to the use of a warp-weighted loom.

In fragments A–D (the relationship between which can be established by the seams and stitching) the two thread-systems run in the same direction; but in fragment E they run at right angles to this.

The fragments are listed as in my forthcoming report, where full details of each may be found (for plan of the fragments see fig. 26). I have confined the description below to the more important features.

Hem (fragments A and B)

The raw edge has been oversewn in simple hemming stitches; there are 5–6 stitches per cm.

Sewing thread: wool (?), 2 weak S-spun strands, S-plied; light in colour.

The threads of the hemming-stitches formed the warp for 6 'weft-threads' in the same yarn which were darned over them in plain weave (fig. 27) (see p. 57).

Seam (fragments A and B, D and E)

A seam joins the cut edges of fragments A and B together; the same seam, less well preserved, joins fragments D and E. The two edges are tacked face to face in plain running stitch, the holes of which are at 2–3 cm. intervals. The sewing thread is as described above. The side of the cloth where the tacking is visible was presumably the inner side of the textile article of which it was a part.

'Button-holes' (fragments B and E)

At the corner formed by the two seams between fragments A and B there is an L-shaped slit, edged in the same darning technique and material as was used in the hem. The stitching is unconnected with the stitches of the seam. The two arms of the slit are c. 4 cm. long. Where the line of running stitches in fragment D reaches the seam between fragments D and E, there are traces of another edged slit of uncertain shape.

Stitching

Across the face of the cloth in fragment C parallel to System (2) and in line with the main seam between fragments A and B ran a line of plain running stitches, of which five survive on the outer face. They appear to be slightly offset in relation to one another. Four hemming stitches were inserted *c.* 6 cm. from the running stitches to hold the outer edge of the pleat (see below). All are in the yarn described above.

Fringe (fragment E)

A straight fringed edge consisting of groups of *c.* 10 warp-threads (System (1)) doubled back upon themselves and twisted together runs parallel to System (2). The looped strands, now in a poor state, are *c.* 1 cm. long. The fringe may represent the warp-threads at the bottom edge of the cloth on the loom.

Starting-border (fragment H)

The border has S-spun double warp-threads (as set up on the band-loom; see p. 63), lighter in colour than the rest of the fabric. There are six pairs, forming a band *c.* 1 cm. wide (fig. 28). The weft of the border (later main warp) is also paired, but the individual threads in each shot separate in opposite directions at the outer edge of the band and join adjacent pairs. During the knitting of the heddles the individual threads of each pair (at the inner, lower edge)

were assigned to a different heddle-rod. This is characteristic of the starting-border of the warp-weighted loom, but might possibly represent a selvedge worked by tablets (see p. 56) on a twill cloth. The spin of the yarns and the fringe, however, speak in favour of a starting-border.

Purpose of the cloth

When found, the cloth had a narrow pleat inserted into it, which would have lain on the underside of the cloth. It was held in position by a single surviving stitch, which still secures a small folded patch of cloth torn away from the pleat. It lies *c.* 2 cm. from the button-hole on the reverse of fragment B. The fold of the pleat visible on the upper surface was fastened by four hemming stitches.

The hem on fragment A is approximately 80 cm. from the fringe of fragment E. The painstaking stitching, the fringe and the nap point to the cloth having been part of a garment or item of soft furnishing. The 'button-holes' may have had a strap passing through them; they are unlikely to be button-holes in the modern sense. Buttons are rare, if not unknown, in the Roman period, except perhaps for leatherwork. In the present state of our knowledge it is not possible to be more precise about the nature of the garment or upholstery.

Dr M. L. Ryder reports: The yarns have a diameter range of 6–36μ (means 12, 13, 5 at 14, and 17μ) and show a skewed to fine distribution. They are unpigmented.

Verulamium Museum, St Albans.

2-OVER-1 TWILL WEAVE

50 CORBRIDGE (FIG. 21)

From the Trajanic hoard; see above, nos. 1–4.

System (1) 10 per cm., Z-spun.
System (2) 8 per cm., Z-spun.

Both yarns are moderately fine. System (1) dominates, but neither system is closely set. All the fragments adhere to pieces of plain-weave cloth; the face which is outermost is in all cases faced with System (1), which may once have been of a different colour from (2).

Faults: At one point on a fragment in Box (10 A) a single thread of System (1) floats over 5 of (2), instead of over 2, under 1 and over 2 (fig. 21).

The textile may be a cushion cover (see above nos. 3, 4).

3-OVER-1 DAMASK

51 HOLBOROUGH (SNODLAND, KENT)

Three small fragments, each of three layers, adhering to the hair of a child in a lead coffin which was a secondary burial in a Roman barrow (fig. 41). The pottery gives a TPQ *c.* A.D. 250, confirmed by stylistic dating of the sarcophagus and its parallels.

System (1) warp ?, 50–60 per cm., Z-spun, light-brown in colour.
System (2) weft ?, 50–60 per cm., practically unspun, slightly darker than yarn (1).
About 7.5 sq.cm. of stuff survive.

The weave is a simple geometric damask, with full displacement in the warp, partial in the weft. Weaving required 8 sheds, and the thread-up of the pattern was based on 8 warp-threads.

The warp and weft appear to have been of different colours; the cloth would have been a tartan with a minute check pattern (fig. 41). The entire repeat-pattern cannot now be reconstructed. The squares and rectangles of the pattern are alternately warp-faced and weft-faced, and would have cast light in different directions.

Faults

(1) A thread of the warp (Z-spun) floats over 15 weft-threads where normal shedding would have required it to pass under 3 weft-threads at points on its length. A heddle-leash may have broken, or the warp may have become tangled.

(2) A weft-thread floats over 5 warp-threads, one of which it should have passed under; the latter is the same warp-thread as is concerned in fault (1). Accordingly, while this fault is the *reverse* of fault (1), the two mistakes may be mechanically connected.

Report on the fibre: Manchester Chamber of Commerce Testing House state that it is probably of animal origin.

Maidstone Museum and Art Gallery (noted in *Arch. Cant.* LXVIII (1954), 19; my report *Arch. Cant.* LXXX (1965), 246 ff.).

TABLE A

NETTING TECHNIQUES

52 CHESTER (BRIDGE ST. 1911)
Adhering to coin of Trajan.

Grosvenor Museum, Chester.

FELT

53 NEWSTEAD
Felt lining of helmet from Pit xxII in south annexe of fort; probably late-first-century. Identified as wool by A. F. Tagg.

NMA (Curle (1911), 360; Toynbee (1963), 167 cat. no. 99).

MISCELLANEOUS FRAGMENTS

54 BARTLOW HILLS (ASHDON, ESSEX)
'Some cloth or linen' covering a series of bronze vessels in Barrow No. V (*VCH*) with mid-second-century samian ware. Destroyed by fire 1847.

(*Archaeologia*, xxvIII (1840), 1 ff.; *VCH Essex*, III (1963), 42.)

55 BECKFOOT (CUMBERLAND)
Charred fragments of wool, apparently the stuffing of a mattress from a funeral couch. The rite (cremation) suggests a date within the first two centuries A.D.

(*CW*, N.S. LIV (1954), 51–4.)

56 CAERWENT
A piece of woollen fabric from House I N in the Roman town; no indication of date or character.

(*Archaeologia*, LX (1908), 460.)

57 HUSTHWAITE (E.YORKS)
Remains of a bag 'quite decayed', which held a small coin hoard. The latest coins were of Valens and Theodosius. Probably linen.

(Kitson Clark (1935), 94.)

58 LANGLEY (KENT)
Remains of a coarse cloth covering bronze vessels in a cremation burial. There is now no trace of it.

Vessels in Maidstone Museum and Art Gallery (*JBrit. AA*, XXII (1959), 27).

59 LONDON (ROYAL EXCHANGE)
Fragments of wool.

(Roach Smith (1859), 142–3.)

60 SANDY (BEDS.)

'Urn containing burnt bones divided by layers of cloth, a silver ring and a copper coin.'

(*VCH Beds.* II (1908), 10.)

61 SOUTHFLEET (KENT)

Remains of 'a dress reduced to tinder' in a sarcophagus.

(*JBrit. AA*, XXII (1959), 30; *Archaeologia*, XIV (1808), 37–9, 221–3.)

CLOTH IMPRESSIONS WITH NO DETAILS

62 CHATHAM (KENT)

Oxydised remains or impressions of cloth on iron knife in late-Roman inhumation.

(*Arch. Cant.* XXIII (1898), 16.)

63 PUTLEY (HEREFORD)

Tile from Roman villa bearing cloth impression.

(*JBrit. AA*, XXXII (1876), 250; *Trans. Woolhope FC* (1881–2), 258; *VCH Hereford*, I (1908), 193.)

PLAIN-WEAVE

Wool

1 CONTHEY (WALLIS)

Small fragment of plain-weave woollen cloth adhering to layers of fine silk in a late-Roman sarcophagus. Both systems have 15 threads per cm. Marta Hoffman ((1964), 389, note 3) thought that one edge might be a simple (starting ?) border. However, a selvedge did not appear to be present when I saw it. See silk, no. 85.

Schweiz. LM, 32075.

2 KÖLN (JACOBSTR.)

Oxydised remains on iron blades of barber's double knife; late third or early fourth century.

Both systems about 9 per cm., but wide set; yarns loosely woven.

R-G Mus., 29.1853-4 (*Germ.* 16 (1932), 129 f. Abb. 1, 10).

3 KÖLN (SEVERINSKIRCHE)

Oxydised fragment on blade of knife; TPQ *c.* A.D. 270, on coins.

System (1) *c.* 15 per cm., length *c.* 1.5 cm.
System (2) *c.* 15 per cm., length *c.* 2.5 cm.
Yarn (2) thicker than (1), almost covering it.

R-G Mus., 25,885 (*BJb*, 131 (1926), 297, Abb. 10, Grab. XXVII).

Cloth with colour effects from Mainz

Mainz—The findspots

The textiles from Mainz owe their survival to the marshy terrain on which much of the legionary camp and town were built. The following findspots lie within the area of the late-Roman town, and probably antedate its major building phase of *c.* A.D. 300; they are adjacent to the road leading north:

Schillerplatz (1850 and later). The material discovered 16 ft. deep was associated with Roman artefacts, pottery, etc. A selection of the textiles are now in the Städtisches Alter-tumsmuseum, Wiesbaden, and in the Musée des Antiquités Nationales, St Germain-en-Laye.

Corner of Emmeranstrasse and Gr. Langgasse, 1963. Excavations of Bauherr Kolb; material in R-G ZM, Mainz.

Gr. Emmeranstrasse. Textiles in the Mittelrheini-sches Landesmuseum, Mainz, once in private collection of Dr Fr. Fremersdorf. Others from here were destroyed in the war.

Findspots within the earlier legionary camp:

Universitäts-Kliniken, 1963. Excavations of Bauherr Kolb, material in R-G ZM, Mainz.

Indefinitely located finds:

'*Moorschicht 1855*' perhaps near Schillerplatz. Textiles found at depth of 18 ft. 'with coins of

Adrian, sandals, leather and pottery'. Now in Rijksmuseum G. M. Kam, Nijmegen.

4 EMMERANSTR.–GR. LANGGASSE, 1963

Two-colour cloth, poorly preserved

System (1) c. 10 per cm., Z-spun; yarn dark-brown, length c. 0.9 cm.

System (2) c. 20 per cm., Z-spun, yarn light-brown, length c. 3.5 cm.

Dark mainly covered by light yarn.

5 SCHILLERPLATZ

Light-brown cloth with chocolate-brown band.

System (1) warp ?, 8 per cm., Z-spun, fine yarn, length 17 cm.

System (2) weft ?, 28 per cm., Z-spun, fine yarn, close set, length 10 cm.

Band in direction (2) consists of 28 dark threads of (2), finer than the rest, covering (1).

Wiesbaden.

8 SCHILLERPLATZ

Band (?) with tablet-woven selvedge (fig. 32).

System (1) warp, 22 per cm., Z-spun, length 4 cm., light-brown yarn.

System (2) weft, 6 per cm., Z-spun, length 16 cm., dark-brown yarn.

Yarn (3) extra warp in selvedge, 2 threads (one selvedge only survives), strong Z-spun, dark-brown, coarse—possibly doubled.

Outer two warp-threads of selvedge woven on a tablet using two holes; full turn of tablet, then reversed. Main warp may have been woven on tablets, half-turns, then reverse. Roughly cut slit for 'button-hole'?

6 MOORSCHICHT 1855

Slightly felted two-colour *check* in coarse yarns.

System (1) 7 per cm., Z-spun, all dark brown, length 3.2 cm.

System (2) 7–8 per cm., Z-spun, length 4 cm.

//6+light/12 dark/6+light//

Nijmegen, no. 4.

7 GR. EMMERANSTR.

Tattered fragment with *speckled* effect.

System (1) warp ?, strong Z-spin, 9–10 per cm., light brown, length c. 11 cm.

System (2) weft ? weak Z-spin, c. 20 per cm., black, length c. 9 cm.

Mittelrheinisches Landesmuseum, Mainz, no. 2 W (F.1505).

Bands from Mainz

Wiesbaden (*Nass. Ann.* 15 (1879), 35, Nr. 6, Patrone 8).

9 EMMERANSTR.–GR. LANGGASSE

Band, medium-brown, both (simple) selvedges preserved (fig. 30).

Fragment 1

System (1) warp, 26 per cm., Z-spun, length 21 cm.

System (2) weft, 7 per cm., strong Z-spun, wide-spaced, length 5 cm., i.e., width of band complete.

Warp somewhat coarser than weft.

R-G ZM, Mainz, 0, 37906.

Fragment 2

System (1) warp, 20–25 per cm., Z-spun.
System (2) weft, 8 per cm., Z-spun, length
5 cm.

R-G ZM, Mainz, 0, 37907.

10 EMMERANSTR.–GR. LANGGASSE

Band, light-brown, both (simple) selvedges
preserved.

System (1) warp, 24 per cm., Z-spun,
length 10.5 cm.
System (2) weft, 7 per cm., Z-spun, length
5.6 cm., i.e. width of band.

R-G ZM, Mainz (no number).

11 EMMERANSTR.–GR. LANGGASSE

Band fragment (no selvedges), dark-brown.

System (1) warp ?, 18–20 per cm., Z-spun,
length 5 cm., good even yarn.
System (2) weft ?, 7–8 per cm., Z-spun,
wide set, length 5 cm.

R-G ZM, Mainz (no number).

12 EMMERANSTR.–GR. LANGGASSE

Small fragment of band, black, c. 1 sq.cm.

System (1) c. 24 per cm., weak Z-spun, fine
and much felted.
System (2) c. 8 per cm., strong Z-spun.

R-G ZM, Mainz (no number).

13 MOORSCHICHT 1855

Dark-brown, slightly felted fragment of
band (?)

System (1) c. 20 per cm., Z-spun, fairly fine,
evenly spun, yarn, length 3.5 cm.

System (2) 11–12 per cm., Z-spun, length
4 cm.

Nijmegen, no. 3.

14 EMMERANSTR.–GR. LANGGASSE

Possibly band fragment, dark-brown.

System (1) 24–25 per cm., weak Z-spun,
close set, length 8.5 cm.
System (2) 7 per cm., strong Z-spun, spaced
out, length 4 cm.

R-G ZM, Mainz, 0, 37905.

15 SCHILLERPLATZ

Two fragments of dark-brown band.

System (1) 20 per cm., Z-spun, coarse yarn
close set, length 19.5 cm.
System (2) 4 per cm., Z-spun, fairly fine
yarn, length 8 cm.

Wiesbaden (*Nass. Ann.* 15 (1879), 36, Nr.10,16).

16 SCHILLERPLATZ

Fragment of band (?), dark-brown.

System (1) 24 per cm., S-spun, length
5.5 cm.
System (2) 8 per cm., Z-spun, length c.
3 cm.
Both yarns of fine quality.

Wiesbaden (*Nass. Ann.* 15 (1879), 35, Nr. 2,
Patrone 6).

17 SCHILLERPLATZ

Seven fragments, now mislaid. Spin-direction
and the measurements were not published.

1 (1) 22 per cm. (2) 8 per cm.
   Nass. Ann. 15 (1879), 35, Nr. 5.
2 (1) 22 per cm. (2) 9 per cm. *Ibid.* Nr. 7.

3 (1) 26 per cm. (2) 9 per cm. *Ibid.*, Nr. 8.
4 (1) 28 per cm. (2) 7 per cm. Fine light-brown yarns. *Ibid.* Nr. 9.
5 (1) 16 per cm. (2) 7 per cm., length 5.5 cm., with selvedge? *Ibid.* Nr. 14.

6 (1) 24 per cm. (2) 8 per cm., length 5.5 cm., with selvedge? *Ibid.* Nr. 15.
7 (1) 24 per cm. (2) 8 per cm. *Ibid.* Nr. 17.

Plain-weave from Mainz with no distinguishing features

18 SCHILLERPLATZ

Cloth with ornamentally stitched edge (fig. 31).

System (1) 13 per cm., Z-spun, length 4.5 cm.
System (2) 36 per cm., Z-spun, length 6 cm.
Yarn (3), couching-thread, coarse wool, S-spun.
Yarn (4), sewing-thread, S-spun, light-brown.

The couching-thread (3) was held against the raw edge of the cloth (parallel to (1)) and sewn into that position by a series of embroidered ornamental stitches in yarn (4), which cross and decorate the outer six threads of System (1). No sign of the original colour of the stitching.

Dr M. L. Ryder reports: Yarn (*a*), unpigmented, has a diameter range 10–32µ (mean 19.3) and a symmetrical distribution—a true fine wool. Yarn (*b*), unpigmented, has a diameter range 10–32µ (mean 20.97) and a symmetrical distribution—a true fine wool.

Wiesbaden (*Nass. Ann.* 15 (1879), 37, Nr. 22, Patrone 9).

19 SCHILLERPLATZ
(Weft-faced fragments)

Fragment 1 (1) 13 per cm. (2) 46 per cm.

Nass. Ann. 15 (1879), 36, No. 13.

Fragment 2 (1) 13 per cm. (2) 60 per cm.

Ibid. 36, Nr. 18.

20 GR. EMMERANSTR. 8
Weft-faced cloth.

System (1) 6 per cm., spin?, length *c.* 3 cm.
System (2) *c.* 20 per cm., spin?, perhaps S, length 9 cm.

Details from drawing in Inventory.

Mittelrheinisches Landesmuseum, Mainz, 4092 (lost in war).

21 GR. EMMERANSTR.
Weft-faced cloth, black.

System (1) warp ?, 14 per cm., Z-spun, very fine yarn, length 21 cm.
System (2) weft ?, 50–60 per cm. (variable), weak Z-spun, length 11 cm.

Mittelrheinisches Landesmuseum, Mainz, I.W. (F. 1504).

22 SCHILLERPLATZ
Dark-brown fragment.

System (1) 11 per cm., S-spun, length 8.3 cm.
System (2) 12 per cm., Z-spun, length 4.5 cm.
Even quality yarns.

Wiesbaden (*Nass. Ann.* 15 (1879), 36, Nr. 11).

23 SCHILLERPLATZ

Fragment 1 (1) singles, 9 per cm., S-spun.
(2) doubles, 7 pairs per cm., S-spun.

Ibid. 35, Nr. 1, Patrone 5.

Fragment 2 (1) 10 per cm. (2) 8 per cm.

Ibid. 35, Nr. 4.

24–25 UNIVERSITÄTS-KLINIKEN 1963

Two layers of woollen cloth sewn together; perhaps a lining.

24 *Fragment* 1. Very coarse light brown stuff, heavily felted on both sides.

System (1) *c.* 7 per cm., Z-spun, well spaced, medium-fine yarn, length 8.5 cm.
System (2) *c.* 8 per cm., Z-spun, close set thick yarn, length 7 cm.

25 *Fragment* 2. Black unfelted cloth, cut aslant to weave and sewn on top (?) of (1), covering it.

System (1) 8 per cm., Z-spun, length 6 cm.
System (2) 8 per cm., Z-spun, length 7 cm.
Stitching: two rows of running-stitches at each side, parallel to System (1), 0.4 cm. from edge; holes 0.4 cm. apart. Yarn S-spun, fine; fibre probably wool.

R-G ZM, Mainz, 0, 37903.

26 SCHILLERPLATZ

Dark-brown cloth.

System (1) 2-ply, 8 per cm., Z-spun, S-plied, length 8 cm.
System (2) 2-ply, 8 per cm., Z-spun, S-plied, length 14 cm.

Wiesbaden.

27 SCHILLERPLATZ

Fragment 1 (1) 6 per cm., (2) 7 per cm.

Ibid, 36, Nr. 20.

Fragment 2 (1) 5 per cm. (2) 6 per cm.

Ibid. 35, Nr. 3.

28 SCHILLERPLATZ

Coarse sacking, light-brown.

System (1) 6 per cm., Z-spun, length 10 cm.
System (2) 5 per cm., Z-spun, length 15 cm.

Wiesbaden (*Ibid.* 36, Nr. 19).

29 SCHILLERPLATZ

(1) 4 per cm., (2) 5 per cm.

Ibid. 36, Nr.12.

30 SAALBURG-KASTELL (BAD HOMBURG)

Jacobi ((1897) 1, 161, 483) records fragments of woollen cloth from Wells no. 17 and 18 of the vicus of the Limes-fort. They are not dated, but must fall into the period A.D. 83–260. There are at least five fragments of the same textile (plate v *b*).

Characteristics

System (1) warp (?), singles, 5–6 per cm., Z-spun.
System (2) weft (?), singles, 18–20 per cm., S-spun.

Dr M. L. Ryder reports: Yarn (*a*) (System (2)) has a diameter range 12–32μ (mean 19μ) with a symmetrical distribution and is a true fine wool. Yarn (*b*) (System (1)) has a range 12–40μ (mean 24μ) with a skewed to fine distribution and is generalised medium-fine wool.

Saalburg Museum (Wild (1967 *d*) for full account).

31 VINDONISSA (SCHUTTHÜGEL)

From the first-century rubbish-dump; fine unfelted woollen cloth, stained uniformly dark-brown. Seven fragments in all.

System (1) warp ?, singles, 10 per cm., Z-spun, well spaced out, length 6 cm.

System (2) weft, singles, 14–15 per cm., weak Z-spun, length 12 cm.

Faults: doubles instead of singles in System (2) in largest fragment: 16+singles/2 doubles/9s./2d./2s./2d./2s./2d./17+singles.

Vindonissa-Museum, Brugg.

32 VINDONISSA
Backing of leather object from E.–W. drain in N.–S. street of the fort; probably first-century in date.

System (1) 5 per cm., length 2 cm. (spin not recorded).

System (2) 5 per cm., length 2 cm.

Vindonissa-Museum, Brugg, 44: 55 (*Ges. Vindonissa* (1957–8), 175, Abb. 3, 5).

33–34 XANTEN (KR. MOERS)
Fragments in plain-weave, dark-brown in colour, from a rubbish-pit associated with military occupation; TAQ A.D. 69.

33 *Textile 1*
System (1) singles, 12–13 per cm., strong Z-spun, length 23 cm.

System (2) singles, 26–27 per cm., Z-spun, length 8.8 cm.

Yarn (2) practically conceals (1); the quality of (2) is uneven.

Faults: in System (2) 15 cases of double threads, 2 of three threads, instead of one.

34 *Textile 2*
Two pieces (6.6 by 7 cm., 6 by 6.5 cm.).

System (1) warp ?, singles, 5–6 per cm., strong Z-spun, wide spaced.

System (2) weft ?, doubles, 10–11 pairs per cm., weak Z-spun.

One edge cut and oversewn in plain hemming stitch; yarn, wool, dark-brown, S-spun. Remains of 4 stitches. In two cases a new ball of weft (System (2)) may have been started; the end is visible in the cloth. It may on the other hand be merely a result of later damage.

Dr M. L. Ryder reports: Textile 1—Yarn (a), pigmented, has a diameter range 10–40μ (mean 22.7) and a skewed to fine distribution; generalised medium-fine wool. Yarn (b), pigmented, 10–40μ (hairs 52 and 60μ) (mean 20.7μ), skewed to fine distribution; generalised medium-fine wool. Textile 2—Yarn (a), pigmented, 10–44μ (mean 25.6). Yarn (b) pigmented, 14–44μ (mean 22.7); both have a skewed to fine distribution, and are generalised medium-fine wool.

LMB 18738 (further pieces in the Stadtmuseum, Xanten, 3360, 3426–28) (mentioned in *BJb*, 116 (1907), 325, Schnitt XXVI; report in *BJb*, 165 (1965), 275).

Silk

35 CONTHEY (WALLIS)
Silk cloth in plain-weave with one selvedge from a late-Roman burial.

System (1) warp, 20–25 per cm., well spaced out, length 21 cm.

System (2) weft, c. 40 per cm., length 15 cm.

Selvedge: the 12 (or less likely, 18) extra warp-threads of the selvedge appear to be of two yarns; one was probably wool, probably purple-dyed, the other (now missing) may have been a bast fibre. The count is *c.* 10 per cm. One woollen warp-thread is followed by one (or possibly two) of the (?) bast. It is a plain selvedge in construction.

I am indebted to Dr M. L. Ryder for the identification of the silk.

Schweiz. LM, Zürich.

Bast fibres

36 ALZEY

Small fragment of hemp cloth associated with a coin hoard; TPQ A.D. 259.

System (1) 15 per cm., Z-spun.
System (2) 17–18 per cm., Z-spun.

Identified by W. von Stokar.

Museum, Alzey (*MZ*, 33 (1938), 63, 67, Abb. 8).

37 CHUR (RAETIA)

Large piece of basket-weave cloth (plate VII *a*) from Roman settlement at Welschdörfli near Chur; found in bog conditions; late-second-century on pottery evidence.

System (1) warp, doubles, 7 pairs per cm., Z-spun, close set, length 28 cm.
System (2) weft, doubles, 3–4 pairs per cm., Z-spun, mainly covered by (1), length 12 cm. plus 8 over seam.

Both systems are now very dark-brown, in yarns of uneven quality.

Two selvedges, tacked together in simple running stitch down the centre of the piece; holes at 1 cm. intervals. Two-ply sewing thread, Z-spun, S-plied. The selvedge is plain, but the outermost warp-thread is a single, not a double. Three pairs of warp-threads running side by side are uniformly finer than the rest; this suggests that one ball of yarn only was used in warping.

Faults (fig. 33): a single pair of warp-threads together with *one* thread from the adjacent pair are on the wrong side of one shot

of weft. Probably a leash-fault or a warp-thread accidentally caught up.

Dr M. L. Ryder reports that it is a bast fibre.

Schweiz. LM, Zürich, 46258; portions also in the Rätisches Museum, Chur.

38 DORWEILER (KR. EUSKIRCHEN)

Oxydised remains of plain-weave linen (?) adhering to bronze fittings of a small basket from a sarcophagus; fourth-century in date.

LMB 43,143 (not accessible) (*BJb*, 149 (1949), 90, Taf. 50, 2).

39 KÖLN (KÖNIGIN-LUISE-SCHULE)

Several small fragments of a pale-coloured plain-weave fabric (probably linen) from a gypsum burial; TPQ *c.* A.D. 300 (coin of Maximian).

Both systems weak Z-spun, *c.* 15 by 15 per cm., well spaced.

R-G Mus., 57,263, Foto Nr. 180 (*KJb*, 5 (1960–1), 87).

40 KÖLN (SEVERINSKIRCHE)

Minute fragment of plain-weave (linen?) adhering to inside of handle of a pair of shears (iron) from a burial: TPQ A.D. 270 (coins).

Count c. 30 by 30 per cm.

R-G Mus., 25,884 (*BJb*, 131 (1926), 297, Grab XXVII, Abb. 10; *PZ*, XVIII (1927), 283).

41 MOYLAND (BEI KLEVE)

Two cloth fragments adhering to outside of rim of a bronze dish from a Roman barrow; mid-first century A.D.

System (1) *c.* 7 per cm., length 3.2 cm. (larger fragment).
System (2) *c.* 7 per cm., length 2.5 cm.

Yarns very unevenly spun, white in colour; linen?

Museum of Society of Arts and Sciences, Utrecht, 3479. (*Arch. Traiectina*, III (1959), 12, no. 4, pl. V, 3 (details from photograph)).

42 QUINT (KR. TRIER)

'Very coarse, well preserved linen cloth' wrapping bones in a glass container from a burial: TPQ A.D. 69 (coin).

Lost (*TJhber.* (1872–3), 66, 88).

43 TRIER (ST MATTHIAS)

Minute fragment of coarse linen at feet of child buried in gypsum; fourth century.

Count *c.* 9 by 9 per cm. No spin visible.

LM Trier, A 4, 61, 60; Fundnr. 27. (*TZ* forthcoming).

44 TRIER

Remains of fine linen round lead sarcophagus of child; fourth century.

System (1) 15 per cm., hard Z-spun.
System (2) 20 per cm., weak Z-spun.

Body of child inside coffin wrapped in linen bands (now only impressions), the structure of which is not clear.

LM Trier (*TZ* forthcoming).

45 TRIER (ST. MATTHIAS)

Minute fragments of linen from fourth-century burial.

System (1) warp ?, 20 per cm., Z-spun, spaced out.
System (2) weft ?, 40 per cm., Z-spun, close set.
Fine spun, even yarns.

LM Trier, Fundnr. 44 (*TZ* forthcoming).

46 TRIER (ST. PAULINUS)

From coffin of St Paulinus; small fragment of gauze-like cloth. Vegetable fibre. See silk, nos. 86–8.

System (1) warp ?, S-spun, *c.* 22–25 per cm., fine yarn, well spaced out, length 6 cm.
System (2) weft ?, S-spun, *c.* 25–28 per cm., coarser yarn, length 5 cm.

Bischöfliches Museum, Trier (*BJb*, 78 (1884), 178).

Union fabrics in plain-weave

47 VINDONISSA (E.–W. DRAIN OF N.–S. STREET OF FORT, 1935)

Appears to be open plain-weave attached to leather backing.

System (1) bast fibre, warp.

System (2) wool, weft.

No spin directions clear, no counts given.

Vindonissa-Museum, Brugg, 44: 62 (*Ges. Vindonissa* (1957–8), 175, Abb. 4, 6, 8).

Impressions of plain-weave cloth

48   TRIER (ST MATTHIAS)

Textile impressions on gypsum of late-Roman burial.

(*TZ*, 24–6 (1956–8), 452.)

49   TRIER (ST MATTHIAS, NAVE)

Impressions of a towel (*mappa*) used to wrap body of a child in a gypsum burial; fourth century.

System (1) warp ?, 20 per cm., no spin visible.

System (2) weft ?, 20 per cm.

The short fringe of the towel runs down the left side of the child from the region of the shoulder.

The fell of the cloth (fig. 34) is followed (in this order) by a gap free of weft (1.5 cm. wide), a band with weft (0.8 cm., or *c.* 15 weft-threads) and the fringe (2.3 cm. long). The width and length of the complete *mappa* are unknown.

LM Trier, A 4, 61, 60; Fundnr. 27 (*TZ* forth-coming).

PLAIN 2-OVER-2 TWILL

50   KÖLN (SEVERINSKIRCHE)

Lining of a purse (?) from a stone burial cist; TPQ A.D. 270 on coins, but rite (cremation) suggests this is the date of deposition.

System (1) 12 per cm., Z-spun, length 7.5 cm.
System (2) *c* 12 per cm., Z-spun, length *c.* 8 cm.

Yarn (2) is slightly coarser and closer set than (1).

The cloth is now brown, saturated with iron oxides, and brittle. It is double; two parallel raw edges (cut) are turned back and tacked together with running stitches; the sewing-thread has vanished.

R-G Mus., 25,876 (film no. 621) (*BJb*, 131 (1926), 297, Grab XXVII, Abb. 10, 8; *PZ*, XVIII (1927), 283).

51   KÖLN (JACOBSTR.)

Oxydised remains of cloth wrapping barber's double shears; the neighbouring graves are

dated to the late third and early fourth centuries.

System (1) *c.* 13 per cm.
System (2) *c.* 14 per cm.

R-G Mus., 29,1853–54 (*Germ.* 16 (1932), 129 f., Abb. 1, 9; *ibid.* 14 (1930), 107, 249, Grab 171).

52   MAINZ (MOORSCHICHT 1855)

Fine quality cloth, now peat-brown.

System (1) 19–20 per cm., Z-spun, length 4.5 cm.
System (2) 20 per cm., S-spun, length 6 cm.
Yarn (1) closer set, slightly coarser than (2).

Rijksmuseum G. M. Kam, Nijmegen, no. 6.

53   MAINZ

Medium-fine quality cloth, peat-brown; one large, two smaller fragments.

System (1) *c.* 18 per cm., Z-spun, length 12 cm.

System (2) *c.* 14 per cm., S-spun, length 10 cm.

R-G ZM, Mainz (D. D. Herr Schaffer).

54–58 MAINZ (CORNER EMMERANSTR.–GR. LANGGASSE, 1963)

All pieces found at depth of 6 metres.

54 *Textile 1.* Medium quality cloth, light-brown, slightly felted in patches.

System (1) 10–11 per cm., strong Z-spun, length 12 cm.

System (2) 11–12 per cm., strong Z-spun, length 20 cm.

55 *Textile 2.* Medium-fine cloth, badly pre-served, in three small pieces.

System (1) 12–14 per cm., Z-spun, fine yarn, length 4 cm., 3 cm., 3 cm.

System (2) *c.* 15 per cm., Z-spun, length 4.5 cm., 3 cm., 3 cm.

Yarn (2) fine, but unevenly spun.

56 *Textile 3.* Poorly preserved fragments, peat-brown in patches.

System (1) 12 per cm., Z-spun, length 5 cm., 6 cm.

System (2) 18–20 per cm., Z-spun, length 10 cm., 2.5 cm.

57 *Textile 4.* Medium cloth of good quality.

System (1) warp ?, 12–14 per cm., Z-spun, length 11 cm.

System (2) weft ?, 12–14 per cm., weak S-spun, length 7.5 cm.

All the above at R-G ZM, Mainz (D.D. Bauherr Kolb).

58 *Textile 5.* Medium-fine cloth, now black.

System (1) *c.* 15 per cm., Z-spun, length 13 cm.

System (2) *c.* 14–15 per cm., Z-spun, length 8.5 cm.

Both yarns of high quality.

R-G ZM, Mainz, 0, 37904.

59 MAINZ (SCHILLERPLATZ) (FIGS. 35, 37)

Check twill with tablet-woven (?) selvedge.

System (1) warp, 11 per cm., Z-spun, length 10 cm.

System (2) weft, 11 per cm., Z-spun, length 10 cm.

The pattern is of dark-brown glossy stripes on a lighter background. Counting from the selvedge: 2 dark warps, 40 light (3.5 cm.), 6 dark, 10 light, 8 dark. Weft direction: 2 dark weft-threads, 40 light (3.5 cm.), 6 dark, 10 light, 8 dark. The pattern is regular, but the full repeat is not preserved. The hollow selvedge is con-structed round 8 pairs of warp-threads (each pair is equivalent in the weaving pattern to *one* warp) grouped to form a tube. Each weft-thread is carried through from the fell of the cloth (in 2-over-2 twill), passes (in plain-weave) round the circumference of the tube, and back into the cloth. Hence the selvedge has the appearance of widely spaced plain-weave, since only alternate weft-threads are visible at any given point on its surface. The selvedge is likely to have been woven on tablets, which in turn suggest the use of a warp-weighted loom.

Wiesbaden (*Nass. Ann.* 15 (1879), 37, Nr. 28, Patrone 11).

60 MAINZ (GR. EMMERANSTR.)

Two pieces of same cloth from an early-Roman context.

Fragment 1. Medium peat-brown.

System (1) warp, 11 per cm., strong Z-spun, length 26 cm.

System (2) weft, 10 per cm., strong Z-spun, length 14 cm.

Warp evenly spun; more variation in weft. Hollow selvedge (badly damaged), plain-weave over 8 warp-threads (singles) (Z-spun). Length of selvedge 26 cm.

Fragment 2. No selvedges; other details including measurements, same.

Mittelrheinisches Landesmuseum, Mainz, 4 W (F. 1799) (Frag. 1); Nr. 5 W (F. 1800) (Frag. 2). From former Fremersdorf Collection.

61–70 MAINZ (SCHILLERPLATZ)

A number of fragments of twill cloth.

61 *Textile* 1. Soft woollen cloth, felted.
  System (1) warp ?, singles, 14 per cm., strong Z-spun.
  System (2) weft ?, singles, 64 per cm., weak Z (?)-spun.

Wiesbaden (*Nass. Ann.* 15 (1879), 38, Nr. 29).

62 *Textile* 2. Medium cloth.
  System (1) 9 per cm., Z-spun, length *c.* 10 cm.
  System (2) 9 per cm., Z-spun, length *c.* 10 cm.
  Both yarns very unevenly spun.

Wiesbaden (*Nass. Ann.* 15 (1879), 38, Nr. 30).

63 *Textile* 3. Fine dark-brown cloth.
  System (1) 22–24 per cm., Z-spun, length 8 cm.
  System (2) 22–24 per cm., Z-spun, length 3.5 cm.
  Fine, evenly spun yarns.
  Dr M. L. Ryder reports: Yarn (*a*) has a

diameter range 12–38μ (mean 20.4); yarn (*b*) 10–36μ (mean 19.4); both have a skewed to fine distribution, and are generalised medium or fine wools.

Wiesbaden (*Nass. Ann.* 15 (1879), 38, Nr. 31).

64 *Textile* 4. Medium-fine dark-brown cloth.
  System (1) warp ?, 12 per cm., Z-spun, length 2.5 cm.
  System (2) weft?, 16–17 per cm., Z-spun, length 13 cm.
  System (1) closely set; fine evenly spun yarns.

Wiesbaden (*Nass. Ann.* 15 (1879), 38, Nr. 32).

65 *Textile* 5. Medium-fine cloth.
  System (1) 13–14 per cm., Z-spun, length 11 cm.
  System (2) 13–14 per cm., Z-spun, length 7.5 cm.
  Good even yarns.

Wiesbaden (*Nass. Ann.* 15 (1879), 38, Nr. 33).

66 *Textile* 6. Medium cloth, dark-brown.
  System (1) warp ?, 11 per cm., Z-spun, well spaced, length 5 cm.
  System (2) weft ?, 11 per cm., Z-spun, length 7 cm.
  Yarn (1) seems to be darker than (2) on one side; but this was possibly accidental.

Wiesbaden (*Nass. Ann.* 15 (1879), 38, Nr. 34).

67 *Textile* 7. Light-brown medium fabric, well beaten up and slightly felted; 5 fragments in all.
  System (1) 10 per cm., Z-spun, length 7 cm.
  System (2) 10 per cm., Z-spun, length 9.5 cm.

TABLE B

Coarse, even yarns.

Dr M. L. Ryder reports: Yarn (*a*), unpigment-ed, has a diameter range 10–38μ (mean 18.5); yarn (*b*) 12–38μ (mean 19.3); both have a skewed to fine distribution pattern, and are generalised medium or fine wools.

Wiesbaden (*Nass. Ann.* 15 (1879), 38, Nr. 35).

68   *Textile 8.* Dark-brown medium cloth of good quality.
  System (1) 12 per cm., Z-spun, length 3.5 cm.
  System (2) 11 per cm., Z-spun, length 3.5 cm.
  Both evenly spun yarns.

Wiesbaden (*Nass. Ann.* 15 (1879), 38, Nr. 36).

69   *Textile 9.* Medium cloth.
  System (1) 11 per cm.
  System (2) 11 per cm.

Not seen by me; possibly at Wiesbaden (*Nass. Ann.* 15 (1879), 38, Nr. 37).

70   *Textile 10.* Small fragment of medium cloth with check pattern.
  System (1) 8–9 per cm., Z-spun.
  System (2) 8–9 per cm., Z-spun.

Stripes, light (undyed yarn) and dark-brown, alternating in both warp and weft; the exact size is uncertain, but the stripes were at least 3 cm. wide; probably a regular check. The yarns are very coarse and heavy.

Wiesbaden (*Nass. Ann.* 15 (1879), 38, Nr. 38).

71   MAINZ (GR. EMMERANSTR. 8)
Drawing of 2-over-2 plain twill in the Inventory under Inv. Nr. 4093 (Mittelrheinisches Landesmuseum, Mainz); the material was destroyed in 1945.

72   MAINZ (GR. EMMERANSTR.)
Small fragment of coarse twill.
  System (1) *c.* 7–8 per cm., Z-spun.
  System (2) *c.* 7–8 per cm., Z-spun.

Warp and weft same yarns, but wool blended before spinning from black and light-brown fibres, probably dyed in the fleece.
Mittelrheinisches Landesmuseum, Mainz, 3 W (F. 1506); former Fremersdorf Collection.

73   VINDONISSA (SCHUTTHÜGEL)
Two fragments of twill joined together by a single thread (plate VII *b*). Uniformly dark-brown. First century in date.
  System (1) 9–10 per cm., strong Z-spun, length 6 cm.
  System (2) 9–10 per cm., strong Z-spun, length 5 cm. and 3 cm.

Vindonissa-Museum, Brugg.

2-OVER-2 TWILL IMPRESSION

74   SAALBURG-KASTELL (BATH-BLOCK)
Impression of 2-over-2 plain twill on a broken tile of the Legio VIII made at Strassburg-Königshofen *c.* A.D. 125–139; built into baths.
  System (1) *c.* 8 per cm., length *c.* 15 cm.
  System (2) *c.* 8–10 per cm., length *c.* 14 cm.

No spin direction visible. Fault or damage in System (1): one thread runs 3-over-1 for 2 cm., then corrects itself.

Saalburg Museum, S 1/XIII 3c; squeeze kindly provided by Dr D. Baatz (to be published in *S-Jb.*).

TABLE B

2-OVER-2 DIAMOND TWILL WEAVE

75 MAINZ (SCHILLERPLATZ) (FIG. 38)
Light-brown, medium-fine twill.

System (1) warp ?, 16 per cm., Z-spun, length 12 cm.
System (2) weft ?, 16 per cm., Z-spun, length 14 cm.
Good, fine, evenly spun yarns.

Displacement in both warp and weft (directions suggested by Icelandic mode of knitting heddles). There are minor errors in the published draft.

Wiesbaden (*Nass. Ann.* 15 (1879), 39, Nr. 40 Patrone 13).

76 MAINZ (SCHILLERPLATZ) (FIG. 39)
Two fragments of fine diamond twill, light-brown.

System (1) warp ?, 26 per cm., strong Z-spun, length 9 and 9.5 cm.
System (2) weft ?, 26 per cm., weak S-spun, length 7 and 12 cm.

There is displacement in the warp-direction (System (1)) and reversal after 12 warp-threads; in the weft there is point repeat, reversing after 23 weft-threads (including the point).

Dr M. L. Ryder reports: Yarn (*a*) (System (1)), unpigmented, has a diameter range of 14–34μ (mean 20.4); yarn (*b*) (System (2)) unpigmented, 14–36μ (mean 21.2); both have a

symmetrical distribution, and are therefore true fine wools.

Wiesbaden (*Nass. Ann.* 15 (1879), 38, Nr. 39, Patrone 12 (inaccurate)).

77 MAINZ (MOORSCHICHT, 1855)
Peat-brown, fine cloth fragment.

System (1) warp ?, 20 per cm., Z-spun, length 7 cm.
System (2) weft ?, 19–20 per cm., S-spun, length 2 cm.

There is full displacement in both systems. Reversal in System (1) is after 14 warp(?)-threads, in System (2) after 8 weft (?)-threads.

Nijmegen, no. 2.

78 MAINZ (MOORSCHICHT, 1855) (FIG. 40)
Dark-brown, medium-fine cloth

System (1) warp ?, *c.* 15 per cm., Z-spun, length *c.* 5 cm.
System (2) weft ?, 10 per cm., S-spun, length 5.5 cm.

System (1) has full displacement, with 18 threads before reversal of the slope; System (2) has point-repeat, with 8 threads before reversal (including the points).

Nijmegen, no. 1.

TABLE B

2-OVER-1 TWILL WEAVE

79–83 MAINZ (SCHILLERPLATZ)

A series of fragments:

79 *Textile* 1. Light-brown, slightly felted.

System (1) warp ?, 8–10 per cm., Z-spun, length 5 cm.
System (2) weft ?, 8–10 per cm., Z-spun, length 7 cm.
Yarn (2) coarser than (1), closer set; System (1) well spaced out.

Wiesbaden (*Nass. Ann.* 15 (1879), 37, Nr. 25).

80 *Textile* 2. Dark-brown fragment, tattered.

System (1) 12 per cm., Z-spun, length 10 cm.
System (2) 12 per cm., Z-spun, length 10 cm.
Yarns very unevenly spun.

Wiesbaden (*Nass. Ann.* 15 (1879), 37, Nr. 23).

81 *Textile* 3. Light-brown cloth.

System (1) 9 per cm., Z-spun, length 11 cm.
System (2) 9 per cm., Z-spun, length 9 cm.
Yarns coarse, but evenly spun.

(*Ibid.*, 37, Nr. 24.)

82 *Textile* 4. Light-brown cloth.

System (1) 11 per cm., Z-spun, length *c.* 6 cm.

System (2) 9 per cm., Z-spun, length *c.* 6 cm.
Yarn (1) finer than (2), which is unevenly spun.

Dr M. L. Ryder reports: Yarn (*a*) has a diameter range of 14–40μ (mean 22.3); yarn (*b*) 14–44μ (mean 22.9); both have a skewed to fine distribution, and are generalised medium or fine wools.

(*Ibid.* 37, Nr. 26.)

83 *Textile* 5. Irregularly torn, light-brown cloth, slightly felted.

System (1) 13 per cm., Z-spun, length 7 cm.
System (2) 13 per cm., Z-spun, length 10 cm.

(*Ibid.* 37, Nr. 27.)

84 MAINZ (MOORSCHICHT, 1855)

Dark-brown, fairly coarse cloth, felted on both sides.

System (1) warp ?, *c.* 10 per cm., Z-spun, length 3 cm.
System (2) weft ?, *c.* 13–14 per cm., Z-spun, length 5 cm.
Both yarns are thick and unevenly spun.

Nijmegen, no. 5.

2-OVER-2 DAMASK TWILL WEAVE

85 CONTHEY (KT. WALLIS) (FIG. 43; PLATE VIII)

A number of small fragments of damask silk from a late-Roman burial. They may have been the remains of a tunic such as that worn by the Lullingstone Christian *orans*.

System (1) warp, 55–60 per cm., Z-spun.
System (2) weft, 44–60 per cm., unspun.

The cloth is in 2-over-2 twill, and the simple rectilinear pattern is created by the reversal in the slope of the twill. There is no indication of the original colour.

The weaving would require 12 complete separate sheds. The slope of the weft reverses on points, while the warp appears to have full displacement. Unfortunately Emil Vogt did not publish a detailed weaving-plan, but his drawing of the overall pattern shows that the basic element in the design is repeated after 1.4 cm. (weft-direction) and 1.65 cm. (warp-direction).

I have checked the spin and count, but drawn the other details from the publication.

Schweiz. LM, Zürich (*Germ.* 18 (1934), 202 ff., Taf. 24, Abb. 1–3, Textabb. 4). I am grateful to Professor Vogt for allowing me access to this material.

86 TRIER (FIG. 44)

Silk cloth, found both inside and outside the cedar-wood coffin of St Paulinus, whose remains were interred in Trier in A.D. 395.

The colour is now a pale yellow with a geometric pattern of rectangles and crosses.

System (1), warp, *c.* 50 per cm., Z-spun.
System (2), weft, 50–60 per cm., unspun.

The pattern is formed by reversal in the direction of the slope of the twill. There is full displacement in both systems. 16 sheds are required for the weaving.

The original publication is inadequate and the diagrams inaccurate.

Through the kindness of the Director of the Bischöfliches Museum, Trier (where the fabric is) I hope to publish a full account of this cloth later. (*Zeitschr. Christ. Kunst*, XXIII (1910), 279 (Stoff 2), Abb. S. 347; *BJb*, 78 (1884), 185, Taf. VII; Kempf & Reusch (1965), 179, Nr. 3, Foto opp. p. 178 (colour).)

Embroidery

Embroidered on the silk with a sliver of hide (established under a microscope) is the factory mark JORENTIAOF. The best interpretation is probably FLORENTIA OFFICINA on analogy with potters' stamps on *terra sigillata*.

(*Zeitschr. Christ. Kunst*, XXIII (1910), 282, 347 with photograph.) Now lost.

87 TRIER

A small black fragment of the same type of silk damask from the same context as the above. No details at present available.

Bischöfliches Museum, Trier.

3-OVER-1 COMPOUND CLOTH IN TWO-FACED WEAVE

88 TRIER (FIG. 46)

Silk damask from the same context as the above.

System (1), warp, well spaced out, 40–50 per cm., Z-spun, length 12 cm.
System (2), weft, unspun, *c.* 40 per cm. (?), thicker yarn covering warp to great extent, length 24 cm.

Wefts, alternating dark (purple?) and light (undyed?), facing opposite sides of the cloth.

The pattern of circles and crosses created solely by the weft is the same on both sides of the cloth, the colours being reversed. The weave is basically 3-over-1, but breaks its regularity to accommodate the pattern.

The published account and diagrams are

inadequate; I hope to be able to republish the cloth at a future date.

Bischöfliches Museum, Trier. (*Zeitschr. Christ. Kunst.* XXIII (1910), 279 (Stoff 1); *BJb*, 78 (1884), 171, Taf. VII (bottom left); Kempf & Reusch (1965), 179, Nr. 3, Foto opp. p. 178.)

89 TOURNAI (LA CITADELLE)
Textile impression, possibly of damask; from fourth-century burial of a Germanic *foederatus*.

'Une étoffe, dont le décor était constitué de têtes de clous, formant probablement un motif géometrique.'
Faider-Feytmans (1951), 39 Tombe D refers to 'une étoffe grossière', but this is probably not the same fabric.

(Amand & Eykens-Dierickx (1960), 80 Tombe D; *Latomus*, X (1951), 39, Tombe D.)

TAPESTRY-WEAVING IN GOBELIN TECHNIQUE

90 CONTHEY (KT. WALLIS) (FIG. 47)
From a fourth-century Roman burial; oval medallion in wool, originally sewn to a silk tunic (?), no. 85 above.

Warp, 16–20 per cm., well spaced out, but almost all perished; possibly linen.
Weft (tapestry), varying, max. *c.* 120 per cm., Z-spun, fine yarn closely beaten up to cover warp.

The pattern consists of contiguous circles and aligned crosses, the outlines of which are accentuated by groups of *c.* 5 weft-threads woven in Gobelin technique round the contours. Further decoration may have been added in

linen (?) with a needle during the process of weaving ('*fliegende Nadel*').
Spin and count noted by the writer through the kindness of Professor Emil Vogt.

Schweiz. LM, Zürich (*Germ.* 18 (1934), 198 ff., Stoff A, Abb. 1, Taf. 23, 1, 2).

91 CONTHEY
From the same context as the above; band in wool, sewn to tunic (?). No details of spin or count given. Design composed of ovolo-band and circles containing crosses.

(*Germ.* 18 (1934), 202, Abb. 3.)

EMBROIDERY

92 MAINZ (GR. EMMERANSTR. 8)
Zig-zag line embroidered in stitch resembling *reverse tent stitch*. There are six rows of stitches in the line. The width of it is *c.* 0.6 cm., the length of each leg of the zig-zag 1.7 cm., the length of the whole *c.* 8 cm.

The nature of the cloth on which it is worked is unknown. Details taken from excellent drawing in the Old Inventory of the Mittelrheinisches Landesmuseum, Mainz; the fabric was destroyed in 1945. Inv. No. 4091.

NETTING AND PLAITING TECHNIQUES

Sprang

93 VINDONISSA (SCHUTTHÜGEL)
(PLATE IX B)

Remains of an open-work hair-net (?) of first-century date. Extended, it measures 18 by 10 cm.

Very fine wool yarn, S-spun, now dark-brown. A portion of the side and centre survive, but the other edges are lost. There were once more than 120 warps (no weft), twined round each other three times at the points of contact. On one side of the centre line the warps are S-twined, on the other Z-twined. The point where the centre was secured to prevent it unravelling is lost; at the point where the centre line meets the outer edge, a number of warps have been left un-twined.

Vindonissa-Museum, Brugg.

94 MAINZ (NEUTOR)

Remains of a hair-net found *in situ* round the plaits of (female) hair in a late-Roman burial. No details were recorded, and the material has since been destroyed. Sprang?

(*Korr. bl. WZ*, II (1883), Para. 222, 223.)

BOBBIN-WORK

95 ESCH (NEAR 'S-HERTOGENBOSCH)

From a woman's tomb of late-second-century date (fig. 50). A woollen cord composed of four threads, plaited together by a means analogous to modern so-called 'bobbin-work'.

The threads: wool, *c.* 1 mm. thick, S-plied from several strands. Two fragments survive.

Details kindly supplied by Prof. J. E. A. Bogaers and Mr L. van den Hurk of Amersfoort, who is to publish the finds.

FELT AND STUFFING

96 AARDENBURG (ZEELAND)

Traces of woollen felt inside a shoe (A.D. 150–250).

(*Ber. Rijksdienst*, 9 (1959), 73, Nr. 4, 77.)

97 BASEL (PETERSBERG)

Complete sole of felt made from hares' fibres; late-Roman habitation site.

Sole *c.* 2 mm. thick, 11 cm. wide, 18.5 cm. long.

Fibres 15–27μ with coarse hairs up to 42μ. Dyed green, probably with copper lactate.

(A. Gansser-Burckhardt in *ZAK*, 2 (1940), 22, Taf. 5, 5.)

98 VINDONISSA (SCHUTTHÜGEL)

A mass of fibres sticking to a piece of leather from same layer as tile-stamp LEG XXI; mid-first century A.D.

Mostly wool (red-, blue-, green-, brown- and black-dyed), feathers, hair, thin strips of hide and bast fibres. Probably stuffing of a bolster.

(*Ges. Vindonissa* (1957–8), 179, Abb. 9–14.)

99 VINDONISSA (E.–W. DRAIN OF N.–S. STREET OF FORT)

Felted mass of wool and strips of leather; probably first century A.D.

Vindonissa-Museum, Brugg, 44: 56; 44: 57 (*Ges. Vindonissa* (1957–8), 175 ff., Abb. 1–14).

TEXTILES PUBLISHED WITH INSUFFICIENT DETAIL

100 BUDENHEIM (KR. MAINZ)
Impression of a shroud 'perhaps of coarse linen' in a gypsum burial; late third century.

(*MZ*, 1 (1906), 70 Sarg 2 (now lost).)

101 KÖLN (SEVERINSKIRCHE)
Cloth impressions in late-Roman stone coffin.

(*BJb*, 138 (1933), 56, Grab 116.)

102 MAINZ
352 cloth fragments from the town, now lost.

Mittelrheinisches Landesmuseum, Mainz Inv. no. 60–63 (see Lindenschmit, *AuhV*, IV, Taf. 37, 46).

103 MAINZ (SOUTHERN PART OF TOWN)
Coarse cloth in a burial. Cannot be traced.

(*Korr. bl. WZ*, 1 (1882), Para. 221.)

104 MAINZ (FINTHERSTR.)
Cloth fragment on first-century brooch. Cannot be traced.

(*MZ*, 24–5 (1929–30), 150, Grab 30.)

105 MAYEN
Cloth impressions from a grave; TPQ A.D. 370.
LMB, 38,610 (*BJb*, 147 (1947), 282, Grab 27 k).

106 MAYEN
Cloth fragments of mid-fourth-century date.

Eifelmuseum, Mayen, Inv. Nr. 1038, FB. II. 8 (*BJb*, 147 (1947), 267, Grab 1).

107 NIEDEREMMEL (KR. BERNKASTEL)
Cloth impression on coin of Licinius in mint condition; TPQ A.D. 313.

(*TZ*, 19 (1950), 31, Grab II.)

108 TRIER (VIKTORIENSTR.–PHILOSO-PHENWEG)
Remains of 'woollen cloth' in burial; A.D. 200–250. Lost.

(*BJb*, 127 (1922), 306.)

109 TRITTENHEIM (KR. TRIER)
Thick woollen cloth wrapping the upper part of a corpse. The material is now lost, and photographs show no details.

(*BJb*, 127 (1922), 310.)

TABLE B

110 TRITTENHEIM

Fine folded cloth wrapping shoulders of above corpse.

(*BJb*, 127 (1922), 310.)

111 VINDONISSA (SCHUTTHÜGEL, 1906)

Small cloth fragments of well-preserved fine wool.

(*ASA*, N.F. IX (1907), 112.)

112 XANTEN (KR. MOERS)

Traces of coarse cloth in iron rust on rim of pot in first-century burial.

Museum, Xanten, 408 (*Kat. Xanten* (1911), 28, Grab 11).

113 WORMS

Remains of cloth adhering to coin in a third-century grave.

(*Korr. bl. WZ*, XII (1893), Para. 1, Sarg 8.)

TABLE C *Iron wool-combs*

Iron wool-combs with a single row of teeth and slotted handle

	FO	No.	L.	Br.	L. of teeth	No. of teeth	L. of slot	Br. of slot	Context/date	Publication	Museum
1	Caistor-by-Norwich (Norfolk)	1	38	10	?	22	?	?	?	ANL, 6, no. 11 (1960), 262	Norwich, Castle Museum, 152.929
2	Icklingham (Suffolk)	2	c.28	10	c.10	23+	10	3	Unstrat. on villa site	Ibid.	Mildenhall Museum and Moyses Hall, Bury St Edmunds
3	Worlington (Suffolk) (plate 1 b)	2	c.25	10	c.10	23	10	3	Depot-find (undated)	Ibid.	Mus. Arch. Eth., Cambridge

Iron wool-combs with a double row of teeth

	FO	No.	L.	Br.	L. of teeth	No. of teeth	Width of centre	Context/date	Publication	Museum
4	Baydon (Wilts.) (fig. 9)	1	27	9.5	(lost)	27, c.27	3	Iron-working site, poss. depot-find	Cat. Devizes (1911) No. 459, pl. xxviii, 3	Devizes, County Museum
5	Augst (Basel)	1	c.35	10	10-15+	c.50, 31	c.4.5	(Roman town)	(unpublished?)	Römerhaus, Augst, 1960.950
6	Waldfischbach (Kr. Pirmasens)	6	34	10	c.12	c.20, 20	4	Depot-find of late-third century	Sprater (1929), 65, Abb. 59	Historisches Mus. d. Pfalz, Speyer
7	Kastell Kösching (Raetia)	1	6.5+	8.5	2.7+	42, 40	3	Limes-fort TAQ c. A.D. 260	ORL, B, vii, Kast. Nr. 74, Taf. iv, 18	Nat. Mus., Nürnberg, 3726 a
8	Virunum (Noricum)	1	26	9	9	c.22	c.6	Roman baths and workshops (unstrat.)	Kenner (1947), 155, Abb. 135	—
9	Straubing (Raetia)	1	27.4+	11.3	c.10-12	c.40	4	Depot-find A.D. 200-260	Keim & Klumbach (1951), 38, Nr. 63, Taf. 43	Mus., Straubing
10	Uranje (Noricum)							Depot-find of third- or fourth-century date	Jhb. f. Altertumskunde (Wien), III (1909), 5, fig. 5 g.	
	(a)		31-33	9-11	c.12	17, 17	5			—
	(b)		33	11	c.12	28, 24	5			—
	(c)		32	10	c.13	21, 21	4.8			—

TABLE D Rippling(?)-combs

Three wooden (rippling?)-combs with roughly cut teeth from the *Schutthügel* at Vindonissa; now in the Vindonissa-Museum, Brugg (fig. 12)

	Length	Thickness	Br.	L. of teeth	Br. of teeth	No. of teeth	Museum inventory no.
1	14	1–1.5	c. 9	7	0.5	11–12	56.591
2	10.5	c. 1	9.5	4	—	8	9689
3	13	1.2	5+ (broken)	7	—	7+	23.1453

TABLE E Distaffs

Ornamental distaffs of (Whitby?) jet (fig. 15)

	FO	L.	L. of shaft	Br. of shaft	Shaft section	Nature of terminals	Centrepiece	Context/date	Museum	Publication
1	Köln	20.5	8.5	1.2	Spirally carved, round; handle: gold leaf	1. Conical vase 2. Plain knob	—	?	—	*BJb,* 142 (1937), 135, G10, Taf. 34
2	Köln	18+	10	1.4	Spirally carved	1. Spirally carved cone on disc	Plain band	Grave	LMB, 1787	*Ibid.* 135, G 9, 1, Taf. 33
3	Mainz?	8+	?	?	Spirally carved	1. Spirally carved cone on disc	—	?	Germ. Nat. Mus., Nürnberg, F.G.1587	*Ibid.* G 9, 2
4	Köln (Molkestr.)	17	6	1.2	Octagonal	1. Double-handled vase 2. Cone on disc	Plain disc octagonal	Grave	R-G Mus, Köln, 8	*Ibid.* 136, G 13, Taf. 34
5	Köln (St. Gereon)	16.2	—	c. 1.2	Round	1. Saucer containing central column	Plain disc	Female grave	?	*Ibid.* 135, G 8; *Ibid.* 14 (1849), 46, Taf. IV, 3
6	Metz	22.2	9.5	c. 0.8	Round, spirally carved	1. Barrel 2. Plain	Thin disc	Female grave	Metz	*BJb,* 142 (1937), 135, G 5, Taf.33
7	Tongeren	21.5	c. 7.5	c. 1.5	Octagonal	1. Chalice on disc 2. Incised polyhedron	Polyhedron	Frankish grave	—	*Ibid.* 135, G 11, Taf. 34

TABLE E (cont.)

FO	L.	L. of shaft	Br. of shaft	Shaft section	Nature of terminals	Centrepiece	Context/date		Museum	Publication
8 Trier (St Matthias)	18.6	—	max. c.1.3	Octagonal	1. Double-handle vase 2. Carved cube	—	Grave 237	C IV	LM Trier, 04,492 b	Ibid. 135, G 12, Taf. 34; WZ, xxiv (1905), 373, Taf. 12, 6
9 York	15.6	—	—	Octagonal, tapering	Simple cube	—	Grave?	—	Yorks. Museum, H 1098	Eburacum (1962), 143
10 York	14.1	—	0.9–1.2	Spiral	Faceted polyhedron	—	Grave?	—	Yorks. Museum, H 314.2	Ibid. 143, pl. 69
11 York (Railway Sta. Cemetery)	18.7	—	1.25	Octagonal, tapering	Faceted polyhedron	—	Female grave (IV Reg. (c) (ix))		Yorks. Museum, H 314.1	Ibid. 143, pl. 69

Distaffs consisting of pierced amber sections slotted on a central bronze pin

FO	L.	L. of shaft	Br. of shaft	Shaft section	Nature of terminals	Centrepiece	Context/date	Museum	Publication
12 Dorweiler (Kr. Euskirchen)	18.4	4.4	1.4	Round, spirally carved	Saucer and series of discs	3 discs	Rich female burial in sarcophagus; A.D. 300–400	LMB, 43,143 (mislaid)	BJb, 149 (1949), 84 f., Abb. 5, Nr. 2; 87, Abb. 7, 1
13 Stein on Maas (Limburg)	18.5	—	—	Round (24 cylinders)	Simple discs	Simple disc	Female burial (sarcophagus I), late second century	?	Oud. Med. N.S. VII (1926), 12, Abb. 20, 2; 13, 6
14 Worms (Luxemburgerstr.)	19.3	—	1.3	Round, cordoned (14 sections)	Knob disc	Disc	Cist of ashes, prob. third century	Lost	WZ, VIII (1889), 267 Taf. 6, 4

Distaff of octagonal shale discs set on iron pin

FO	L.	L. of shaft	Br. of shaft	Shaft section	Nature of terminals	Centrepiece	Context/date	Museum	Publication
15 Verulamium	c. 20	—	1.3	Octagonal	(Knob)	—	Girl's grave; coin of A.D. 210	Verulamium Museum, St Albans	(Unpublished)

TABLE E (cont.)

FO	L.	L. of shaft	Br. of shaft	Shaft section	Nature of terminals	Centrepiece	Context/date	Museum	Publication
Distaff of plain wood									
16 Vindonissa	33	Handle 8 shaft 25	0.7	Square	Spike 4.5	—	*Schutthügel*, C I	Vindonissa-Mus., Brugg, Aargau	(Unpublished)
17 Mainz	28.4	—	1.2	Square	Spiked	—	C I-III	Mitelrheinisches Landesmuseum, Mainz, 198 (Old invty.) (lost object)	(Unpublished)
Simple stick-distaffs									
18 Vindonissa	22	—	—	(Round)	5 short twigs pointing backwards to handle	—	*Schutthügel*, C I	Vindonissa-Mus., Brugg, Aargau	(Unpublished)
19 Les-Martres-de-Veyre (Puy de Dôme)	20	—	—	(Round)	Plain forked stick, ends tied to form cage	—	Tomb F of young girl, C II?	Musée Bargoin, Clermont-Ferrand	Audollent (1922), 33, item 31, pl. VII, 12
Objects in jet which may be either spindles or distaffs; perhaps more likely to be distaffs									
20 Köln	17.8	17.8	c.1.2	Square tapering to octagonal	Two rills at heavier end	—	—	R-G Mus., Köln	*BJb*, 142 (1937), 135, G 7, Taf. 33
21 Köln	20	20	c. 1.2	Square tapering to octagonal	Two rills at heavier end; small whorl at other	—	—	R-G Mus., Köln, 24, 382	*Ibid.* 135, G 6, Taf. 33. *WZ*, III (1884), 188
22 Worms	12.8+	12.8+	c. 2	Round	Narrows sharply to point at one end	—	—	Städtisches Museum, Worms	?*Korr. bl. WZ*, v (1886), Par. 27
Object of wood with square shaft rounded to point at both ends									
23 Saalburg	31	1		Square...rounded Graffito...MNOP	—	—	With, but not attached to, whorl in well no. 74	Saalburg Museum	*S-Jb*, VIII (1934), 22, Taf. III, Nr. 6

TABLE F *Spindles*

Spindles from Britain

	FO	No.	Material	L.	Br. of bulb	State	Upper terminal	Context/date	Museum	Publication
1	Cirencester	1	Bone	14+	0.8	Broken in antiquity, but used further. Incised decoration	Plain	(Roman town)	Corinium Mus., Cirencester, C 731 *a*	—
2	Cirencester	1	Bone	9+	0.7	Top broken	—	(Roman town)	Corinium Mus., C 731 *b*	—
3	Corbridge	1	Bone	13	0.8	—	Plain	—	Corbridge Mus.	—
4	London	1	Wood	19	0.8	—	Plain	—	London Mus., 29.183	*Wheeler* (1930), 107, pl. XLVI, 2.
5	London (Moorgate St.)	1	Wood	14	0.5	—	Plain	—	London Mus., A 4691	*Ibid.* pl. XLVI, 1.
6	London (Tokenhouse Yard)	1	Bone	13.5	0.8	Broken	Plain	—	London Mus., A 28343	*Ibid.* pl. XLVI, 3
7	London (Poultry)	1	Wood	18	0.9	—	Plain	—	London Mus., A 27942	*Ibid.* pl. XLVI, 4
8	London (Bank of Lond. and S. America)	1	(No details)			—	—	Well, TAQ *c.* A.D. 100	Guildhall Mus.	*JRS*, XLIV (1955), 138
9	London (129–30, Upper Thames St.)	1	(No details)				—	*c.* A.D. 75–100	Guildhall Mus. (found 1931)	Home (1948), 237–8
10	London (Bank of England) (plate III *b*)	1	Bone	15.2	—	Fixed whorl 4 cm. diam.	Knob	—	BM, 1928.7–13.26	*BM Guide* (1958), 50, III, d, 3, fig. 23
11	London	1	Wood	16	0.8	Top broken	—	—	BM, 56.7–1.1071	*Ibid.* 50, III, d, 2, fig. 23
12	London (Royal Exch.)		Several wood	15–20	—	Wool attached still	Plain	Rubbish in Roman gravel-pit. Severan?	—	Roach Smith (1859), 143 with fig.
13	Newstead	2	Wood	8.5, 6.25	—	—	—	Pit LIV; Flavian?	N.M.A., Edinburgh, FRA 461	Curle (1911), 290, pl. LXVIII, 7

TABLE F (cont.)

Spindles from the continental provinces

	FO	No.	Material	L.	Br. of bulb	State	Upper terminal	Context/date	Museum	Publication
14	Augst	1	Bone	20	0.6	—	Arrow-shaped with triangular section	(Roman town)	Römerhaus, Augst, 268.2061	—
15	Augst	1	Bone	14	c. 1	—	—	(Roman town)	Römerhaus, Augst	—
16	Köln	7	Wood	c. 15–22	c. 0.5–1	Many broken	Plain	Stream bed on edge of Roman harbour; c. 150–c. 250	R-G Mus., Köln, 24,440+	Germ. x (1926), 53, Abb. 11 (no scale or dimensions)
17	Köln	1	Bone	7.7	0.7	Broken	(Missing)	Roman harbour	R-G Mus., Köln	BJb, 153 (1953), 119, Abb. 4, Nr. 197, Taf. 10, Nr. 197
18	Mainz (Legionslager)	1	Bone	16.8	0.6	Decorated	Plain	Well no. 4 Prob. C III	Mittelrheinisches Landesmuseum, Mainz, 397	MZ, vi (1911), 109, Abb. 26,27; 118, Nr. 27
19	Mainz	1	Bone	17	—	Plain	Whorl in situ	C I–C III	Mainz, 2338 (lost)	—
20	Rottweil	1	Bone	11.4+	0.8	—	Plain	(Small town) TAQ c. A.D. 260	Stadtmuseum, Rottweil	Führer Rottweil (1928), Taf. xxii Nr. 6
21	Vindonissa (Brugg, Aargau)	1	Bone	14	1	Broken	(Missing)	Schutthügel; C I	Vindonissa-Mus., Brugg, 1942.147	—
22	Vindonissa	1	Bone	13.3	1	—	Two incised rills both ends	?	22.229	—
23	Vindonissa	1	Bone	13	0.8	Top broken	—	?	35.576	—
24	Vindonissa	1	Bone	13	0.6	Broken	—	?	5357	—
25	Vindonissa	1	Bone	12.5	1.2	Roughed out with knife, but not smoothed	—	?	27,307	—
26	Vindonissa	1	Bone	12.5	0.8	—	—	?	5398	—
27	Vindonissa	2	Bone	12	1	—	Rills both ends	?	42,417, 22,229	—
28	Vindonissa	1	Bone	10.5+	1	Broken	Rills both ends	?	23,2015	—

TABLE F (cont.)

FO	No.	Material	L.	Br. of bulb	State	Upper terminal	Context/date	Museum	Publication
29 Vindonissa	c. 35	Wood	under 20	c. 1	—	Plain	*Schutthügel*	Vindonissa-Mus.	—
30 Vindonissa	c. 20	Wood	over 20	c. 0.6	—	Plain	*Schutthügel*	Vindonissa-Mus.	—
31 Vindonissa	1	Wood	13.5+	0.6	Broken	—	*Schutthügel*	2873	—
32 Vindonissa	1	Wood	16+	1.0	Both ends broken	—	*Schutthügel*	Vindonissa-Mus.	—
33 Vindonissa	1	Wood	17+	0.6	Top broken	—	*Schutthügel*	23,1533	—
34 Vindonissa	1	Wood	18+	0.6	Bottom broken	Plain	*Schutthügel*; C I	Vindonissa-Mus., Brugg, 4771	—
35 Vindonissa	1	Wood	19+	1	Top broken	Bottom marked by whorl	*Schutthügel*; C I	Vindonissa-Mus., Brugg, 1942.93	—
36 Xanten (Kr. Moers)	1	Bone	8.5	—	—	Plain	*Brandgrab*; late first–early second century	Museum, Xanten, 401	*Kat. Xanten* (1911), 28, Grab 9, Taf. I, 186; *Mschr. Ges. WD*, IV, 1878, 367
37 Zugmantel	1	Wood	—	—	—	—	TAQ *c.* A.D. 260	—	*S-Jb*, III (1912), 32
38 Zugmantel	1	Bone	17	1	—	—	TAQ *c.* A.D. 260	Saalburg Museum	*Ibid.* I (1910), 58, Taf. x, 11.

TABLE G *Bobbins*

Bone bobbins made of the metatarsals and metacarpals of sheep and/or goats (fig. 16)

	FO	L.	Br.	Hole	Markings	Context	Museum	Publication
1	Chesters (Northumber.)	11.5	1.2	Centre	Centre polished	(Roman fort)	Chesters Museum, 472	Arch. Cant. xxii (1897), 71
2	Darenth (Kent)	—	—	—	—	(Roman villa ?)	—	—
3	Mumrills (Stirling)	6+	1.5	Centre	—	(Antonine fort)	—	PSAS, lxiii (1928–9), 567, fig. 131a
4	Woodcuts (Dorset)	12.5	1.4	Near distal end; drilled vertically into proximal end	—	(Village, Roman?)	—	Pitt-Rivers (1887), 175 with fig. 1
5	Woodcuts (Dorset)	11.5	1.2	Centre and into proximal end	—	(Village)	—	Ibid. fig. 2.
6	Woodcuts (Dorset)	11	1.2	Centre	—	(Village)	—	Ibid. fig. 3.

TABLE H *Gold thread*

Gold thread from the Roman provinces

	FO	Classification*	Width (mm.)	Core	Context/date	Museum	Publication
1	St Aldegund (Kr. Zell)	3, Z-spun. Gold and silver	0.25	(Silk?)	Rich female burial in sarcophagus; A.D. 300–350	Staatliches Amt. für Vor- und Frühgeschichte, Koblenz	*Germ.* 39 (1961), 131
2	Bingen	'Goldfäden'	—	—	Sarcophagus; third or fourth century A.D.	?	*MZ*, 50 (1955), 108
3	Dorweiler (Kr. Euskirchen)	'Goldfäden'	—	—	Female grave (sarcophagus); A.D. 300–400	LMB, 43, 143 (not now available)	*BJb*, 149 (1949), 88, Nr. 4c; 85, Abb. 5, 4
4	Essenheim (Mainz)	'Goldfäden'	—	—	Sarcophagus of woman; fourth century A.D.	Lost in war	*MZ*, 30 (1935), 84, Sarg 1
5	Horburg, Colmar (Alsace)	'Goldfäden'	—	—	Tile-grave—Roman?	—	*Korr. bl. WZ*, IV (1885), Par. 2
6	Mainz (Zahlbacher Weg)	3	—	—	Rich female grave, prob. of third century or late second (cf. *MZ*, 8–9 (1913–14), 47, Grab. 376 for date).	Lost in war	*MZ*, 20–21 (1925–6), 96, Abb. 9, 5; *Germ.* 9 (1925), 131, Abb. 2, 5
7	Trier (St Paulinus)	3	—	Poss. absent	Sarcophagus of St Paulinus; c. A.D. 395	—	*BJb*, 77 (1884), 238 ff.; 78 (1884), 171
8	Trittenheim (Kr. Trier)	'Goldfäden'	—	—	Sarcophagus; third or fourth century A.D.	Photographs only survive; LM Trier	*BJb*, 127 (1922), 310
9	Worms	'Goldfäden'	—	—	Cist for ashes; second century?	Städtisches Museum, Worms.	*Korr. bl. WZ*, IV (1885), Par. 145
10	(Unknown) (Lower Germany?)	2 or 3	—	—	'Roman grave'	Rijksmuseum van Oudheden, Leiden	*Birka*, III, 70, Anm. 2
11	Verulamium (St Albans)	3	c. 0.25	Missing	Girl's grave TPQ A.D. 210	Verulamium Mus., St Albans	(Unpublished)

TABLE H (cont.)

Gold thread; comparative material (listed according to date)

FO	Classification*	Width (mm.)	Core	Context/date	Museum	Publication
12 Gieshübel (Württemberg)	—	—	—	Late-Hallstatt *Fürstengrab*	—	*Germ.* 30 (1952), 38
13 Koropi (Athens)	Silver-gilt metal strip 3	—	Silk or linen missing	Embroidery on linen; fifth century B.C.	V and A, London	*ILN*, 23 January, 1954, 114
14 Kerch (Crimea)	2 or 3	—	—	Grave-mound of third century B.C.	—	*C-R. Comm. Imp.* (1877–9), Erklärung, S.135; *Atlas* (1878–9), Taf. v, 4
15 Lexden (Essex)	3	—	Missing	Tumulus of Cunobelinus (?); 17 B.C.–c. A.D. 40	—	*Archaeologia*, LXXVI, 251, pl. LXII, fig. 1
16 Dura-Europos (Syria)	3	—	Missing	Roman town/fort; TAQ A.D. 256	—	*Dura* (1945), 60
17 Palmyra (Syria) (a)	3 (Z-spun)	0.33	Z-spun silk	Mausoleum—late Roman? poss. TAQ c. A.D. 273	—	Pfister (1934), 18
18 Palmyra (Syria) (b)	Gilt organic strip	0.31	Z-spun silk	Mausoleum—late Roman? poss. TAQ c. A.D. 273 (prob. Han import)	—	*Ibid.* 45
19 Köln	3	c. 0.4–0.8	Silk	'Singer's grave'; A.D. 600–650	—	*Ver. Inst. VF*, 7 (1945), 4, Abb. 3
20 Rome (Vatican) (a)	4	—	Vegetable fibre	'Tomb of St Peter'	—	Guarducci (1965), Tav. 43
21 Rome (Vatican) (b)	3	—	Z-spun wool	'Tomb of St Peter'	—	*Ibid.* Tav. 9

* Classification of gold thread: (1) gold wire, (2) spirally spun gold wire, (3) spun gold ribbon, (4) gilt organic strip.

TABLE I *Thimbles*

Thimbles of bronze

FO	No.	L.	Br.	Date	Museum	Publication
1 Avenches	2	1.5	1.5	Roman?	Musée rom., Avenches, 6030; 5061	—
2 Gerpinnes (Hainaut)	1	—	—	Roman?	—	de Maeyer (1940), 1,64
3 (Trier?)	1	1.2	1.8	Roman?	LM Trier	—
4 Verulamium	1	1.7	1.9	Roman?	Verulamium Mus., St Albans	—

TABLE J *Pin-beaters of Iron-Age type in Roman Britain*

FO	L.	Br.	Context/date	Publication
1 Langton (E. Yorks.)	11.5	—	Ditch of early fortlet; possibly Iron Age	Corder & Kirk (1932), fig. 19, 1
2 Langton (E. Yorks.)	9	—		Ibid. fig. 19, 2
3 Langton (E. Yorks.)	6 (broken)	—		Ibid. fig. 19, 4

TABLE K *Cigar-shaped pin-beaters*

	FO	L.	Br.	Context/date	Museum	Publication
	Cigar-shaped pin-beaters in Roman Britain (fig. 16)					
1	Corinium (Cirencester)	14.2	1	(Roman town)	Corinium Mus., Cirencester, B789	—
2	Eastington (Glos.)	14.6	0.9	A.D. 50–200 (?)	Stroud Museum	*Proc. Cott. C*, XXIV (1930–2), 170, pl. XXIII, B
3	Richborough (Kent)	8 (broken) notched at one end		Unstrat. on fort site	Site Museum, Richborough	*Richborough*, IV, 132, no. 141, pl. XXXIX
4	York (Railway Station Cemetery)	8	0.9	Female grave with comb (H. 315.1) Fourth century?	Yorks. Museum, York	?
5	York	18	1.2	Roman?	Museum of Antiquities, Newcastle-upon-Tyne, 1956, 112.A	—
	Cigar-shaped pin-beaters in the continental provinces					
6	Elewijt (Belgium)	—	—	Roman well	—	*Ant. Class.* 23 (1954), 445
7	Hofheim (Maintaunuskr.)	10	—	Fort, Claud.-Vesp.	Städtisches Mus., Wiesbaden, 17117	*Nass. Ann.* XXXIV (1904), 105, Abb. 614, 106, Nr. 9
8	Rottweil	12.6	1.4	Town, TAQ *c.* A.D. 260	Stadtmus., Rottweil	*Führer Rottweil* (1928), Taf. XXII, 3
9	Speyer	10	0.9	(Roman?)	Historisches Mus. d. Pfalz, Speyer	—
10	Stein on Maas	9.5	—	Villa, TAQ *c.* A.D. 250	—	*Oud. Med.* N.S. IX (1928), 32, Afb. 17 B, no. 7
11	Stein on Maas	13	—	Villa, TAQ *c.* A.D. 250	—	*Ibid.* Afb. 17 B, no. 8
12	Strasburg	16.5	1	(Roman?)	Château des Rohan, Strassburg, 6670	—
13	Worms	13.5 16.5	0.6 0.6	(Roman?) (Roman?)	Städt. Mus., Worms	— —

TABLE L *Bone and antler weaving-combs*

Bone and antler weaving combs of Iron-Age type in Roman Britain (fig. 16)

	FO	No.	L.	Br.	No. of teeth	Class	Context/date	Museum	Publication
1	Caerwent	1	—	—	—	—	House XVII N in town	—	Archaeologia, LXII (1910), 2; Henshall (1950), 160
2	Camelon (Stirling)	1	10.7	4	9	4	Antonine fort	—	PSAS,[3] xxxv (1900–1), 410, fig. 50
3	(Carlisle)	1	12.7	4	7	4	Antonine fort	Tullie House, Carlisle	Ibid. fig. 51; Henshall (1950), 160
4	Chesters (?)	1	(Broken)	—	—	—	Fort?	Chesters Museum, 631	—
5	Chesters (?)	1	—	—	—	3	Fort?	Chesters Museum, 630	—
6	Corbridge	5	—	—	—	—	(Roman fort)	Site Museum, Corbridge	Henshall (1950), 160; AA,[3] VIII (1912), 207 (one)
7	Housesteads	(Broken)	—	—	—	—	(Roman fort)	Chesters Museum	Henshall (1950), 160.
8	Ickleton (Cambs.)	1	—	—	—	—	Roman villa	—	Arch. J, vi (1849), 17
9	Newstead	1	12	4	8	3	Pit LIX, N. of fort; late first–early second century	NMA, Edinburgh	Curle (1911), 290, pl. LXVIII, 4
10	Newstead	1	13	3.5	7	4	Inner ditch of E. Annexe	NMA, Edinburgh	Ibid. pl. LXVIII, 3
11	Newstead	1	12	4	9	4	Ditch of early fort	NMA, Edinburgh	Ibid. pl. LXVIII, 2
12	Newstead	1	15	4	8	3	Pit XXXVII, in S. Annexe	NMA, Edinburgh	Ibid. pl. LXVIII, 1
13	Piercebridge (Co. Durham)	1	13.3	5	10	1	Fort, TPQ c. A.D. 300	—	Trans. AAS, 9 (1939–43), 64; Henshall (1950), 160
14	South Shields	1	(Stump only)	—	9	—	Fort	South Shields Museum	—
15	Wallsend	1	8 (broken)	—	9	—	Fort (Post-Hadrianic)	Museum of Antiquities, Newcastle-upon-Tyne, 1956, 176.A	—
16	Wroxeter	1	c. 12	c. 4	13	1	(Town)	—	Wroxeter, iv, 33, pl. XXII, fig. 1, 1
17	York	2	—	—	12	3	Roman?	Yorks. Mus., York	Henshall (1950), 160

TABLE M *Loom-weights*

Loom-weights in Britain

	FO	Material	Shape	Size/weight	Context/date	Museum	Publication
1	Bourton-on-the-Water (Gloucestershire)	Limestone	Globular with hole	2.5 kg.	Settlement? TAQ third century A.D.	—	Trans. BG, LVI (1934), 120, no. 13, fig. 11.
2	Gillamoor (Kirkby Moorside, Yorks.)	Limestone	Roughly globular	12.5 high	Hut site; late-Roman	—	YAJ, XXXIII (1936–8), 227
3	Middleton-on-the-Wolds (Yorks.)	Chalk	Pear-shaped, with groove for string	0.9 kg.	(Roman)	Hull Museum	Trans. ERAS, XXIV (1923), 84 fig. 2
4	Silchester	Clay	?	'Small'	From Roman town	Reading Museum	Boon (1957), 194
5	West Blatchington (Hove, Sussex)	Clay	Pyramidal (?)	c. 7.5 high	Late-third or fourth century	—	Sussex AC, LXXXIX (1950), 53 fig. 18 A, no. 3

Loom-weights of clay from the continental provinces

	FO	No.	Shape	L.	Br. at base	W.	Context/date	Museum	Publication
6	Arentsburg (Westland)	2	Triangular (I A type)	—	—	—	Auxiliary fort; C I–II	Rijksmuseum van Oudheden, Leiden	Cat. Leiden (1908), 166, 11–12
7	Augst	1	Pyramidal	11	6	—	(Roman town)	Römerhaus, Augst, 1908. 2642; 1923.390	—
8	Augst	1	Pyramidal	9	6	—			
9	Bonn (Koblenzerstr.)	8	Pyramidal, conical	c. 7	—	—	Found together in house in cannabae	—	BJb, 26 (1858), 190
10	Brühl (Lkr. Köln)		—	—	—	—	Roman well, second or third century	LMB, 42, 189	BJb, 148 (1948), 383
11	Engehalbinsel (Bern)	1	Pyramidal	11	5.5	—	Settlement of La-Tène to Roman date	Hist. Mus., Bern, 29774	—
12	Engehalbinsel (Bern)	1	Pyramidal	9.5	5.5	—	With spindle-whorls	28604	—

TABLE M (cont.)

	FO	No.	Shape	L.	Br. at base	W.	Context/date	Museum	Publication
13	Engehalbinsel (Bern)	1	Pyramidal	9	5.5	—	With spindle-whorls	29152	—
14	Givry (Hainaut)	1	Triangular with one hole (I A shape)	9.4	3.3	—	Roman villa	Mus. royale d'art et hist., Brussels	de Maeyer (1940), 65
15	Givry (Hainaut)	1		9	3.7	—	—	—	—
16	Givry (Hainaut)	1		11	3	—	—	—	—
17	Givry (Hainaut)	1		12.3	3.4	—	—	—	—
18	Givry (Hainaut)	1		10.9	3	—	—	—	—
19	Hofheim (Maintaunuskr.)	1	Pyramidal (chalk)	12	7 by 5	—	Auxiliary fort, Claudian to Vespasian	Städtisches Mus., Wiesbaden, 17111	Nass. Ann. 34 (1904), 107, no. 3, Abb. 62
20	Holdoorn	1	Pyramidal	—	—	—	(Roman?)	Rijksmuseum van Oudheden, Leiden	Cat. Leiden (1908), 166, v 1,3
21	Köln-Müngersdorf	1	Pyramidal	13	5	—	Suburban Roman villa	—	Fremersdorf (1933), Taf. 27, Nr. 12
22	Köln-Müngersdorf	2	Pyramidal	14.8	4.5	—	Suburban Roman villa	—	Ibid. Taf. 42, A, 5, 6
23	Köln-Müngersdorf	1	Pyramidal	12	5.5	—	Suburban Roman villa	—	Ibid. Taf. 30, 1
24	Köln-Müngersdorf	1	Pyramidal	11	4	—	Suburban Roman villa	—	Ibid. Taf. 30, 2
25	Naaldwijk (Westland)	16	Pyramidal	—	—	—	Found together in vicus of fort at Arentsburg; first or second century	—	Oud. Med. N.S. xvii (1936), 35, Afb. 22
26	Ressen (Betuwe)	1	Triangular (I A type)	15	15	—	Vicus of early Roman fort	—	Ibid. N.S. xxx (1949), 29, Afb. 7, 1:
27	Vechten	7	Triangular	—	—	—	Vicus of early Roman fort	Rijksmus. v. Oud, Leiden	Cat. Leiden (1908), 166, 4–10
28	Zugmantel	40	Pyramidal	15–18	8	800–1300 gr.	Together in pit in vicus of fort; TAQ c. A.D. 260	Saalburg Museum	S-Jb, iii (1912), 65, Abb. 24
29	Zugmantel	2	Pyramidal	—	—	—	—	Saalburg Museum	Ibid. 67

TABLE N Netting-needles of bronze

	FO	No.	L.	L. of prongs	Angle*	Context/date	Museum	Publication
	Netting-needles from Britain (fig. 65)							
1	Gloucester (Kingsholm Sq.)	1	14	—	—	First or second century	City Museum, Gloucester, A 2983	Trans. BG, LXXII (1953), 154
2	Kenchester	1	13	—	(None)	(Bone) Roman?	—	JRS, xv (1925), 229; Ant. J, v (1925), 174
3	London	4	—	—	—	—	London Museum, A 4849, A 2903, A 4850, A 4852	Wheeler (1930), 105, 11–14, pl. XLII
4	Richborough	1	14	—	—	—	—	Richborough, I, 46, no, 22
5	Wroxeter	1	15.3	—	—	(Iron) Roman	Rowley's House Museum, Shrewsbury	Wroxeter, II, 13, fig. 5, no. 9
	Netting-needles from the continental provinces							
6	Andernach (Kr. Mayen)	1	c. 6	—	—	Augustan female grave	—	BJb, 86 (1888), 167, Grab 15, Taf. VIII, 28
7	Augst	1	13	1.8	90°	(Roman town)	Römerhaus, Augst	—
8	Engehalbinsel (Bern)	1	16.6	3.2	90°	From La-Tène and Roman settlement	Hist. Mus., Bern, 29599	—
9	Heddernheim	1	16.6	2.3	90°	Second-century grave, Nr. 169	—	Heddernheim, v (1911), 32, Abb. 7, 7
10	Heddernheim	2	c. 7	—	—	Second-century grave, Nr. 169	—	Ibid. Abb. 7, 6
11	Köln	1	13.5	2	(None)	Roman, from harbour	—	BJb, 153 (1953), 119, Taf. 10, Nr. 162, Abb. 4, 162
12	Köln (?)	1	13.7	—	90°	Köln ? Roman?	—	Niessen (1911), 207, Nr. 3960

TABLE N (cont.)

	FO	No.	L.	L. of prongs	Angle*	Context/date	Museum	Publication
13	Köln	1	13.4	—	90°	Köln? Roman?	—	Ibid. Nr. 3961
14	Köln	1	12.4	—	90°	Köln? Roman?	—	Ibid. Nr. 3962
15	Köln	1	12.2	—	90°	Köln? Roman?	—	Ibid. Nr. 3963
16	Köln	1	10.3	—	90°	Köln? Roman?	—	Ibid. Nr. 3964
17	Köngen	1	17.5+	2	(None)	(Iron) from W. tower of fort; TAQ c. A.D.150	—	ORL, B, v, 1 Kast. 60, 38, Nr. 32, Taf. v, 10.
18	Mainz	1	14	2	—	From legionary fort; prob. second century	—	MZ, 8 (1912), 89, Abb. 5, 11
19	Mainz	1	10+	—	—		—	—
20	Nijmegen	2	18	—	90°	Vicus W. of fort; c. A.D. 200–250	Rijksmuseum G.M. Kam, Nijmegen	—
21	Saalburg	1	16.6	3	90°	(Iron) from fort; TAQ c. A.D. 260	Saalburg Museum	Jacobi (1897), 454, Abb. 71, 12
22	Trier	1	21	1.5	90°	(Roman?)	LM Trier	—
23	Trier	1	17.5	1.3	90°	(Roman?)	LM Trier, G 1478	—
24	Vechten	3	—	—	—	(Roman?)	Rijksmus. v. Oud., Leiden	—
25	Vindonissa	1	12	0.8	90°	C I	Vindonissa-Mus., Brugg, 481	—
		1	14.7	2.8	90°	C I	2183, 87	—
		1	19	3	90°	C I	73, 21	—
		1	14.5	1.3	90°	C I	32, 2066	—
		1	15	2	90°	C I	23, 16	—
		1	14.5	3	(None)	(Iron) C I	56, 263	—
31	Zofingen (Kt. Aargau)	1	20.6	—	90°	Roman villa site	—	Urschweiz, XIII (1949), 26, Abb. 17

* The word 'angle' denotes the angle between the planes of the prongs (see fig. 65)

TABLE O *Tablets*

Tablets in Roman Britain (figs. 63–4)

	FO	No.	Shape	Material	Holes	Wear on holes	Size	Ornament	Context/date	Museum	Publication
1	Alchester (Oxford)	2	Square	Bone	6(4 used)	Mod.	3.8 × 3.8	Incised rings	Roman, but undated	Ashmolean Mus., Oxford	*Ant. J,* IX (1929), 134, pl. XI, I
2	Caerleon	1	Square	Bronze	4	Heavy	3.8 × 3.8	—	(Roman)	Legionary Mus., Caerleon, C 159	—
3	Caister-by-Yarmouth	1	Triang.	Bone	3	Heavy, repaired	5 × 5	—	Unstrat., but prob. Roman	Castle Mus., Norwich, 155,948	*NArch.* XXVI (1935–7), 180, pl. p. 179
4	Corbridge	1	Triang.	Bone	3	None	2.5 × 4.6	Plain	Roman, from fort	Site Mus., Corbridge	*AA.*³ IV (1908), 299
5	Corbridge	1	Triang.	Bone	3	Mod.	2.5 × 4.6	Incised rings			
6	Corinium (Cirencester)	1	Triang.	Bone	3	Mod.	—	—	From Roman town	Corinium Mus., Cirencester, C 187	*Trans. BG,* LXXVIII (1959), 63, no.17, fig. 10
7	Holbury (Wilts.)	1	Square	Bone	5	Mod.	—	—	(Roman)		*WAM,* XIII (1872), 40
8	London (Bank of England)	2 (?)	Triang.	Bone	3	Heavy	4 × 4	—	(Roman)	BM, 1928.7–13.15	*BM Guide* (1958), 48, fig. 23, III, d, I
9	Richborough	5	Triang.	Bone	3	—	4 × 4	—	Topsoil, but prob. Roman	Site Mus., Richborough	*Richborough* IV, 151 pl. LVI, no. 267
10	Richborough	1	Square	Bone	4	—	3.5 × 3.5	—	(Roman)		*Ibid.* 151, pl. LVI, no. 268
11	Silchester	2	Triang.	Bone	3	—	3.7 × 3.7	—	(Roman)	Reading Mus.	Boon (1957), 195
12	Tingewick (Bucks,)	1	Square	Bone	4	—	—	—	Prob. Roman	—	*VCH Bucks.* II (1908), 13
13	Wroxeter	1	Square	Bone	4	Linear	3.2 × 3.2	Plain	Unstrat., but Roman	Rowley's House Mus., Shrewsbury	Atkinson (1942), 231, pl. 51, C 188
14	Wroxeter	1	Square	Bone	4	Heavy	4 × 4	Linear	Prob. second century		*Ibid.* 231, pl. 51, C 189
15	Wroxeter	1	Triang.	Bone	3	Heavy, broken	4.8 × 4.8	—	Prob. second century		*Ibid.* C 187
16	Wroxeter	1	Triang.	Bone	3	None	5.1 × 5.1	—	?		?

TABLE O (cont.)

Tablets from the continental provinces

	FO	No.	Shape	Material	Holes	Wear on holes	Size	Ornament	Context/date	Museum	Publication
17	Bingen	1	Triang.	Bone	3	—	—	—	Roman?	Museum, Bingen, 2537	Behrens (1954), 26, Abb. 36
18	Boos (Kr. Kreuznach)	2	Square	Bone	4	Mod.	4 × 4	—	Roman-occupied cave; Roman?	—	Behrens (1925), 46, Abb. Nr. 1, 2
19	Hermsheim (Mannheim)	2	Square	Bone	4	—	—	(Linear)	Roman?	Mus, Mannheim	Behrens (1954), 26
20	Koblenz	4	Triang.	Bone	3	—	—	—	(Roman)	Städt. Amt. f. Vorgeschichte, Koblenz, 1960	Ibid.
21	Mainz	1	Square	Bone	4	Mod.	4.4 × 4.4	Line and circle	(Roman)	Mittelrheinisches Landesmuseum, Mainz, 2401 (lost)	—
22	Mainz	1	Square	Bone	4	—	3.4 × 3.4		(Roman)	Mittelrheinisches Landesmuseum, Mainz	Behrens (1925), 47, 46, Abb. 6
23	Planig	1	Square	Bone	4	Heavy	3 × 3	Linear	Roman?	Städt. Mus., Worms.	Ibid. Abb. 5
24	Planig	1	Square	Bone	4	Heavy	4 × 4	Linear	Roman?		Ibid. Abb. 3
25	Planig	1	Square	Bone	4	Heavy	3.7 × 3.7	Linear	Roman?		Ibid. Abb. 4
26	Trier (Böhmerstr.)	1	Triang.	Bone	3	V. heavy	6 × (now) 4	Circles	Roman?	LM Trier	Ibid. Abb. 8
27	Trier (St Barbara)	1	Triang.	Bone	3	Heavy	5.6 × 5.6	Plain	From Roman baths?	LM Trier	Ibid. Abb. 7
28	Vindonissa	1	Triang.	Bone	3	—	—	—	First century, from fort?	Vindonissa-Mus., Brugg, 28, 1800	Behrens (1954), 26

TABLE P *Northern dyestuffs*

Dyestuffs	Colours	Ancient source	Evidence for plant in Roman Britain	Possible mordants
Woad (*Isatis tinctoria*)	Blue	Caesar, *B.G.* v, 14	Godwin (1956), 342—earliest find Anglo-Saxon	Substantive dye
Whortleberry (*Vaccinium*)	Blue	Pliny, *N.H.* xvi, 77	Godwin (1956), 150	Substantive; purple–blue with alum
Whelks (*Purpura haemostoma*)	Scarlet-red	'Black' acc. Vitruvius, viii, 13, 1–3	—	Substantive dye
Archil (lichen) (*Rocella tinctoria*)	Red-purple	Pliny, *N.H.* xxii, 2	None	Substantive dye, but alum sometimes used
Madder (*Rubia tinctorum*)	Red-purple-brown	*Ibid.* xix, 47	—	Alum for red, iron for purple-brown

BIBLIOGRAPHY

AMAND & EYKENS-DIERICKX (1960). M. Amand & I. Eykens-Dierickx, *Tournai Romain, Diss. Arch. Gandenses*, V.

ARBMAN & STRÖMBERG (1934). H. Arbman & E. Strömberg, *Äslevanten*.

ATKINSON (1942). D. Atkinson, *Report on Excavations at Wroxeter, 1923–1927*.

AUDOLLENT (1922). A. Audollent, *Les Tombes Gallo-Romaines à Inhumation des Martres-de-Veyre', Mémoires présentés à l'Académie des Sciences et Belles Lettres*, XIII.

BAATZ (1962). D. Baatz, *Mogontiacum: neue Untersuchungen am römischen Legionslager in Mainz, Limesforschungen*, 4.

BEHRENS (1925). G. Behrens, 'Brettchenweberei in römischer Zeit', *Germ.* 9, 45 f.

BEHRENS (1946–8). G. Behrens, 'Eiserne Webschwerter der Merovingerzeit', *MZ*, XLI–XLIII, 138 ff.

BEHRENS (1954). G. Behrens, *Die Binger Landschaft in der Vor- und Frühgeschichte*.

BIEK (1963). L. Biek, *Archaeology and the Microscope*.

VON BLANCKENHAGEN (1940). P. H. von Blanckenhagen, *Flavische Architektur und ihre Dekoration*.

BLÜMNER (1912). H. Blümner, *Technologie und Terminologie der Gewerbe und Künste bei Griechen und Römern*, 2te Auflage.

BOESSNECK (1958). J. Boessneck, *Zur Entwicklung vor- und frühgeschichtlicher Haus- und Wildtiere Bayerns im Rahmen der gleichzeitigen Tierwelt Mitteleuropas*.

BOON (1957). G. C. Boon, *Roman Silchester*.

BOYD et al. (1964). J. Morton Boyd et al. 'The Soay Sheep of the Island of Hirta, St Kilda. A Study of a Feral Population', *Proceedings of the Zoological Society of London*, **142**, 129–63.

BRADBURY (1920). F. Bradbury, *Flax Culture and Preparation*.

BRØNSTED (1960). J. Brønsted, *Jernalderen, Danmarks Oldtid*, III.

BROWN & WARE (1958). H. B. Brown & J. O. Ware, *Cotton*, 3rd edition.

BRUNSTING (1937). H. Brunsting, *Het Grafveld on der Hees bij Nijmegen*.

BULLEID & GRAY (1911), (1917). A. Bulleid & H. St. George Gray, *The Glastonbury Lake Village*, I, 1911; II, 1917.

CARCOPINO (1956). J. Carcopino, *De Pythagore aux Apôtres*.

CARTER & NEWBERRY (1904). H. Carter & P. E. Newberry, *The Tomb of Thoutmosis IV, Catalogue Général des Antiquités Egyptiennes du Musée du Caire*.

CASTELLANI (1964). O. Castellani, 'La Momie de la Grotta Rosa', *Revue Archéologique du Centre*, III, Fasc. 2, 138 ff.

CHADWICK & KILLEN (1964). J. Chadwick & J. T. Killen, *The Knossos Tablets, Institute of Classical Studies Bulletin, Supplement* 15.

CHILDE (1935). V. G. Childe, *The Prehistory of Scotland*.

CHILDE (1947). V. G. Childe, *Prehistoric Communities of the British Isles*, 2nd edition.

CHRIST (1913). H. Christ, 'Das Vorkommen des Buchsbaumes in der Schweiz, Europa und Vorderasien', *Verhandlungen Nat. Ges. Basel*, XXIV, 46 ff.

CLARK (1947). J. G. D. Clark, 'Sheep and Swine in the Husbandry of Prehistoric Europe', *Antiquity*, XXI, 122 ff.

CORDER & KIRK (1932). P. Corder & J. L. Kirk, *The Roman Villa at Langton near Malton, E. Yorkshire*.

CROWFOOT (1931). G. M. Crowfoot, *Methods of Hand Spinning in Egypt and the Sudan, Bankfield Museum Notes*, Series II, 12.

CROWFOOT (1936–7). G. M. Crowfoot, 'Of the Warp-weighted Loom', *BSA*, XXXVII, 36 ff.

CROWFOOT & GRIFFITHS (1939). G. M. Crowfoot & J. Griffiths, 'Coptic Textiles in Two-faced Weave with Patterns in Reverse', *JEA*, XXV, 40 ff.

CROWFOOT (1955). G. M. Crowfoot *apud* D. Barthelmy, J. T. Milik, *Qûmran Cave I, Discoveries in the Judaean Desert*, I.

CROWFOOT (1962). G. M. Crowfoot *apud* P. Benoit, J.T. Milik, R. de Vaux, *Les Grottes de Murabba'at, Discoveries in the Judaean Desert*, II.

CURLE (1911). J. Curle, *Newstead, a Roman Frontier Post and its People*.

CURTIUS (1929). L. Curtius, *Die Wandmalerei Pompejis*.

DIHLE (1965). A. Dihle, *Umstrittene Daten: Untersuchungen zum Auftreten der Griechen am Roten Meer, Wissenschaftliche Abhandlungen der Arbeitsgemeinschaft für Forschung des Landes Nord-Rhein-Westfalen*, 32.

DIMAND (1924). M. Dimand, *Die Ornamentik der ägyptischen Wollwirkereien: Stilprobleme der spätantiken und koptischen Kunst*.

ENDREI (1958). W. G. Endrei, 'A Lábitós Szövőszék Kialakulása és Feltűnése Európában', *Történelmi Szemle*, 331 ff.

ENDREI (1961). W. G. Endrei, 'Der Trittwebstuhl im frühmittelalterlichen Europa', *Acta Historica*, VIII, 107 ff.

EYDOUX (1962). H. P. Eydoux, *La France Antique*.

FILIP (1960). J. Filip, *Keltská Civilisace a její Dedictri* (English translation 1962).

FORBES (1956). R. J. Forbes, *Studies in Ancient Technology*, IV.

FORBES (1930). W. T. M. Forbes, 'The Silkworm of Aristotle', *Classical Philology*, XXV, 22 ff.

FORRER (1898). R. Forrer, *Die Kunst des Zeugdrucks*.

FOX (1932). C. F. Fox, *The Personality of Britain*.

FREMERSDORF (1933). Fr. Fremersdorf, *Der römische Gutshof Köln–Müngersdorf*.

FREMERSDORF (1950). Fr. Fremersdorf, *Neue Beiträge zur Topographie des römischen Köln*.

GANSSER-BURCKHARDT (1942). A. Gansser-Burckhardt, *Das Leder und seine Verarbeitung im römischen Legionslager Vindonissa, Veröffentlichungen der Gesellschaft Pro Vindonissa*, I.

GARBSCH (1965). J. G. Garbsch, *Die norisch-pannonische Frauentracht im 1. und 2. Jahrhundert, Münchener Beiträge zur Vor- und Frühgeschichte*, II.

GEIJER (1939). A. Geijer, 'Ett svenskt textilfynd från romersk järnålder', *Fornvännen*, **34**, 190 ff.

GODWIN (1956). H. Godwin, *The History of the British Flora*.

GODWIN (1967). H. Godwin, 'The Ancient Cultivation of Hemp', *Antiquity*, XLI, 42 ff., 137 ff.

GRIFFITH & CROWFOOT (1934). F. L. Griffith & G. M. Crowfoot, 'On the early use of cotton in the Nile Valley', *JEA*, XX, 5 ff.

GUARDUCCI (1965). M. Guarducci, *Le Reliquie di Pietro*.

HAHNE (1915). H. Hahne, *Moorleichenfunde aus Niedersachsen, Vorzeitfunde aus Niedersachsen*, B.

HAJNAL (1965). M. L. Hajnal, 'Textiles from the graves of late Roman Brigetio', *Acta Antiqua*, XIII, 259–66.

HALD (1934). H. Hald, 'Le tissage aux plâques dans les trouvailles préhistoriques du Danemark',

Mémoires de la Société Royale des Antiquaires du Nord, 389 ff. (Danish text in *Aarbøger*, 1930, 277 ff.)

HALD (1946). M. Hald, 'Ancient textile techniques in Egypt and Scandinavia', *Acta Arch.* **17**, 49 ff.

HALD (1950). M. Hald, *Olddanske Tekstiler, Nordiske Fortidsminder*, v.

HALD (1961). M. Hald, 'Dragtstudier', *Aarbøger*, 37 ff. with English summary p. 76 ff.

HALD (1962). M. Hald, *Jernalderens Dragt* (Guide to the National Museum, Copenhagen).

HALD (1963). M. Hald, 'Vaevning over Gruber', *Kuml*, 88 ff.

HAMILTON (1956). J. R. C. Hamilton, *Excavations at Jarlshof, Shetland, Ministry of Works Archaeological Report*, 1.

HENSHALL (1950). A. S. Henshall, 'Textiles and weaving appliances in prehistoric Britain', *PPS*, NS, XVI, 130 ff.

HENSHALL (1951–2). A. S. Henshall, 'Early Textiles found in Scotland', *PSAS*, LXXXVI, 1 ff.; LXXXVIII, 1954–6, 22 ff.

HOFFMANN (1958). M. Hoffmann, *En Gruppe Vevstoler på Vestlandet*.

HOFFMANN & TRAETTEBERG (1959). M. Hoffmann & R. Traetteberg, 'Teglefunnet', *Stavanger Museums Årbok*, 41 ff.

HOFFMANN (1964). M. Hoffmann, *The Warp-Weighted Loom*.

HOME (1948). G. Home, *Roman London*.

HOUGEN (1935). B. Hougen, *Snartemofunnene, Norske Oldfunn*, VII.

HOUGEN (1940). B. Hougen, 'Osebergfunnets billedvev', *Viking*, IV, 85 ff.

HUNDT (1959). H.-J. Hundt, 'Vorgeschichtliche Gewebe aus dem Hallstätter Salzberg', *Jhb. R-GZM*, **6**, 66 ff.

HUNDT (1960). H.-J. Hundt, 'Vorgeschichtliche Gewebe aus dem Hallstätter Salzberg', *Jhb. R-GZM*, **7**, 126 ff.

HUNDT (1961). H.-J. Hundt, 'Neunzehn Textilreste aus dem Dürrnberg in Hallein', *Jhb. R-GZM*, **8**, 7 ff.

HUNDT (1964). H.-J. Hundt, 'Eine leinumwickelte Schwertscheide der Hallstattzeit', *Mainfränkisches Jahrbuch für Geschichte und Kunst*, **15**, 180 ff.

HUNDT (1966). H.-J. Hundt *apud* R. Christle, 'Das alamannische Reihengräberfeld von Marktoberdorf in Allgäu', *Materialhefte zur Bayerischen Vorgeschichte*, **21**, 93 ff.

HUNDT (1967). H.-J. Hundt *apud* P. Paulsen, 'Alamannische Adelsgräber von Niederstotzingen (Kr. Heidenheim)', *Veröffentlichungen d. Staatl. Amtes f. Denkmalpflege Stuttgart*, **12**/II,7 ff.

JACKSON (1953). K. H. Jackson, *Language and History in Early Britain*.

JACOBI (1897). L. Jacobi, *Das Römerkastell Saalburg*.

JESSEN & HELBAEK (1944). K. Jessen & H. Helbaek, *Cereals in Great Britain and Ireland in Prehistoric and Early Historic Times*.

JOHL (1917). C. H. Johl, *Die Webestühle der Griechen und Römer* (Kiel University diss.).

JONES (1960–1). A. H. M. Jones, 'The Cloth Industry under the Roman Empire', *Economic History Review*, XIII, 183 ff.

KEIM & KLUMBACH (1951). J. Keim & H. Klumbach, *Der römische Schatzfund von Straubing, Münchener Beiträge zur Vor- und Frühgeschichte*, 3.

KEMPF & REUSCH (1965). Th. K. Kempf & W. Reusch, *Frühchristliche Zeugnisse im Einzugsgebiet von Rhein und Mosel*.

KENNER (1947). H. Kenner, *Der Bäderbezirk von Virunum.*

KILLEN (1963). J. T. Killen, 'Some adjuncts to the SHEEP ideogram on Knossos tablets', *Eranos*, LXI, 69 ff.

KITSON CLARK (1935). M. Kitson Clark, *A Gazeteer of Roman Remains in East Yorkshire.*

LA BAUME (1931). W. La Baume, 'Die vorgeschichtliche Handspindel und ihr Gebrauch', *Mannus*, Erg.-Band VIII, 71–3.

LA BAUME (1955). W. La Baume, *Die Entwicklung des Textilhandwerks in Alteuropa.*

LA BAUME (1961). W. La Baume, *Frühgeschichte der europaischen Kulturpflanzen, Giessener Abhandlungen zur Agrar- und Wirtschaftsforschung des europaischen Osten*, 16.

LAUFFER (1964). S. Lauffer, 'Zu Diokletians Höchstpreisedikt', *Akte des IV Internat. Kongresses f. gr. u. lat. Epigraphik, Wien*, 214 ff.

LEWIS (1943). H. Lewis, *Yr Elfen Ladin yn yr Iaith Gymraeg.*

LIVERSIDGE (1955). J. E. A. Liversidge, *Furniture in Roman Britain.*

DE MAEYER (1940). R. de Maeyer, *De Overblijfselen der romeinsche villa's in Belgie.*

MAIURI (1956). A. Maiuri, *Pompeii* (English text, 8th edition).

MAIURI (1958). A. Maiuri, *Ercolano. I nuovi Scavi (1927–58).*

MAIURI (1960). A. Maiuri, *Pompeii* (Instituto Geografico de Agostini).

MAIURI (1963). A. Maiuri, *Pittori di Pompeii, Monumenti d'Arte Italiana*, 4.

MANNING (1966). W. H. Manning, 'Caistor-by-Norwich and the *Notitia Dignitatum*', *Antiquity*, XL, 60 ff.

MAU (1908). A. Mau, *Pompeji in Leben und Kunst*, 2te Auflage.

MOMMSEN & BLÜMNER (1893). Th. Mommsen & H. Blümner, *Der Maximaltarif des Diocletian.*

MURPHY (1910–11). W. S. Murphy, *The Textile Industry: a Practical Guide to Fibres, Yarns and Fabrics*, 8 vols.

NAGY (1935). L. Nagy, *Aquincumi Múmiatemetkezések, Diss. Pannonicae*, Ser. 1, Fasc. 4, 35 ff.

NIESSEN (1911). *Die Sammlung römischer Altertümer von C. A. Niessen in Köln a. Rh.* 3te Auflage.

OVERBECK (1884). J. Overbeck, *Pompeji in seinen Gebäuden, Alterthümern und Kunstwerken*, 4te Auflage.

PFISTER (1932). R. Pfister, *Tissus coptes du Musée du Louvre.*

PFISTER (1933). R. Pfister, 'Les débuts du vêtement copte', *Mélanges Linossier.*

PFISTER (1934). R. Pfister, *Textiles de Palmyre.*

PFISTER (1935). R. Pfister, 'Teinture et alchimie dans l'Orient hellénistique', *Seminarium Kondakovianum*, VII, 1 ff.

PFISTER (1937). R. Pfister, *Nouveaux Textiles de Palmyre.*

PFISTER (1940). R. Pfister, *Textiles de Palmyre*, III.

PFISTER (1951). R. Pfister, *Textiles de Halabiyeh (Zenobia), Bibliothèque arch. et hist. de Beyrouth*, XLVIII.

PITT-RIVERS (1887). A. Pitt-Rivers, *Excavations on Cranborne Chase*, I.

PITT-RIVERS (1892). A. Pitt-Rivers, *Excavations in Bokerly and Wansdyke, Dorset and Wilts*, III.

POTRATZ (1942). H. A. Potratz, *Das Moorgewand von Reepsholt, Kr. Wittmund, Ostfriesland, Veröffentlichungen d. urges. Sammlung d. Landesmuseum Hannover*, VII.

VON POST et al. (1924). L. von Post, E. von Walterstorff, S. Lindqvist, *Bronsåldersmanteln från Gerumsberget i Våstergötland, K. Vitterhets Hist. och Antikv. Akad. Monogr.* 15.

BIBLIOGRAPHY

PRALLE (1921). H. Pralle, *Tabletweaving* (translated and revised by H. H. Peach).

PRITCHARD (1954). M. E. Pritchard, *A Short Dictionary of Weaving*.

RICHMOND (1958). I. A. Richmond (ed)., *Roman and Native in North Britain*.

RIEK & HUNDT (1962). G. Riek & H.-J. Hundt, *Der Hohmichele, Römisch-Germanische Forschungen*, 25.

ROES (1963). A. Roes, *Bone and Antler Objects from the Frisian Terp-mounds*.

ROSTOVTZEFF (1931). M. I. Rostovtzeff, *Skythien und der Bosporus*, I.

LING ROTH (1906). H. Ling Roth, *Hand Woolcombing, Bankfield Museum Notes*, Ser. I, 6 (c. 1906).

LING ROTH (1934). H. Ling Roth, *Studies in Primitive Looms*.

LING ROTH (1951). H. Ling Roth, *Ancient Egyptian and Greek Looms*, 2nd edition.

RYDER (1959). M. L. Ryder, 'Sheep of the Ancient Civilisations', *Wool Knowledge*, IV, **12**, 10 ff.

RYDER (1962). M. L. Ryder, 'The Histological Examination of Skin in the Study of the Domestication of Sheep', *Zeitschrift f. Tierzüchtung und Züchtungsbiologie*, **77**, 168 ff.

RYDER (1964*a*). M. L. Ryder, 'The History of Sheep Breeds in Britain', *Agricultural History Review*, XII, 1 ff., 65 ff.

RYDER (1964*b*). M. L. Ryder, 'Parchment: its History, Manufacture and Composition', *Journal of the Society of Archivists*, II, 391 ff.

RYDER (1965). M. L. Ryder, 'Report of Textiles from Çatal Hüyük', *Anatolian Studies*, XV, 175–6.

RYDER (1966). M. L. Ryder, 'Coat Structure in Soay Sheep', *Nature*, **211**, 1092–3.

RYDER & STEPHENSON (1968). M. L. Ryder & S. K. Stephenson, *Wool Growth*.

SCHEFOLD (1957). K. Schefold, *Die Wände Pompejis*.

SCHEUERMEIER (1956). P. Scheuermeier, *Bauernwerk in Italien, der italienischen und rätoromanischen Schweiz*, II.

SCHLABOW (1939). K. Schlabow, 'Das Spinngut des bronzezeitlichen Webers', *Offa*, 4, 109 ff.

SCHLABOW (1941–2). K. Schlabow, 'Nochmals: Das Spinngut des bronzezeitlichen Webers', *PZ*, XXXII–XXXIII, 325 ff.

SCHLABOW (1951). K. Schlabow, 'Der Thorsberger Prachtmantel, der Schlüssel zum altgermanischen Webstuhl', *Festschrift G. Schwantes*, 176 ff.

SCHLABOW (1957). K. Schlabow, *Die Kunst des Brettchenwebens*.

SCHLABOW (1961). K. Schlabow, *Trachten der Eisenzeit, Wegweiser durch die Sammlung des Schleswig-Holsteiner Museums vorgeschichtlicher Altertümer*, 5.

SCHLABOW (1962). K. Schlabow, *Gewebe und Gewand zur Bronzezeit, Veröffentlichungen des Fördervereins, Textilmuseum Neumünster*, 3.

SINGER & HOLMYARD (1954), (1956). C. Singer & E. J. Holmyard et al. *A History of Technology*, I, 1954; II, 1956.

SMITH (1859). C. Roach Smith, *Illustrations of Roman London*.

SNOOK (1963). B. Snook, *Embroidery Stitches*.

SPINAZZOLA (1953). V. Spinazzola, *Pompei alla luce degli scavi nuovi di via dell'Abbondanza (anni 1910–23)*.

SPRATER (1929). F. Sprater, *Die Pfalz unter den Römern*, I.

STAEHELIN (1948). F. Staehelin, *Die Schweiz in Römischer Zeit*, 3te Auflage.

VON STOKAR (1934). W. von Stokar, 'Die mikroskopische Untersuchung vorgeschichtlicher Webarbeiten', *Mannus*, **26**, 309 ff.

VON STOKAR (1938). W. von Stokar, *Spinnen und Weben bei den Germanen, Mannus-Bibliothek,* 59.

VON STOKAR (1939–40). W. von Stokar, 'Die bronzezeitlichen Schafwollen', *PZ,* XXX–XXXI, 404 ff.

TAYLOR (1967). C. C. Taylor, 'Late Roman Pastoral Farming in Wessex', *Antiquity,* XLI, 304 ff.

TOYNBEE (1963). J. M. C. Toynbee, *Art in Roman Britain,* 2nd edition.

TOYNBEE (1964). J. M. C. Toynbee, *Art in Britain under the Romans.*

TROW-SMITH (1957). R. Trow-Smith, *A History of British Livestock Husbandry to 1700.*

VISTRAND (1899–1900). G. Vistrand, 'Gnidstenar i Nordiska Museet', *Meddelanden från Nordiska Museet 1899–1900,* 13 ff.

VOGT (1937). E. Vogt, *Geflechte und Gewebe der Steinzeit, Monogr. zur Ur-und Frühgeschichte der Schweiz,* I.

WALDE & HOFMANN (1938). A. Walde & J. B. Hofmann, *Lateinisches Etymologisches Wörterbuch,* 3te Auflage.

WEDLAKE (1958). W. J. Wedlake, *Excavations at Camerton, Somerset.*

WEISGERBER (1966–7). L. Weisgerber, 'Frühgeschichtliche Sprachbewegungen im Kölner Raum', *Rheinische Vierteljahrsblätter,* **31,** 197 ff.

WHEELER (1930). R. E. M. Wheeler, *Roman London* (Catalogue 3 of the London Museum).

WHEELER (1943). R. E. M. Wheeler, *Maiden Castle, Dorset, Report of the Research Committee of the Society of Antiquaries of London,* XII.

WHITE (1962). L. T. White, *Mediaeval Technology and Social Change.*

WILD (1964). J. P. Wild, 'The Textile Term *Scutulatus*', *CQ,* NS, XIV, 263 ff.

WILD (1965 *a*). J. P. Wild, 'A Roman damask silk from Kent', *Arch. Cant.* LXXX, 246 ff.

WILD (1965 *b*). J. P. Wild, 'Zwei Textilproben aus Xanten', *BJb,* **165,** 275–7.

WILD (1966). J. P. Wild, 'Mantus', *Zeitschrift f.vergleichende Sprachforschung,* **80,** 247 f.

WILD (1967 *a*). J. P. Wild, 'Soft-finished textiles in Roman Britain', *CQ,* NS, XVII, 133–5.

WILD (1967 *b*). J. P. Wild, 'Two technical terms used by Roman tapestry-weavers', *Philologus,* **III,** 151 ff.

WILD (1967 *c*). J. P. Wild, 'The *gynaeceum* at Venta and its context', *Latomus,* XXVI, 648 ff.

WILD (1967 *d*). J. P. Wild, 'Römische Textilreste im Saalburgmuseum', *S-Jb,* XXIV, 77 f.

WILD (1968). J. P. Wild, 'The Roman flax-hackle (*aena*)', *Museum Helveticum,* **25,** 139 ff.

WILLIAMSON & BOYD (1960). K. Williamson & J. M. Boyd, *St Kilda Summer.*

WILSON (1933). L. M. Wilson, *Ancient Textiles from Egypt in the University of Michigan Collection.*

WILSON (1938). L. M. Wilson, *The Clothing of the Ancient Romans.*

WINLOCK & CRUM (1926). H. E. Winlock & W. E. Crum, *The Monastery of Epiphanius at Thebes.*

WINTER & YOUTIE (1944). J. G. Winter & H. C. Youtie, 'Cotton in Graeco-Roman Egypt', *AJP,* LXV, 249 ff.

WIPSZYCKA (1965). E. Wipszycka, *L'Industrie Textile dans l'Egypte Romaine.*

DE WIT (1959). J. de Wit, *Die Miniaturen des Vergilius Vaticanus.*

YADIN (1963). Y. Yadin, *The Finds from the Bar Kokhba Period in the Cave of Letters, Judaean Desert Studies* (separate texts in English and Hebrew).

YOUATT (1837). W. Youatt, *Sheep, Their Breeds, Management and Diseases.*

ZEUNER (1963). F. E. Zeuner, *A History of Domesticated Animals.*

GLOSSARY

Band   Decorative linear ornament woven in coloured weft to contrast with the body of
the cloth is known as a *band* to differentiate it from a *stripe* which is the same
feature woven in the warp-direction.

Cross   The point at which the two halves of a loop, formed round a peg by a single
warp-thread during warping, intersect.

Displacement Displacement occurs where two adjacent threads (of warp or weft) in a twill
weave follow completely different courses instead of overlapping (see fig. 62.)

Heddle   A loop of string (leash), one of a series which connect selected warp-threads on
the loom to a rod for the opening of a shed.

Roving   A loose 'rope' or sliver of fibres prepared ready for spinning.

Shed   The gap created between two systems (rows) of warp-threads into which the weft
is passed.

Shed-rod   A rod fixed to the uprights (or sometimes free) of the loom behind selected
warp-threads to keep a permanent (natural) shed. It has no heddles attached.

Warp, weft   The warp-threads, the main system, run vertically on the warp-weighted loom;
the weft-threads are interlaced with them horizontally.

FIGURES

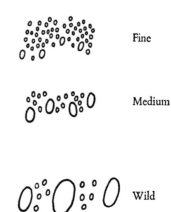

1 Scale structure of a wool fibre
(scale 300:1)

2 Follicle distribution in three
types of fleece

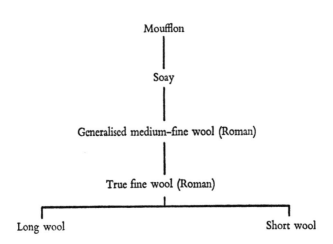

3 Probable stemma of early British sheep breeds

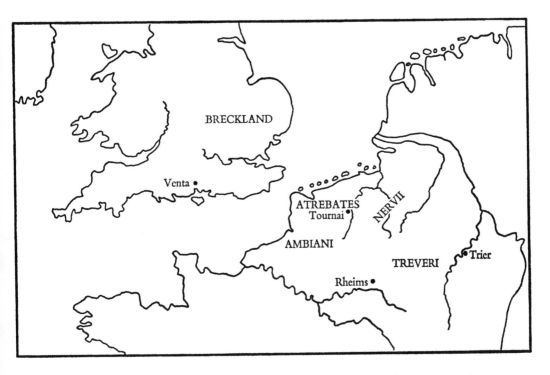

4 Main wool-producing areas in the western provinces (scale 1:8,000,000)

5 Leaf and boll of modern *Gossypium herbaceum*

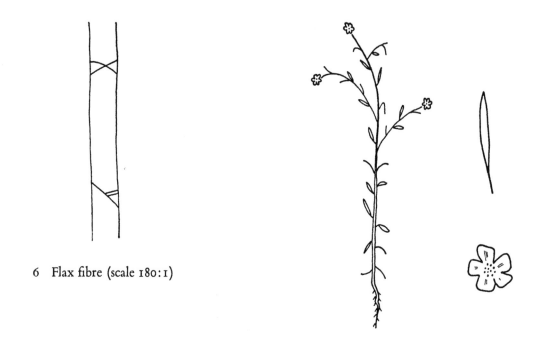

6   Flax fibre (scale 180:1)

7   Flax plant

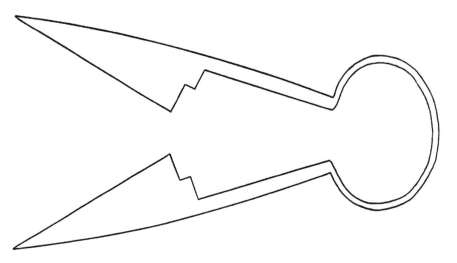

8   Modern sheep shears (scale 1:3)

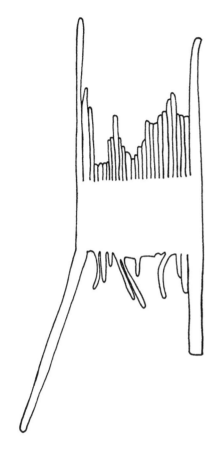

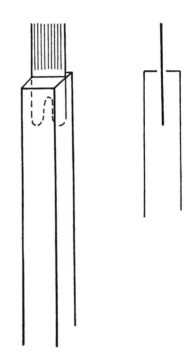

10 Reconstruction of the method
of mounting the wool-combs of
East Anglian type

9 Two-ended wool-comb from Baydon,
Wiltshire (scale 1:3) (table C 4)

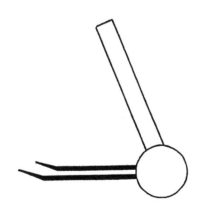

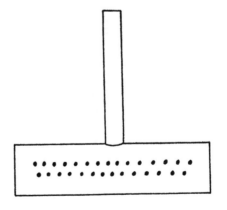

11 Structure of a nineteenth-century wool-comb (scale 1:3)

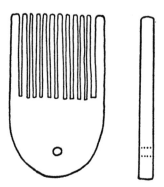

12 Wooden rippling-comb (?) from Vindonissa,
Switzerland, with right-hand side restored
(scale 1:3) (table D 3)

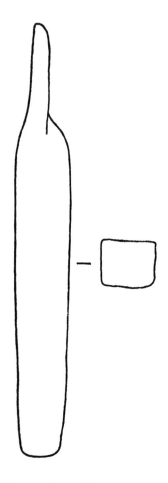

13 Neolithic scutching-blade from the
Swiss *Pfahlbauten* (scale 1:6)

14 Neolithic hackle from the Swiss *Pfahlbauten*
with right-hand side restored (scale 1:3)

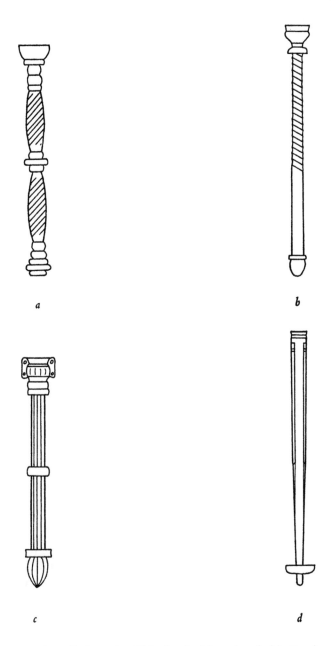

15   Distaffs from the Rhineland: (*a*) amber (table E 12),
(*b–d*) jet (table E 1, 4, 21) (scale 1:3)

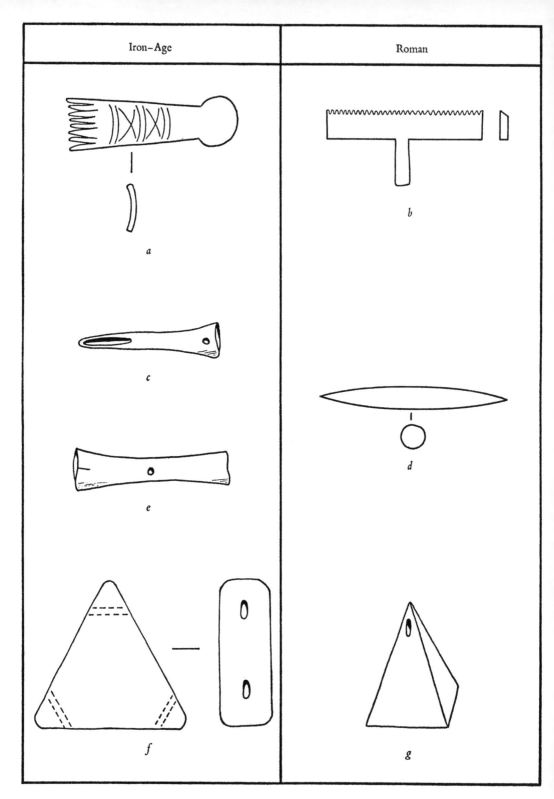

| Iron–Age | Roman |

16   Comparative diagram of Iron-Age and Roman weaving implements: (*a, b*) weaving-combs; (*c, d*) pin-beaters; (*e*) bobbin; (*f, g*) loom-weights (scale 1:3; except *b*, 1:6)

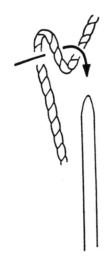

17   Possible methods of knotting the thread on the top of the spindle

18   Spin-direction

19 Half-basket weave from
Newstead (table A 9)

20 2-over-2 twill weave from
Caerwent (table A 40)

21 2-over-1 twill weave from Corbridge
(table A 50) (⊠ fault: system 1 on surface
incorrectly)

22 Basket-weave from Cambridge
(table A 11)

23 Weaving-plan of herringbone
twill from Falkirk (table A 42)

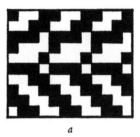

a

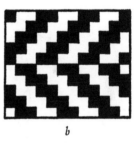

b

25 Faults in the herringbone twill from
Huntcliff (table A 43): (*a*) faults in the
weft-direction; (*b*) corrected plan. Paired
threads are drawn here as a single thread.

24 Weaving-plan of the diamond twill from
Balmaclellan, Kirkcudbright (table A 45)

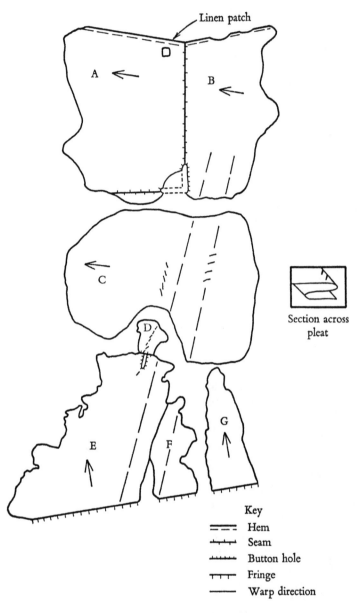

Linen patch

A

B

C

D

E

F

G

Section across
pleat

Key

Hem

Seam

Button hole

Fringe

Warp direction

26   Outline of the cloth fragments from Verulamium after unfolding (scale 1:6) (table A 49)

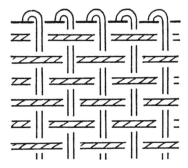

27 Diagram of the darned edge on the cloth from Verulamium

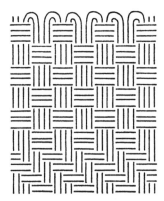

28 Weaving-plan of the starting-border from Verulamium

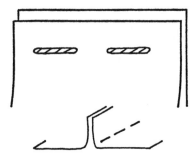

29 Seam on the cloth from Verulamium

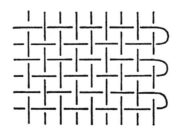

30   Plain selvedge on a band from Mainz (table B 9)

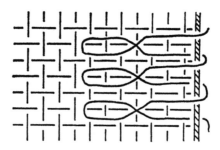

31   Couching from Mainz (table B 18)

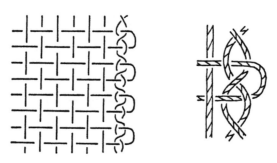

32   Tablet-woven (?) selvedge on a band from Mainz (table B 8)

33 Faults in the cloth from Chur,
Switzerland (table B 37) (⊠ faults:
warp on surface incorrectly)

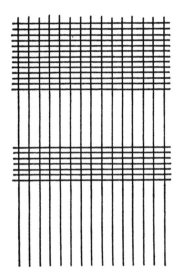

34 Fringe on the towel from Trier
(scale 1:1) (table B 49)

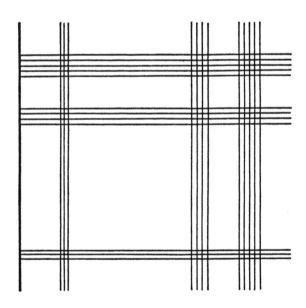

35 Scheme of a check fabric from Mainz, showing selvedge on
the left-hand side (scale 1:1) (table B 59)

II-2

36   Hollow selvedge from the Hallstatt salt mines

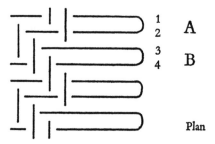

Plan

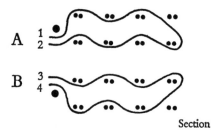

Section

37   Simplified plan and cross-section of the hollow
selvedge from Mainz (table B 59)

38 Diamond twill from Mainz
(table B 75)

39 Diamond twill from Mainz (table B 76)

40 Diamond twill from Mainz (table B 78)

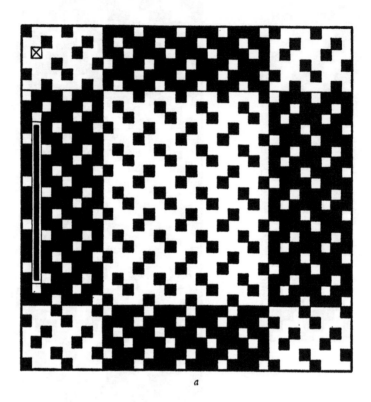

a

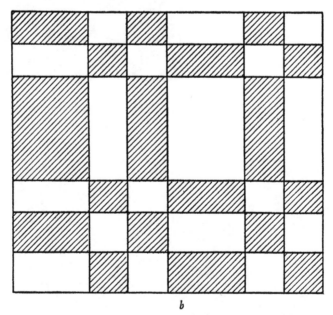

b

41 Damask silk from Holborough, Kent (table A 51): (*a*) weaving-plan (⊠ fault: warp should be on surface); (*b*) general pattern (scale 6:1)

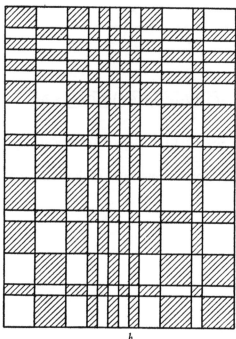

42   Damask silk from Palmyra: (*a*) weaving-plan; (*b*) general pattern (scale 4:1)

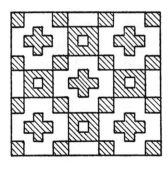

43 General pattern of damask silk
from Conthey, Switzerland
(scale 1:1) (Table B 85)

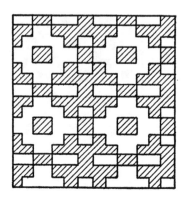

44 General pattern of the 2-over-2
damask twill silk from Trier
(scale 4:3) (table B 86)

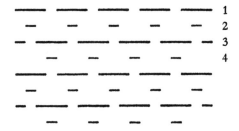

45 Structure of 3-over-1 compound cloth in plan and cross-section

46 General pattern of the 3-over-1 compound cloth from Trier (scale 4:3) (table B 88)

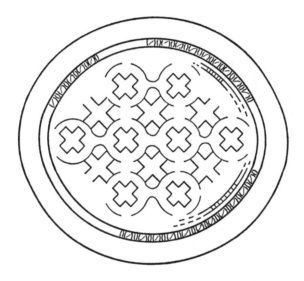

47 Plan of the tapestry roundel from Conthey, Switzerland (table B 90)

48 Check pattern of the herringbone twill from Falkirk (table A 42)

49 Diagram of the *cordeline* principle

50 'Bobbin-work' from Esch, 's-Hertogenbosch, Holland (table B 95)

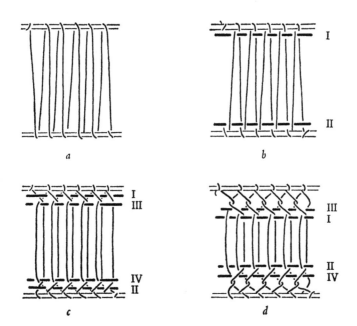

a

b

c

d

51   Technique of *sprang*

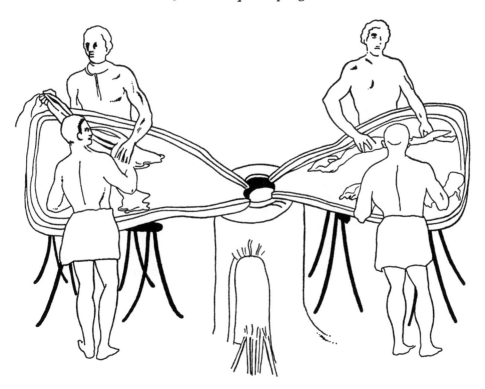

52   Feltmakers from a wall-painting outside Verecundus' workshop in Pompeii

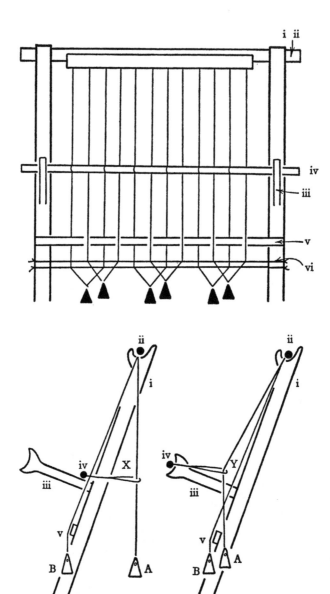

53　Principle of the warp-weighted loom

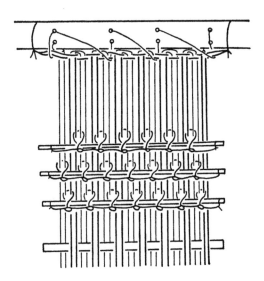

54   Knitting the heddles for twill by the Icelandic method

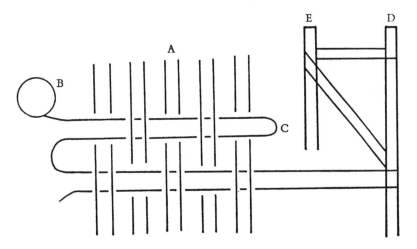

55   Weaving the starting-border from Verulamium (table A 49)

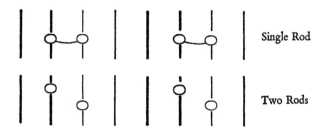

Single Rod

Two Rods

56 Possible knitting of the heddles to account for the Huntcliff weft-faults

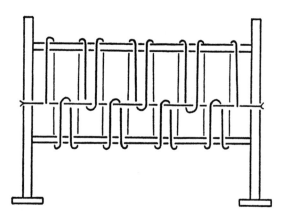

57 Two-beam loom in Iron-Age Denmark, as reconstructed by Dr M. Hald

58 Dolly of weft

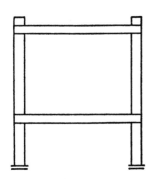

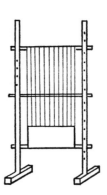

59 Two-beam loom from the
Forum of Nerva, Rome

60 Two-beam loom in MS *Vergilius
Vaticanus Latinus* 3225

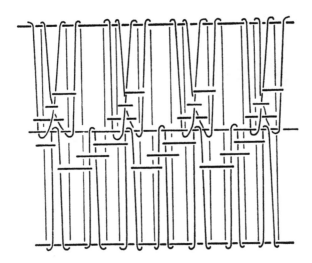

61 Weaving twill on a two-beam loom, as reconstructed by Dr M. Hald

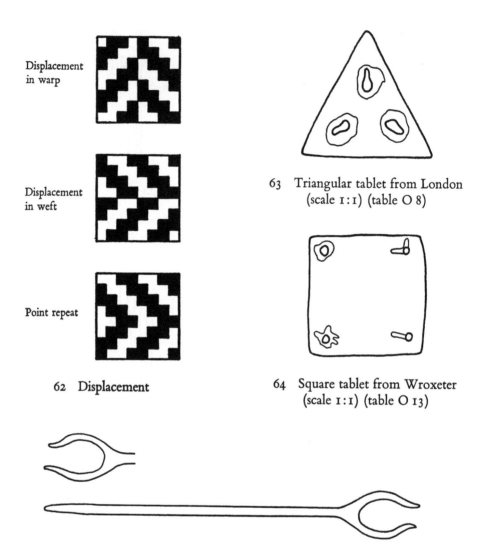

Displacement
in warp

Displacement
in weft

Point repeat

62 Displacement

63 Triangular tablet from London
    (scale 1:1) (table O 8)

64 Square tablet from Wroxeter
    (scale 1:1) (table O 13)

65 Standard type of netting-needle with planes of prongs set at right angles

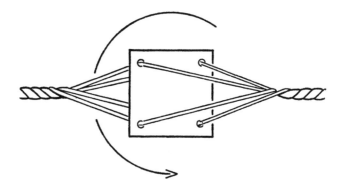

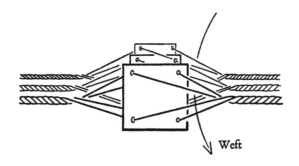

66 Principle of tablet-weaving

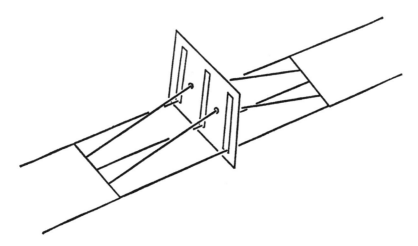

67 Use of the heddle-frame or rigid heddle

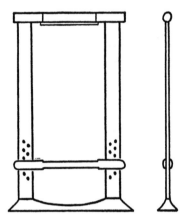

68   Loom from the Oseberg ship (scale 1:22)

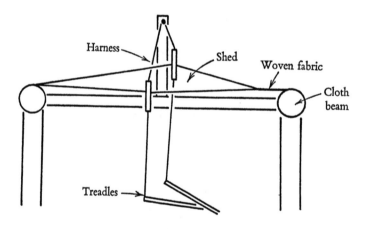

69   Principle of the harness on a modern handloom

70   Principle of draw-loom device

178

71 Dyer (?) from a funerary monument
at Arlon, Belgium

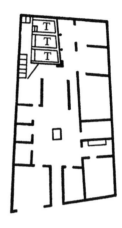

72 Plan of a Pompeian *fullonica*
(VI. 8. 20) (T denotes tank)

a

b

73 Scenes from a fuller's tombstone from Sens, Yonne: (*a*) treading cloth, (*b*) cropping nap

12-2

a   b

74 Wall-painting from Pompeii (VI. 8. 20) showing interior of *fullonica*: (a) use of *aena*,
(b) equipment for bleaching cloth

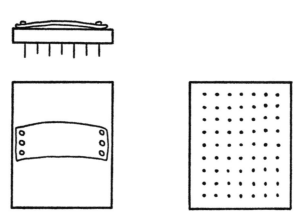

75 Reconstruction of *aena fullonia*

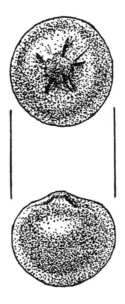

76 Glass linen-rubber from South Shields
(scale 2:3)

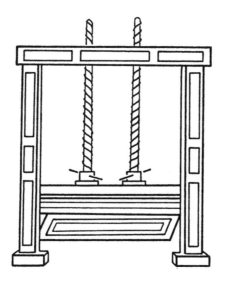

77 Clothes-press from a wall-painting in Pompeii (VI. 14. 21)

PLATES
INDEXES

1*a* Two-year-old Soay ram from the flock at the Animal Breeding
Research Station, Roslin (April 1964)

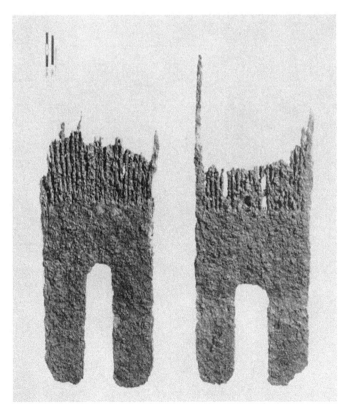

1*b* Wool-combs of East Anglian type from Worlington, Suffolk (scale 1:3.5) (table C 3)

II Wool-comber from a wall-painting outside the workshop of Verecundus in Pompeii

IIa   Reconstructed scene of a nineteenth-century wool-
comber at work in the Bankfield Museum, Halifax

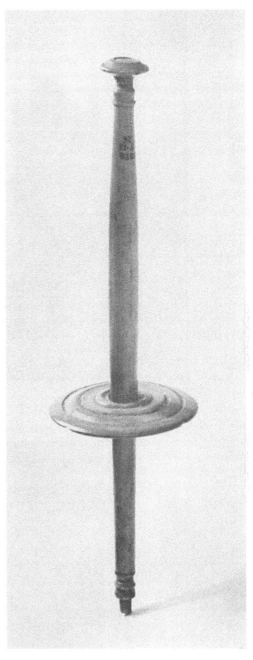

IIIb   Spindle of bone from London
(scale 1:1) (table F 10)

IV *a* Spinsters on a relief from the Forum of Nerva, Rome

IV *b* Examining cloth on a relief from the Forum
of Nerva, Rome

V*a* Plain-weave linen from the pipe-burial at Caerleon (scale 1:1.3) (table A 10)

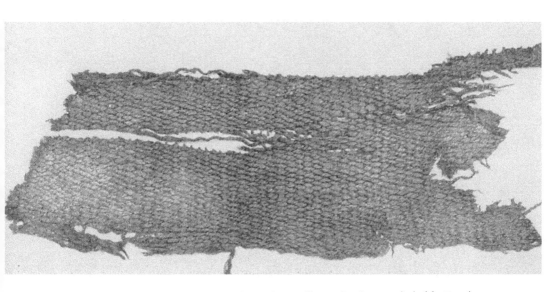

V*b* Plain-weave wool cloth from the Saalburg (scale 1.5:1) (table B 30)

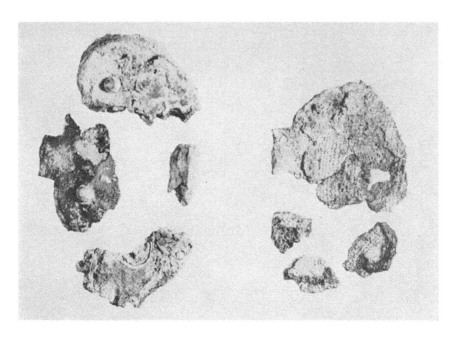

VI*a* Basket weave on a buckle from Silchester (scale 1.5:1) (table A 24)

VI*b* Herringbone twill from Falkirk (scale 2:1) (table A 42)

VII*a*　Basket-weave cloth in a bast fibre from Chur, Switerland (scale 1:2.7) (table B 37)

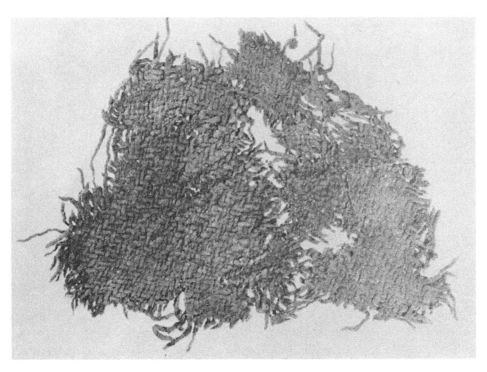

VII*b*　2-over-2 twill from Vindonissa, Switzerland (scale 1.5:1) (table B 73)

VIII   Fragment of damask silk from Conthey, Switzerland (scale 2:1) (table B 85)

IX a   Heddle-frame from South Shields
(scale 1:1)

IX b   Fragment in *sprang*-technique from
Vindonissa, Switzerland (scale 1:2) (table B 93)

X*a*   Beating up the weft on a warp-weighted
loom in western Norway

X*b*   Attaching the weights on a Lappish
warp-weighted loom

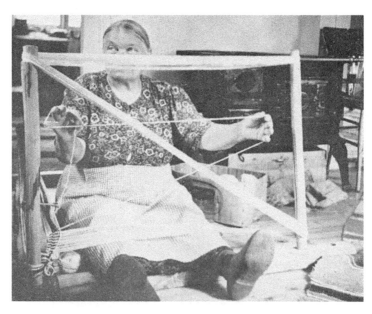

X*c*   Weaving the starting-border in Lappish Norway

XI*a* Two-beam loom from the Forum of Nerva, Rome

XI*b* Two-beam loom from the *hypogeum* of the Aurelii, Rome

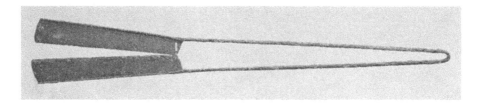

XII*a*   Pair of cropping-shears from Great Chesterford, Cambridge
(scale 1:12)

XII*b*   Reconstruction of a nineteenth-century cropper's workshop
in the Bankfield Museum, Halifax

XII*c*   Model of a wool bale
from Dun an Iardhard,
(scale 1.2:1)

XII*d*   Glass linen-rubber
from South Shields
(scale 1:1.3)

INDEX OF PLACES

GENERAL INDEX

For EU product safety concerns, contact us at Calle de José Abascal, 56–1°,
28003 Madrid, Spain or eugpsr@cambridge.org.

www.ingramcontent.com/pod-product-compliance
Ingram Content Group UK Ltd.
Pitfield, Milton Keynes, MK11 3LW, UK
UKHW030901150625
459647UK00021B/2688